Christmas 1996

Dear David,
    Love you —
        Bette

# GOING BIGTIME

# GOING BIGTIME

## The Spectacular Rise of UMass Basketball

MARTY DOBROW

*Summerset Press | Northampton, Massachusetts | 1996*

*For CAREY,*
*a standout guard*
*who was born on May 9th;*

*and SARAH,*
*who gave wonderful new meaning*
*to the term "March Madness"*
*in the 1995-1996 season*

# ACKNOWLEDGMENTS

**G**oing Bigtime would never have reached the rim were it not for the enormous generosity of many people.

Jim Kaplan of Summerset Press coached with patience and a writer's perspective from the beginning. Readers gave tremendous amounts of themselves. My wife Carey displayed a tenacity and unselfishness from tipoff to final buzzer. The Dobrow family came through, as always. Unending thanks to Alan and Vida, Julie and Joe. Jim Degnim took enormous interest in this project, handing off one assist after another. Peter Neumann, the truest of teammates, continued to be a literary springboard. Susan Kan helped beat the press with her careful ballhandling. John Bowman snared some key rebounds. Jay Neugeboren helped launch this shot all the way from the backcourt. Andrew Ayres and Edward Kubosiak Jr. played some suffocating defense.

Colleagues at the *Daily Hampshire Gazette* were instrumental in allowing this project to reach fruition. The patience and support of Jim Foudy and Deborah Oakley meant a lot to me. Dave Perlmutter helped me scrap for many a loose ball. Thanks also to Rick Seto and Stan Moulton. And, of course, Milt Cole taught me everything I know. So he tells me.

Fellow reporters covering UMass helped me set the halfcourt offense. Ron Chimelis, my alleged competitor at the *Union–News* in Springfield, provided a constant voice of reason, as well as an ongoing example of journalistic integrity. Joe Burris, Mark Murphy, Tony Massarotti and Jim Clark helped shape my thinking through lengthy discussions. Thanks also to Marc Vandermeer and George Miller for setting some jarring picks.

Numerous people at UMass provided help. John Calipari inspired, entertained and essentially created the basis for this book with enormous passion for his job. Above all, he never interfered with my path to the hoop, respecting my desire to write an honest book. Assistant coaches Bruiser Flint, John Robic, Ed Schilling and Bill Bayno all made contributions. Bonnie Martin and Brian Gorman also knocked down some key shots from the perimeter.

Players were consistently open and generous with their time and their stories. Special thanks to the Padilla family, a true inspiration.

Jack Leaman was magnificent. Mike Milewski helped me navigate my way through plenty of archives. Kay Scanlan responded to several requests with great efficiency. The members of Bill Strickland's Media Relations team went beyond the call of duty. Special thanks to Kathy Connors, Scott McConnell, Charlie Bare, Kate Mulligan, Mike McComiskey and Ruthie Drew.

Dan Wetzel and Dave Scott are the Edgar and Carmelo of journalism. They helped me get after it.

When it came to research, Eric Lekus demonstrated unlimited range on his jump shot.

Dozens of sources from earlier eras of UMass basketball contributed in a large way. Of particular note were conversations with Mike Pyatt, Ray Ellerbrook, Tom Witkos, Matt Capeless, Mike Haverty and Rick Pitino.

Michael Gray provided a balance of competence and compassion that I will never forget. In the calendar year 1996, he helped me in times of both emergence and emergency.

Designer Lisa Diercks helped open my eyes to a brand new world. Marie Rodgers came off the bench at the end of the game to give me a tremendous boost.

Lots of role players pitched in during critical moments. Thanks to dogged Doug Banks and Amy Heidenreich, Denise Green and Wayne Feiden, Karen Romanowski and Dan Kaplan, Larry Vale and Julie Zagars, Harry Gural and Dick Benjamin, the late Ethel Cali and Greg Godak, Vince and Donna Calipari, Howie Davis and Bill Doyle, Emily Kozodoy and Richard Parks, Bob Marcum and Glenn Wong, John Feudo and Ralph Savarese, Brooks Robards and Jack Handler, Mordecai Gerstein and Sharon Pilcher, Linda Minoff and Andy Steckel, Ralph Graves and Justin Smith. Many others, unnamed here, sank important baskets, keeping the game close, giving us a chance at the buzzer. In this game you can't ask for more than that.

# Contents

# FOREWORD: "IN BETWEEN FALLS REALITY"

**Summer, 1996**

"Things are never quite as good as they seem," John Calipari often preached during his eight–year stint as basketball coach at the University of Massachusetts. "Things are never quite as bad as they seem. In between falls reality."

Some fans of college sports in general, and of UMass basketball in particular, consider their sporting passions an unadulterated good. There is purity and passion in the college game, they argue; it is unpolluted by the big egos and enormous salaries that have sullied professional sports. These fans view UMass as an old-fashioned American success story. After all, the Minutemen were one of the very worst teams in the nation during the eighties; in the nineties they became one of the very best. Calipari is seen as a modern–day Horatio Alger, a man who rose from modest roots to the very top of his profession through an unrelenting work ethic. His "Refuse to Lose" slogan and emphasis on "teaching life skills" are thought to be the embodiment of college sports' highest ideals.

Others feel that college sports have become a sewer, and that UMass is merely the scum floating on the top. To them, the games played by college kids are a ruthless business, all about money and exploitation, compromising the mission of our institutions of higher learning. This is, after all, the era of the Tostitos Fiesta Bowl, and a CBS television contract of almost $2 billion to televise the NCAA basketball tournament for eight years. These folks see Calipari as a greedy whiner, willing to step on anything or anyone to get his way. In their eyes, he is a jockish Michael Milken whose "Refuse to Lose" bespeaks nothing but arrogance, and whose emphasis on life skills demonstrates only slick self–promotion.

This book is not really for either group. It aims for shades of gray, the luster as well as the warts. Both are true. College sports represent one of our culture's most noble enterprises—a genuine attempt to integrate mind and body—*and* a startlingly hypocritical business that puts bucks ahead of books. UMass *is* an old-fashioned American success story. But it is also a modern success story, replete with compromise and painful loss of innocence. And John Calipari? Suffice to say, he is a complicated man.

The University of Massachusetts basketball program provides a colorful lens through which to look at the changes in college sports. Back in the sixties and seventies, UMass was a regional power in an era long before The Road to the Final Four, sneaker contracts and trademarked mottos. College basketball was merely a popular extracurricular activity, played in ancient New England gyms by student-athletes who had to get at least one thousand on their SATs. Coach Jack Leaman—long on sincerity, short on flash—was an old–fashioned disciplinarian, the prototype of "coach as father figure." His teams, which included Julius Erving and Rick Pitino, won in a vacuum, because outside of the university not many people cared.

With the arrival of the made–for–television Big East Conference and ESPN in the late seventies, college basketball began to change. By the eighties it was a genuine "product" that generated huge national interest and enormous amounts of money. Universities built shining arenas. Stylish and charismatic coaches became the stars of the game. UMass, though, did not get with the program. The Minutemen floundered through the decade, going through four coaches and compiling an 86–190 record, ranking 259th of 267 Division I teams. They were an embarrassment.

Calipari arrived in 1988 at the age of twenty–nine with absolutely no head-coaching experience. Handsome and confident, he told a small gaggle of reporters who showed up at his introductory press conference that his goal was to "create a love affair" between his team and the local community. It was a preposterous statement.

It was an omen.

A marketing major with an evangelical flair, Calipari quickly became the prototype of the modern "coach as salesman." He sold school officials on the Gospel of College Hoop, telling them that basketball could be the front porch of a great university. Indeed, applications and donations started to rise as the basketball team began to win. Money began to flow. The whole image of an oft–beleaguered university palpably improved. Calipari sold fans on the Minutemen.

They filled enough seats to build a new arena, and many actually bowed with tongue–in–cheek appreciation when the great Coach Cal graced them with his presence. In certain parts of campus he became known by a telling one–word nickname: "Himself." Calipari sold recruits on UMass, a place many of them hadn't heard of before. They would become better players and better people, he insisted. And they came. Once they became members of the Minutemen, players bought into Calipari's tenacious approach. They became infused with his will. Even Calipari's harshest critics concede that the Minutemen played unbelievably hard. The "Refuse to Lose" slogan defined his teams perfectly.

The selling act worked because the product was a winner—entertaining and stunningly successful. By Calipari's second year, he had produced UMass's first winning team in over a decade. By his fourth year, he had the Minutemen in the NCAA tournament for the first time in thirty years. In the six seasons played so far in the nineties, UMass's 166 wins ranks second in Division I, trailing only Kentucky's 170. Kentucky coach Rick Pitino, former point guard at UMass under Jack Leaman, refers to Calipari's work as "the greatest building job in college basketball history."

With success, though, came a shadow. Controversy swirled around the UMass program. Some of it was directed at Calipari himself: accusations that he would try to win at all costs. Critics questioned the university's priorities. Was UMass selling its soul for a winner? Issues of academic integrity and exploitative agents—two of the biggest problems in college sports today—visited the university in painful fashion. Some of the controversy, to be sure, was trumped up. Certain people, certain interests, were threatened by UMass's success. In an ultracompetitive business like college basketball, jealousy and pettiness are common. Fair and unfair alike, the controversy provided those close to the UMass basketball program with a clear sense that going bigtime had both advantages and disadvantages. Even before the 1995–96 season tipped off, UMass had seen what sportswriters of the day call the "total package."

But it was in 1995–96 that the University of Massachusetts had the defining modern college sports experience.

The Minutemen enjoyed a season for the ages. Featuring both the National Player of the Year and the National Coach of the Year, they spent most of the season ranked as the Number 1 team in the country. They made a spirited run at the first undefeated season in Division I in twenty years. Lacking the overall talent and depth of several top teams, the Minutemen seldom overpowered opponents. Often they were pushed to the edge—big deficits, four overtime games. Always they seemed to find a way, summoning their togetherness and fighting spirit when they needed it most. They pushed the year all the way to the sport's ultimate weekend, the Final Four, and came tantalizingly close to the national championship they so coveted.

For one memorable winter, the UMass Minutemen were college basketball's version of "America's Team." Their games were nationally televised twenty–five different times. They were featured on the front page of *USA Today*. Calipari put in a bravura performance on *Good Morning America*. President Bill Clinton called to heap praise on the coach.

It wasn't just that this team won. There was a human element to the Minutemen that was undeniably appealing.

Star player Marcus Camby came across as the quintessential role model. On the court he was a multitalented force, and fundamentally, a team player. Off it, he was suffused with a refreshingly boyish innocence. He smiled shyly when asked about his work tutoring middle school students and his desire to be a principal after his playing days were over. Frequently going back to his dilapidated old neighborhood of Bellevue Square in Hartford, he never notified the media of his work with kids. It wasn't for show; it was for real.

In mid–season, Camby mysteriously collapsed and lost consciousness for ten minutes before a UMass game at St. Bonaventure in Olean, New York. It was a singularly terrifying moment for the Minutemen, who held hands in the locker room while they cried and prayed. Calipari climbed into the back of the ambulance, leaving the game behind. The ending was happy: Camby was fine. The Minutemen banded together and won without him. Four games later he rejoined the team, and the magical season went forward. The Minutemen were Number 1, undefeated, *and* the object of people's sympathy. They had it all.

They were an unlikely collection of players whose lives were filled with heart-warming stories. Edgar Padilla and his deaf parents. Carmelo Travieso and his narrow escape from the ravages of Hurricane David as a young boy in the Dominican Republic. Tyrone Weeks helping his mother overcome her addiction to cocaine. Donta Bright becoming a hero to a child with a brain tumor.

They gelled beyond even the most unrealistic of expectations. UMass's chemistry was its most potent weapon. Rival coaches marvelled at the rare and precious sight of a team fully realized.

"That team is a team," Temple coach John Chaney rhapsodized. "That's what you hope that someday you'll have."

Truly, they were an inspiring bunch. A couple of sportswriters from Boston, veterans of the seedy side of athletics, admitted in separate conversations that the Minutemen had melted some of their cynicism, injecting them with a sense of hope, a reminder that sports can represent something precious.

Then it all came crashing down.

In the first week of June, Marcus Camby poured out a wrenching confession to a *Hartford Courant* reporter that he had broken NCAA rules by accepting money and jewelry from a pair of agents—some of it funneled unknowingly through his friends. Asked by the reporter if he would do it again, Camby stumbled, "I probably would. No, I probably wouldn't. Not right now. I know a lot is at stake right now. I messed with my image. And all the other stuff that's been good so far. You don't know what it's like, man. . . .When everybody is pulling on your shoulder, everybody. 'Marcus, hey Marcus. Hey, we want to be your friend.'"

Later that week—just hours after saying he expected to stay at UMass—Calipari stunned Minuteman fans by accepting a job as head coach, executive vice president and director of basketball operations for the NBA's long–pathetic New Jersey Nets. After fulfilling just one year of a ten–year contract at UMass, Calipari used an exit clause and signed a five–year deal with the Nets for $15 million. The controversy surrounding Camby had nothing to do with his decision, he claimed—he was chasing a dream.

"My goal," he said at his opening press conference, "is to create a love affair between this organization and the people of New Jersey."

In the summer of 1996, a stream of stories about UMass basketball stung fans with the particular pain of disillusionment. The truth was hard to find.

Was it true, for instance, that UMass's spending of $200,000 in NCAA tournament money at the Final Four weekend represented a good–faith effort to reward school supporters and build a greater base

*John Calipari (Photo by Jerrey Roberts)*

for the future? Or was it a lavish weekend of partying by university officials gone mad with basketball?

Was UMass's decision to give free tickets to agents an example of the school's indifference to the exploitation of its athletes? Or did it demonstrate part of the school's agent–education program, an effort to allow player access only to "good agents" who could provide responsible assistance in the future?

Most disturbing of all was the news, first broken by Daniel Golden and David Armstrong in *The Boston Globe*, about Calipari's trademarking of "Refuse to Lose." It turns out the team's motto had become a private industry for the coach. He hadn't coined the term, hadn't even been the first on campus to employ it. (The 1990 UMass football team wore T-shirts that proclaimed the message.) Further, he wasn't even the first to apply for a trademark. Jody Hyden, now the women's tennis coach at Duke, had submitted an application when he was a graduate student at Clemson in 1988. Hyden claims that he sold the rights to Calipari for $3,500 after being pressured by Calipari's business agent Dave Glover. That's the same Dave Glover who served as academic coordinator for the UMass basketball team, and who now serves as an administrator for the New Jersey Nets. Calipari had cashed in on royalties from a wide array of individuals and groups who wanted to make use of the term: everyone from the Seattle Mariners to Champion Products. Potentially, the pirated phrase could pay off in the millions.

It was all perfectly legal, and yet it raised a couple of troubling issues. Glover's dual role as academic coordinator—one he performed with considerable distinction—and copyright–seeking business manager provided an awkward marriage of allegedly amateur athletics and cut–throat capitalism. More troubling still was the fact that a phrase used to define the noble spirit of a special group of college athletes was now being used to pad Calipari's pockets. It wasn't that Calipari hadn't given back to UMass in all sorts of ways, or that he wasn't entitled to private business interests, but the merger of something that had seemed so pure with something that seemed so crass was jarring. That merger, though, defines modern college sports. Both parts of the equation are true.

Indeed, the story of the UMass basketball program provides a window on late twentieth century college sports in America—where it has come from and where it is headed, for better and for worse.

While the precious late summer days shortened, a pair of millionaires named Marcus Camby and John Calipari prepared to begin their careers in the NBA. At the University of Massachusetts, where the two men rocketed to fame, an air of uncertainty hovered over the campus while a new school year approached. Possible NCAA penalties from Camby's dealings with agents were pending. One penalty frequently discussed was the voiding of NCAA tournament games involving the Minutemen. Applied to other teams in other situations, this punishment merely throws the games out the window. Like the "memory holes" made famous in George Orwell's *1984*, the NCAA has the power to act as if the games didn't take place. As if history itself could be expunged.

As if the whole UMass basketball story had never really happened.

# 1: "A Crisis Within the UMass Basketball Program"

November 17, 1995

Amherst, Massachusetts

dgar Padilla tried to make the world quiet again. Holding a white towel over his head, he sat on the end of the bench, a couple of seats from his brother Giddel and as far as possible from UMass coach John Calipari. He didn't want to hear the volcanic blasts of coaching Calipari liked to call "aggressive counseling." There was another sound, though, that he couldn't quite suppress: the deep thudding doubts in his head.

A twenty–year–old junior, Padilla felt that the loss playing out on the floor—a humiliating exhibition defeat to a ragtag team called the Converse All–Stars—was entirely his fault. He was now the point guard, the guy who ran the show, and the show was flopping bigtime. At a place like UMass the job of point guard is essentially that of a choreographer. It is your responsibility to make your teammates better and ensure that the whole is greater than the sum of the parts. You are the coach on the floor. You are the leader. Padilla had worked his whole life for this opportunity. Now here it was, right before him, and he was failing, miserably.

He knew all too well that under Calipari, UMass basketball had climbed the mountain. In the eighties, the Minutemen had been one of the worst teams in America; through the first half of the nineties they had become one of the best. They had grown accustomed not only to winning, but to improving every year. That was easy enough to do in the early days of the Calipari regime because up was the only way to go. Now, however, the Minutemen were coming off an unprecedented year in which they reached Number 1 in the Associated Press poll and made it to the Elite Eight of the NCAA tournament. There was not a lot of room to grow.

Realistically, the 1995–96 team had some major holes. Forward Lou Roe, the school's all–time leading rebounder and second leading scorer, was now a Detroit Piston, the first UMass player in more than twenty years to make it to the NBA. In the backcourt, the Minutemen had been decimated. Gone were Mike Williams, the team's second leading scorer in 1994–95, and Derek Kellogg, a supremely steady point guard.

Sure, UMass had center Marcus Camby, a megatalent ready to blossom. The forward position was well stocked with euphonious seniors Donta Bright and Dana Dingle. But the backcourt, to be charitable, was untested. Edgar Padilla had never started at point guard, and Carmelo Travieso had started only two games in two seasons. There looked to be no depth, no leadership. The hoped–for recruiting windfall had yielded only one eligible player, guard Charlton Clarke. It seemed to many that the Minutemen had peaked. Calipari's Massachusetts Miracle had apparently run its course.

To have any chance of remaining in the national spotlight lots of things had to come together in a hurry. As the seconds ticked down in the Converse exhibition, Padilla knew that the team's biggest question mark was at point guard. That was where all great teams started. Pulling the towel tight over his ears, he tried to smother the doubts and return to a quiet world.

He had grown up in silence. Edgar's father, Mariano, was born deaf. His mother, Milca, lost her hearing to meningitis at age five. They met as teenagers at El Colegio de Gabriel, Puerto Rico's school for the deaf in the city of Santurce. The school taught them sign language, but not much more. Milca never got the formal education she wanted. Mariano enrolled in a vocational program and learned a trade. For twenty years he served as a dental technician, working doggedly to support the family after marrying Milca and having three children in the town of Toa Alta.

Millie, Giddel and Edgar could all hear, but sounds were often jarring things to the Padilla children. They got teased by other kids when Milca came in to school for parent–teacher conferences and spoke in her distorted way. They heard it again and again: *"¡Tu madre es estúpida!"* It was no wonder that Millie, the oldest by two years, didn't talk for a long time at school. Why should she? Words hurt.

At home, things weren't much better. Squadrons of well–intentioned relatives descended on the concrete house. Everybody seemed to know what to do with the Padilla children. At times the support was wonderful, but often it was chaotic. "You really don't want to have thirty moms and forty fathers," Edgar reflected years later.

At night, calm was restored when the house turned quiet and sign language filled the air. Milca and Mariano Padilla told their children to be proud of themselves, to set big goals, to get an education. The kids were stamped with a mixture of tenacity and tenderness.

Millie became an adult long before her time. Before she was even a teenager she was helping her grandmother serve as the liaison to the hearing world. Translating at doctor's offices, doing the shopping, looking after her brothers, she lived a life of considerable sacrifice.

Giddel, two years younger, had a firecracker smile and a taste for adventure. Boisterous and sociable, he needed constant stimulation. Milca tried enrolling him in an art class and then in a swimming program. Nothing worked. "I was a very active kid," Giddel said years later. "I was driving my mom crazy."

Edgar, three grades behind Giddel, benefited from the trial–and–error explorations of his siblings. They went into the world without a road map. His path was easier.

From the start, there was something different about Edgar, an almost visible vulnerability. He seemed to feel things deeply, to get hurt easily. And yet, he was not the least bit fragile. Plunging into challenges with an almost startling determination, the baby Padilla was a portrait of quiet focus. He didn't back away from anything.

Edgar looked up to Giddel with an admiration that bordered on worship. "I always, always wanted to do stuff with my brother," he says. "I wanted to do everything he was doing, no matter what."

So when Giddel finally found basketball to absorb his kinetic energy, the game became the major focus in the lives of both brothers. At first they tossed a rubber ball into an oversized paint can they had hung atop a fence. After every basket they had to turn the can upside down to remove the ball. Improving on that system, they cut the bottom out of a milk crate and tied it to a tree.

Giddel starred in a youth league in Toa Alta and ultimately made the twelve–and–under team for the whole island of Puerto Rico. Playing before a large crowd in San Juan at the big Pan–American youth tournament, Giddel led his team to the gold medal, winning the MVP. His brother looked on with awe. Edgar dreamed about doing the same thing himself. Playing basketball for what he would forever term "my country" seemed like the most glorious thing in the world.

But there was another country that beckoned. The boys' uncle, Neftali Rivera, had moved to the United States a few years before, ultimately settling in Springfield, Massachusetts. He kept returning to Puerto Rico with stories of America. Neftali had gone into business and already saved enough money to buy a house. There were unlimited opportunities, he said. Great things could happen. The American Dream was alive and well. He told his sister and brother–in–law, Milca and Mariano Padilla, that they should move to Springfield. There were plenty of jobs, lots of services for the hearing–impaired. And one other thing, Neftali said, looking Milca in the eye: there would be an opportunity for the kids to go to college.

Few of their neighbors thought the Padillas would move. They didn't know people up there. They didn't speak English. The parents were deaf. Besides, Milca's mother Pina Bonilla pointed out, it was cold in Massachusetts. Milca always thought it was too chilly at Pina's air–conditioned house in San Juan—how was she going to handle a New England winter?

In the summer of 1987, Milca visited her brother in Springfield. Returning a few weeks later, she smiled broadly when she announced to the family, "We're moving to the United States!"

Millie was excited. Going into her senior year of high school, she longed to learn English and expand her world. Giddel, eager for adventure, was thrilled.

Edgar was broken–hearted. "I'm not going," he said.

Here he was, twelve years old, standing up to his family. Determined to play on Puerto Rico's twelve–and–under national team as Giddel had done, Edgar explained that he was following a dream. He had set a big goal for himself. He wasn't going to back away from it.

After much debate, the family relented. Edgar stayed behind with his mom. Mariano took Millie and Giddel to Springfield, moving in with Milca's brother.

Millie went to work almost immediately, first at Burger King, then at McDonald's and ultimately for a long stint at Ponderosa. At every stop she worked feverishly, and ingratiated herself with the management. "I want you to hire my dad," she'd say. "He can't speak, and he can't hear, but nobody will work harder." After a while, it always seemed to work. Mariano distinguished himself as a fine dish washer at Ponderosa, even though he longed to work in his chosen field. Millie called every dental lab she could find in the Yellow Pages, trying to explain. There were no takers. *Maybe the guy can wash dishes, but how the hell are we going to train him?* "No, no, no," said Millie, "you don't understand." She kept calling back, not taking no for an answer, but getting it anyway, repeatedly.

Giddel cherished the new environment as he began to star on the basketball team at Central High School. Everything was new, and for a teenager with restless curiosity the world was wide open. "It was a beautiful experience," he recalled years later. "Me and my dad lived in the attic of my uncle's house. I can still remember the smell of the wood. And the snow. Everything was just so great."

Back in Puerto Rico, Edgar sparked the commonwealth's twelve–and–under team to the gold medal of the Pan–American youth games, played that year in Cuba. Like his brother, Edgar was named the MVP. He had never known a prouder moment.

Staying through the end of junior high school, Edgar moved in with his grandmother when Milca joined the rest of the family in Springfield. Millie convinced the managers at Ponderosa to hire her mom as well. Finally, in the fall of 1989, the stubborn baby brother moved north, almost two years after his siblings. He knew only a handful of words in English, words like "Burger King" and "Ponderosa."

Basketball helped ease Edgar's transition. At Central High School in 1989–90, senior Giddel Padilla scored his thousandth point and translated the instructions of coach Howie Burns to his freshman brother.

Edgar was easy to overlook, even though the skinny six–footer could dunk with authority. He was almost painfully shy, and he had to play in some very long shadows on a great high school team. Giddel was a big–time scorer, and junior point guard Travis Best was flashing talent that ultimately took him to the NBA.

By Edgar's junior year of 1991–92, though, he had emerged as one of the top two or three high school players in Massachusetts. He had quick feet, quicker hands and a fierceness that set him apart. Playing the game with locked–on concentration, he rarely looked as if he were having fun. More serious and intense than his brother, Edgar didn't just want to be the best player that he could. He *needed* to be that player. Basketball seemed uniquely suited to his temperament. He was quick and tough and thoroughly unafraid of the challenges the game presented. *These* were challenges?

That summer of 1992 he earned an invitation to the ABCD Camp[1] in Irvine, California. Padilla said hardly a word to his roommate, an equally shy teenager from Hartford named Marcus Camby. The six–

eleven Camby seemed to sleep all the time when he wasn't playing, so Padilla went down the hall and introduced himself to another Latino guard at the camp, Carmelo Travieso. A little over a year later, in the fall of 1993, all three came to UMass.

Padilla selected UMass for a number of reasons. Watching his sister Millie translate John Calipari's recruiting talk into sign language for his parents, Edgar felt a strong desire to stay close to his family. He realized that he would have the opportunity to play with Giddel, who had landed with the Minutemen as a walk-on. Finally, Edgar knew that UMass was a program on the rise.

In his first two years as a collegian, Edgar Padilla was the third guard on the team. He played mostly at shooting guard, backing up the clutch but controversial Mike Williams. For short stretches he also played the point behind Derek Kellogg. Padilla distinguished himself as a scrapper who played hard every second he was on the floor. Fans at the Mullins Center appreciated his unwavering intensity. Invariably the crowd included a large contingent of Padillas. Millie cheered with a piercing pride. Mariano waved his arms with delight. Milca often saw little of the action; when the games were close she always disappeared to walk around the concession concourse, unable to take the tension. Afterward, she pleaded with Millie for every detail in sign language. What had her baby boy done this time?

Calipari loved Padilla's aggressiveness. Perhaps more than any player he had ever coached, Padilla matched Calipari's ferocity, his iron will, his belief that the game should be played, as Calipari was fond of saying, as if the loser were going to the electric chair. The coach used certain words and phrases to describe his players, terms he would trot out again and again in postgame press conferences. Lou Roe was "a warrior." Donta Bright was "the best finisher in America." Marcus Camby was "a seven-footer with guard skills." The term for Padilla was simple: "fearless."

Padilla's aggressiveness, however, was double-edged. At times he wasn't able to channel it effectively. Offensively he was extremely unselfish, but he sometimes played out of control, forcing passes and turning the ball over far too often for Calipari's tastes. Defensively he overused his quick hands, slapping at the ball and picking up fouls rather than establishing good position with his feet. When UMass played at Maryland in his sophomore year, Padilla tried for a steal seventy-five feet from the basket with one second left before halftime, committing a foul that gave the Terrapins two free throws and momentum going into the locker room. "I wanted to kill him," Calipari said afterward, with only the slightest hint of a smile.

Padilla didn't need anyone coming down hard on him. No one was harder on him than himself. Mistakes got into his head, sometimes affected his play. He knew that he could be his own worst enemy on the court, but he couldn't put his sensitivity on a shelf. It had come with the package, along with the scrappiness.

In March of 1995 at the Palestra in Philadelphia, UMass was playing St. Joseph's in the Atlantic 10 tournament. Late in the first half, Calipari called a play to get the ball in the post to senior star Lou Roe. Padilla saw the St. Joe's zone collapse, giving him an open look for a three–pointer. He didn't hesitate, launching the ball on a parabolic arc toward the hoop. It clanged hard off the rim, and moments later, UMass called a timeout. Calipari bolted out to greet Padilla, his face taut with fury. "What the fuck are you thinking?" Calipari shouted. "You think we called the fucking play for you? What the fuck are you doing?"

As Calipari turned his attention to the huddle, Padilla took a seat on the bench, put a towel over his head and stared at the floor. The cups of water he poured on his face did little to conceal the tears streaming down his cheeks. While the game continued, a tender scene played out on the UMass bench, not the kind of scene you'd expect to see in the hardened world of Division I hoops. Donta Bright, sitting to Padilla's left, gently cupped his teammate's head. From the other side, Marcus Camby draped one long arm around Padilla's shoulder. They had all felt the brunt of Calipari's anger before. They knew. Sure, he was a coaching genius. Yes, he made them far better than they ever thought they could be, made them reach into themselves for more when they didn't think they could muster it. But there were times he just pushed things too far.

Padilla finished his sophomore year as the team's starting shooting guard, playing beside Kellogg after Williams was dismissed from the team for disciplinary reasons. When UMass routed Tulsa in the Sweet Sixteen, Padilla landed hard on an opponent's foot after taking a jump shot. After a day and a half on crutches, he tried to warm up against Oklahoma State in the battle for a Final Four berth, but the inflamed tendons in his left instep were just too painful. Padilla watched the Minutemen go to the locker room with a five–point lead, then self–destruct in the second half. Afterward he sat, like most of his teammates, somber and tearful, in a cramped locker room at the Meadowlands. After a while, he heard the emotion–choked voice of Kellogg piercing the silence: "You younger guys, don't ever forget this. You have to remember how much this hurts, to work so hard for something and to just fall short. Don't ever forget it."

Padilla had always admired Kellogg, a rival from their high school days in Springfield. Kellogg was thought to be too slow and not athletic enough to play at UMass. A Springfield radio commentator had said that Calipari should be fired for wasting taxpayer money on Kellogg's scholarship. But Kellogg proved to be a shrewd player who worked exceptionally hard. Emerging as a three–year starter at the point, he quarterbacked UMass all the way to Number 1. He was neither a penetrator nor a point guard who "created" a great deal, but he almost never made mistakes. What's more, he had that critical point–guard gift of making teammates around him better. That's an intangible thing, but people try to quantify it through a statistic called the assist/turnover ratio. A 2/1 ratio is thought to be the benchmark of effective point guards. Kellogg's was a terrific 2.37/1 as a senior.

Through two years at UMass, Padilla's assist/turnover ratio was a singularly unimpressive 1.23/1. At the end of his sophomore year, he didn't really think of himself as a point guard. In his own mind, his skills were better suited to the shooting–guard role, even though that meant competition with his good friend Carmelo Travieso. Fate pushed him to the point. First, freshman Andre Burks, whose season had dissolved in injury and off–court trouble, decided to transfer to McNeese State. Then Calipari just missed landing a couple of point–guard recruits. Wayne Turner was scooped up by Kentucky, and Terrell Stokes chose Maryland over UMass. Suddenly, Calipari was set to lend the car keys of his offense to Padilla.

The driver was not gushing with confidence at the end of his sophomore year. He didn't know if he could do the job as well as Derek Kellogg. He didn't know if he was vocal enough to be a leader. What he did know was that Calipari, who had played the position himself, was always toughest on his point guards.

In the summer of 1995 Padilla's discomfort was compounded by something he didn't expect: the re–emergence of his brother Giddel.

•

Returning to Puerto Rico as he does every year to play in the rabidly followed "Superior League," Edgar Padilla performed superbly for the

Guaynabo Mets and worked himself into the best shape of his life. His team, however, did not win the Superior League title. Nor did the Morovis Titanes, despite a strong summer from Carmelo Travieso. The championship was won instead by the Bayamón Vaqueros, a squad that featured Giddel Padilla. In the championship game, played before fifteen thousand frenzied fans at the Ruben Rodriquez Coliseum, Giddel pleaded with his coach to insert him in the closing seconds, then responded by tipping home the winning basket.

Giddel had taken a circuitous path since his days of starring for Central High. After a year of prep school, he had gone to Las Vegas in 1991 with stars in his eyes. He dreamed about walking on at UNLV, then the hottest team around. Relishing the high–life adventure of Vegas, he felt ready to leave a home life that had always felt too contained. What he didn't count on was the homesickness that hit him almost immediately. Two months after heading west, he was back, enrolling at the University of Massachusetts.

Joining the Minutemen as a non–scholarship player for the 1992–93 season, Giddel knew it would be a while before he would see significant playing time. First, he had to learn the system of coach John Calipari. The coach's discipline also took some getting used to; Giddel acknowledged that he was late to a couple of practices, that he "missed a few things." Still, in his mind, he could play with any of the UMass guards. He thought he deserved more of a chance. In quiet moments of doubt he wondered about the motivation of the UMass coaching staff in giving him a spot on the roster. Were they just trying to lure Edgar, who was then a hotly recruited high school senior? Giddel buried those thoughts when Calipari told him he would have a chance to compete for more playing time the following season.

In 1993–94, Edgar arrived as a scholarship guard, set to join Giddel on the Minutemen. It was the first time the brothers had played together since Edgar's freshman year at Central High. Edgar was excited: Giddel had always paved the way for him in the past. The huge adjustment to college basketball was going to be so much easier.

A couple of weeks into practice, Giddel quit. The decision had nothing to do with competition from Edgar, he insisted. He felt betrayed by Calipari. He wasn't getting a chance. Sure, there was a logjam of guard talent—juniors Derek Kellogg and Mike Williams and a pair of freshmen, his brother and Carmelo Travieso—but Giddel felt that he wasn't even getting a look in practice. In drills, he was always the fifth guard, the one who sat on the sidelines. "I felt like Calipari lied to me," Giddel said later, "like I couldn't trust him." So Giddel took off once again, moving in with his aunt in the mountains of Puerto Rico. Stunned, Edgar was left to fend for himself.

"Even Giddel says it was a mistake now," sister Millie said years later. "But he was unhappy. No matter what decision my brothers make, I stay behind them. I remember when we made a promise that we would always stick together. Nobody will break us up."

In time Giddel returned, homesick once more and convinced that his college education was too important to waste. Uncomfortable at first, he sat in the stands at the Mullins Center with his mother, father and sister, watching the Minutemen rise all the way to Number 1. "I was more a fan of Edgar," he says, "not of the team."

Life changed, though, when he hit that championship–winning shot in the summer of 1995. For a few days he was the toast of Bayamón. He flashed back to those early days of shooting a ball into a paint can, winning the MVP in the twelve–and–under Pan–American tournament, starring at Central High School. The game had come alive for him yet again. Now twenty–two years old and about to begin his senior year of college, he wanted to come back and play one more time—even if it meant sitting on the bench all year long. At Giddel's request, Edgar went in to talk to John Calipari. "My older brother," he said slowly, "has grown up."

In truth, Edgar had some mixed feelings about playing with his brother once again after all these years. On the one hand, he knew that it would make his family happy. Everyone had moved to Amherst by now to be closer together. Mariano was working as a dental technician, thanks to Millie's determined efforts. The director of a local dental lab had said to her one day, "I'm tired of your calling all the time, Millie. Bring him in for two hours, and we'll see what he can do. And don't be late—I know how you people are." When Millie returned to the lab two hours after dropping Mariano off, she was greeted with a huge smile: "Your father is great. We want him to stay for the whole day." Millie had also helped to get Milca a job as a chambermaid at the Howard Johnson's in Hadley, sometimes cleaning the rooms of basketball teams in town to take on the Minutemen. Millie, now twenty–four, was married and back in school, studying communication disorders. They all wanted to see the family reunited one more time around basketball, the centerpiece of the Padilla clan for many years.

Deep down, Edgar also felt that he owed something to Giddel. His older brother, after all, had taught him the game. Giddel had translated for him in Springfield and encouraged him to come to UMass. And truly, it had always been Edgar's dream to play in the same backcourt as his brother.

Still, Edgar knew it could be an awkward situation. Already he was feeling a tremendous sense of pressure about taking over the point–guard position. The last thing he needed was to be his brother's keeper. What's more, the tables had turned since they last played together six years ago at Central. Edgar would be starting for a nationally ranked program, while Giddel would be buried on the bench. On October 12, toward the end of the team's designated preseason gathering with the media, Edgar sat alone at a table on the third floor of the Mullins Center. Fielding a question about whether it was awkward to eclipse his older brother as a star, Edgar stared to the side for several seconds. "It's not," he began. His voice trailed into silence. Turning to look at a window overlooking the basketball court, his determined brown eyes filled with water.

•

Playing their first exhibition game on November 7 against a Russian team called Dinamo, the Minutemen looked sluggish. The 105–75 victory sounded impressive, until you factored in the night before, when Dinamo lost by fifty–nine points to a University of Rhode Island team coming off a 7–20 season. Disjointed on offense, UMass was hurt by Edgar Padilla's six turnovers. Defensively, the Minutemen allowed Dinamo to connect on fourteen of thirty three–pointers, surrendering one uncontested shot after another to a team that was utterly devoid of quickness.

Surely, though, these were just some first–game jitters. UMass had ten days before the second and final exhibition game against Converse. The real season didn't open until the end of the month. There was still time. When Calipari traveled to Philadelphia on November 9 for Atlantic 10 Media Day and described "a crisis within the UMass basketball program," he was just using the usual coach–speak hyperbole, wasn't he? A crisis?

The next week, UMass took the floor against Converse. The team with the sneaker–company sponsor wasn't really a team in the true sense; it was a barnstorming collection of former college players. Assembled in makeshift fashion in November, they only practiced a couple of times. After a few weeks they would disband completely, once they had served their function: providing some "good runs" for college teams getting ready for their seasons.

The Converse team that showed up at the Mullins Center on Friday night, November 17, had some decent talent. There were several former UMass foes from Atlantic 10 competition: Rick Brunson of archrival Temple, Bernard Blunt of St. Joseph's and Jamal Phillips of Rutgers. The point guard was none other than Derek Kellogg, now working for the state treasurer in Boston.

A team with enough talent to push UMass, Converse was expected to force the Minutemen to work on defense and execute some decent plays in their halfcourt offense. They knew they would have to fight for rebounds and loose balls. It was not expected to be easy. Then again, it was not expected to be that hard. The Minutemen always won at home—they were 30–1 in the three–year–old Mullins Center, and they certainly had never lost an exhibition game there. Further, they had more talent and better size than Converse. They had been practicing together for more than a month. Converse's readiness appeared to be defined by Brunson, who showed up behind the bench just seconds before tipoff wearing street clothes and carrying his gym bag.

The crowd, including regulars Mariano and Milca Padilla, gathered on a chilly evening. They were getting ready to dive into another winter of UMass hoops. They were getting ready for the show.

The show stunk. UMass, not Converse, looked like the team with no practice under its belt. The offense flowed like sludge. Edgar Padilla seemed hesitant running the team. He was not penetrating, nor passing the ball to teammates in a position where they could do anything with it. When he did try to make plays, he forced the action, leaving his feet on a couple of occasions with no real sense of what he was going to do. Defensively, he was careless. With the team's shortage of guards, he knew that he couldn't afford foul trouble—he had to find a way to be both aggressive and in control—but on this night he was committing all kinds of Calipari sins: allowing his man to get into the lane, forfeiting good position in a quest for steals, playing defense with his hands instead of his feet.

With 4:49 left in the game and UMass somehow down by ten, Padilla reached in yet again, picking up his fifth and final foul. The team ran to the bench for the thirty–second break allowed when someone fouls out—running because Calipari had said you always ran as a matter of pride. Edgar Padilla, the best conditioned and most dedi-

*Playing point guard under John Calipari could be a crucible, as Edgar Padilla would learn in the 1995-96 season. (Photo by Kevin Gutting)*

cated athlete on the team, walked with his head down. Taking a seat on the end of the bench a couple of chairs away from Giddel, who had not taken off his warmups all night, Edgar tugged the towel hard over his head.

He watched Converse close out the win with Kellogg running the point. In some ways that made the tough night even tougher. Kellogg was the symbol of how to do it right. The Minutemen had always overachieved with Kellogg at the helm. Now, with Padilla in charge, they were underachieving. They were, for the first time in Calipari's eight years as coach, far less than the sum of their parts. As the final seconds ticked down, Padilla sat somberly with these statistics to think about: five points, five assists, four turnovers, five fouls. Worst of all: Converse 94, UMass 89. When a somber group of Minutemen got to the locker room, the first words they heard from Calipari were these: "Maybe, if we're lucky, we'll get to the NIT."

The postgame press conference at UMass takes place in the Green Room just west of the parquet basketball floor. Representatives of the visiting team come in, answer a few questions, then yield the floor to the Minutemen. Walking into the Green Room together that night were the unlikely bedfellows Kellogg and Brunson, longtime point–guard adversaries in heated UMass–Temple games.

Asked to assess UMass's problems, Brunson was blunt: "They need a leader."

Kellogg was more diplomatic. "Talent–wise, they're as good as anybody we played last year, besides maybe a couple of teams at the top of the ladder," he said. "They were just a little out of sync tonight. I think with a little bit of leadership, getting people in the right spots at the right time, and a little bit of continuity, they're going to be right up there. It might take a little longer, because they don't have any seniors at guard, but I would say that by the time the tournament comes around, they're going to be one of the top teams in the country."

Kellogg wanted his words to be true. He wanted to show support to the program in which he had invested so much of his soul for the past four years. Right now, though, he knew he had a mission to perform. As Converse's portion of the press conference concluded, he excused himself and walked back to his old haunts in the UMass locker room. There, as expected, he found Edgar Padilla sitting alone.

Meanwhile, a dour–looking John Calipari had stepped behind the podium and opened with a statement: "I think everybody will start believing me when I say we've got a ways to go. The biggest thing that I was disappointed in is we've built a program based on an aggressive way of playing basketball, an all–out, everything–you–have, leave–it–on–the–floor type of game. And we're just not doing that now."

Asked specifically about Edgar Padilla and the point–guard situation, Calipari said, "We're going to be all right. The challenge of coaching every year is taking a team and figuring out how you're going to win. Leadership doesn't have to come from the quarterback, but someone has to step up and take over the team. The only way you do that is if you're one of those guys who is a consistent performer, and you're not playing with fear. Let me put it this way. If you're in the army, and your general says, 'Let's go get 'em,' and when he turns around and starts walking you see brown on his butt, you get a little worried, like we must be in trouble here. That's part of being a leader, having the courage to go make plays and not be afraid to make mistakes. We're still trying to find that."

Sure, he later said that Padilla was not the sole reason the team was playing poorly. Padilla "has the capability and the potential to be a terrific point guard," he stated. But for all of Calipari's usual polish and masterful stroking of the media, he had betrayed his darker thoughts. Maybe Edgar Padilla wasn't so fearless after all.

Calipari was about to go home and watch the tape of the Converse game until 2:30 in the morning with first–year assistant coach Ed Schilling ("What did I get myself into?" Schilling admitted thinking a few months later). But first Calipari stared down at the lectern, then raised himself up with a look of defiance. "We've got our work cut out for us, and as a coach, I've got my work cut out for me," he said. "I accept the challenge. This is not going to be easy. But I will say, 'We will win. We will win!' I told the guys that. I'll settle for nothing less than that."

The season was set to begin in just eleven days. The Minutemen would be taking on top–ranked Kentucky—a team whose coach knew a thing or two about UMass basketball.

# 2: "BE REASONABLE: DO IT MY WAY"

March 14, 1970

New York City

R ick Pitino was seventeen years old and absolutely intoxicated with possibility. He was standing at Madison Square Garden, reveling at the sight of intense, hotly competitive college basketball, the kind of thing that made his blood race. An upstart University of Massachusetts team was giving the eighth–ranked Marquette Warriors everything they could handle in the NIT. Pitino sensed the terrific energy from the streams of UMass fans who had come down from Amherst to cheer on their team. He gawked at the little–known sophomore star of UMass, a skinny kid named Julius Erving. And he sat mesmerized by the fiery focus of Jack Leaman: a coach whose penchant for structure and control jarred with Pitino's visions, but someone who clearly loved the game every bit as much as he did.

That very night, standing on the hallowed floor of the Garden, Pitino signed his national letter of intent to come to UMass. He imagined himself as the team's point guard, leading the school to the bigtime.

In a certain sense, that's exactly what happened—just not in the way that Pitino had intended.

•

Jack Leaman was born in Cambridge, Massachusetts, in 1932. He loved all sports, but none more than basketball. At the Huntington Avenue YMCA, he learned to work "hahd" and play with "haht." After a couple of years in the army during the Korean War, he became the first of his family to set foot in a college when he enrolled at Boston University in the fall of 1955.

In an era when freshmen were still ineligible to play varsity, the skinny point guard with the jet–black crew cut made a name for himself on the freshman team. Against Wentworth Institute, the BU Terriers were hit so hard by foul trouble that they had only two players on the court for overtime. But no one could take the ball away from Leaman. When they fouled him, he sank free throw after free throw. Improbably, BU won, playing two on five.

Leaman spent his next three years under the tyrannical tutelage of Matt Zunic. An imposing, bespectacled man of six–four, Zunic had played for Red Auerbach in the dawn of the NBA. As a coach he was Bobby Knight before his time, a hot–headed genius. He was known to hurl clipboards and chairs on the court. Once, by his own admission, he "went berserk" at Providence and needed a police escort to leave the building. His authority over his players was absolute, defined by the sign on his desk—"Be reasonable: Do it my way."

Leaman did just that. He was the consummate point guard, the coach out on the floor, running Zunic's set plays every time downcourt. As a senior he led BU to its first–ever NCAA tournament in the winter of 1959 (the same basketball season when John Calipari was born). The Terriers won a couple of games to advance to what would now be called the "Elite Eight," where they lost a tough 86–82 decision to West Virginia, a squad that was led by thirty–three points from Jerry West. That night, after the game, players on both teams went out bowling together.

The loss to West Virginia marked Boston University's last appearance in the NCAA tournament for twenty–four years. It also marked the last game for Zunic as coach of the Terriers; a few months later he accepted an offer to coach at the University of Massachusetts. It was also the end of the road for Leaman, who finished his career as the third leading scorer in school history. After getting his Master's Degree in counseling and then coaching for a year at little Millis High School, he came to Amherst at age twenty–nine to be Zunic's lone assistant coach.

The UMass that greeted Leaman in the fall of 1961 was brimming with optimism. The buoyancy of the fifties still ruled the day. No one knew about Vietnam. Students were proud to attend the state university of Massachusetts, a commonwealth that had just offered up to the country a president who embodied the vigor and hope of the age. Life was simple. Freshmen wore beanies. Men were not allowed in women's dorms after curfew. Cigarette advertisements in the *Massachusetts Daily Collegian* compared bird–watching to girl–watching. A picture in the fraternity section of the yearbook carried the caption, "Oh Joe, you stinker you." Sports teams were known unapologetically as the Redmen, though the skin of almost all of the 7,019 students enrolled that fall was some shade of white.[1]

Rising amid the corn fields and apple orchards of Amherst, UMass had started nearly a century before as a land–grant institution known as Massachusetts Agricultural College. Even while Emily Dickinson remained secluded in her father's house two miles away, fifty–six students arrived as the pioneer class in the fall of 1867. "Mass Aggie" became Massachusetts State College in 1931 and the University of Massachusetts in 1947. Now, fourteen years later, many people within the state still derided the school as "Cow College." Indeed, the campus was a full twenty miles from a legitimate city. That city was Springfield, a still–thriving manufacturing mecca that was known as the birthplace of basketball. It was here that James Naismith, hoping to provide some winter exercise for his students, first hung his peach baskets at the YMCA in 1891.

When Jack Leaman arrived, basketball in western Massachusetts was still a long way from the bigtime. UMass played its home games in the Curry Hicks Cage, a dingy pit in the center of campus that had opened in 1931. The basketball court was laid out atop a dirt floor, meaning that balls that carried out of bounds often had to be wiped clean by officials. On more than one occasion games had to be delayed when squirrels scurried onto the court. The glass roof sometimes cooked courtside temperatures to one hundred degrees. Leaks often caused puddles, once forcing cancellation of a game.

In that first 1961–62 season, Leaman witnessed what he would forever call "the greatest coaching job I have ever seen."

To be sure, Matt Zunic didn't have much to work with. Like its rivals in the Yankee Conference, UMass relied primarily on homegrown talent, the specter of national recruiting and Nike camps a generation away. The ragtag Redmen included a platoon of gawky six–eight centers: Charlie Fohlin, a bespectacled engineering student from Watertown who used to keep the light on in the back of the bus while hovering over ponderous texts; and Don Black from Athol, who brought his guitar on the road and composed corny songs for his wife. The team had exactly one black player, five–eight sparkplug Peter Bernard from Brockton. (Zunic recalls being called a "nigger lover" by some of the old–timers in Amherst.) The point guard, in the tradition of Leaman, was a tough little competitor from Pittsfield named Mike Mole.

*Matt Zunic (back row, far right) cracked the whip with the 1961-62 Redmen, leading them all the way to the NCAA tournament. UMass wouldn't return for 30 years. (Photo courtesy of UMass Special Collections and Archives)*

Zunic drilled this team relentlessly. During winter break they endured triple sessions, dummying his patterned plays until they dropped and forever refining the nuances of his "Chinese Defense," a forerunner of today's matchup zones. Nothing short of maximum effort was acceptable. After one loss, the Redmen bused home in stony silence, arriving at the Cage at two o'clock in the morning, only to have Zunic lead them through a loose–ball drill, making his players dive on the hard floor over and over again.

They were a malleable crew, and Zunic was ready to nail them at every opportunity. As Fohlin recalls, "He would just push you right to your ultimate all the time."

Traditionally, UMass's arch–rival Connecticut won the Yankee Conference title, earning the league's automatic bid to the NCAA tournament, where the Huskies almost always fell in the first round. In 1961–62, the Redmen did lose to Connecticut both at home and at a building known as "the Torture Chamber" in Storrs, where UMass had not won in twenty–seven years. This, however, was a year in which the

Huskies were vulnerable, picking up three league losses. Thus, UMass could win its first–ever Yankee Conference title with a victory in the season finale against New Hampshire, a team the Redmen had defeated by just two points earlier in the year. A close game was expected.

It never happened. Mole stole the ball off the opening tap and went in for a layup. The rout was on. In the delirium, Zunic even let go of the reins. The *Massachusetts Daily Collegian* reported that reserve guard Cliff Bullock sank "an amazing hook shot from deep in the corner." When the final buzzer sounded, the Redmen had set a school scoring record with a 109–62 victory. The same players who sometimes hated Zunic carried him off the floor.

From his relatively anonymous post of assistant coach, Jack Leaman looked on with awe. Zunic, earning a modest yearly salary of $10,010, had once again led an ordinary group of Massachusetts kids to the NCAA tournament, just as he had three years ago at BU during Leaman's senior year. Even after the Redmen upheld the Yankee Conference tradition of losing in the first round—falling by twenty to a New York University squad that included future NBA players Barry Kramer and Harold (Happy) Hairston—Leaman felt that the future stretched out before him. He was getting the best coaching education he could imagine.

His mentor's coaching days at UMass, however, were numbered. After a 12–12 season the following year, Zunic was fired by athletic director Warren McGuirk, who cited Zunic's petulant behavior toward officials and opposing crowds. Some teams, he claimed, were threatening not to play UMass unless there was a coaching change. Zunic called the charge ridiculous, and said that the firing stemmed from a personality conflict with McGuirk. Some people felt that McGuirk, a big supporter of football, had become jealous of the basketball team's success, limiting Zunic's recruiting budget to a paltry $200.

Leaman stayed on as assistant for three years under the new head coach, Johnny Orr. Employing a more free–wheeling style than his predecessor, Orr enjoyed modest success—a 39–33 record, but no Yankee Conference titles. He was a young, ambitious coach who was excited by the diagrams of a new arena that promised a replacement for the quirky but crumbling Curry Hicks Cage. When he saw no progress on those plans, he left in the spring of 1966.

Orr's departure opened the door for Jack Leaman, who ushered in the first golden age of basketball at the University of Massachusetts.

At thirty-three, Leaman was a trim man with close-cropped black hair, penetrating eyes, and a gap in his teeth from his aggressive days as an athlete. There was a slightly high-pitched and lisped quality to his thick Boston accent, but his air of authority was undeniable. Photos from his coaching days almost invariably show a furrowed brow, an intense glare, a sense of mission.

Right from the start it was clear that Leaman was a disciple of Matt Zunic. Discipline ruled.

On the first day of school in that fall of 1966 freshman Ray Ellerbrook arrived at Hills North, a new dormitory with hideous blue tile-on-brick design. Hot after a five-hour drive from Hawthorn, New Jersey, Ellerbrook stepped out of the car with his shirt untucked, ready to dive into his new life. Before he could even say farewell to his parents, he was intercepted by Leaman. "Young man," Leaman started, his eyes boring in on their target, "pride is something our basketball team is built on. My basketball players keep their shirts tucked in, because if you have your shirt out, that means you don't have pride in your appearance. You will have your shirt tucked in every time you are on this campus. That's what you will do. If you don't, you can get back in the car and go home."

Flabbergasted, Ellerbrook tucked in his shirt. "Back then," Ellerbrook reflected almost thirty years later, "you just said, 'Yes, sir,' and you did it."

If players resented Leaman's intrusion into their lives, they didn't show it. They seemed to recognize that in his gruff way, he cared a lot. If there were a break-up with a girlfriend or some health problems back home, Leaman was there in the cafeteria, an extra glass of iced tea on his tray. "We were Jack's kids," recalls Ellerbrook. "He had a daughter, but we were his sons. He genuinely cared about us. He told my parents that I was going to get a degree, and he meant it. He kicked my ass up and down campus. Anything he had to do to help me make progress, he did."

On the court he was exacting, a stickler for conditioning and hard-nosed, relentless defense. Like Zunic, he believed in The System. In practice the Redmen forever fine-tuned the plays, precise patterns of player and ball movement with names like "Iowa State," and "California Reverse Action." If even a tiny thing was off—a cut that was not sharp enough, a pass that arrived a hair late—Leaman blasted out his favorite dictum: "Goddammit, you play the way you practice!"

Evidently they practiced pretty well. In short order Leaman's Redmen upstaged UConn as the dominant team in the Yankee Conference. They won or shared the league title in eight of Leaman's first ten years, before the team shifted into a new conference in 1976. In crusty New England, Leaman's name stood for coaching excellence. "Jackie was the most professional coach in New England," says Jack Donahue, who coached at Holy Cross in 1965–72, before becoming the longtime coach of the Canadian national team. "He was the guy who did the most with the least. Those first couple of years he didn't have anybody who could bounce a ball. They were the only team that beat us that we didn't think was better than us."

On the national stage Leaman's success remained relatively obscure. The NCAA had taken away the automatic bid for the Yankee Conference in the 1967–68 season, the very year Leaman won his first title. (Privately, Leaman blamed UConn athletic director J.O. Christianson, who wielded some significant clout with the NCAA. In Leaman's eyes, Christianson stopped fighting for the league once the Redmen had eclipsed the Huskies as the YC's premier team.) Still, in the little world of Yankee Conference basketball, the Redmen ruled. The guy Matt Zunic called "Little Man" was well on his way to becoming the school's all-time winningest coach.

In 1969 there was considerable excitement on campus when the basketball season approached. Word was out that a skinny sophomore who had excelled on the freshman team might help the varsity right away. An overflow crowd lined up early to cram into the Curry Hicks Cage for the opener against Providence, regarded as perhaps the best team in New England.

Julius Erving did not disappoint. The quiet kid with the big Afro and the white canvas Chuck Taylor hightops scored twenty–four of his twenty–seven points in the second half as UMass rallied for a 90–85 victory. For good measure, Erving also pulled down twenty–eight rebounds, setting a school record the first time he took the floor.

When Eunice Cole, wife of *Daily Hampshire Gazette* sports editor Milton Cole, heard the name of the new star, she instantly thought of her teenage daughter Marjorie. "Oh good," she said, "a nice Jewish boy from Long Island."

Cole's mistake was understandable. Erving had arrived at UMass with little fanfare. At Roosevelt High School, he had been a slight six–three guard with no outside shot. (At UMass he grew to six–six–and–a–half, leading Leaman to crow in later years, "Now *that's* coaching!")

No one expected big things. "He wasn't a blue–chipper," recalled *Sports Illustrated*'s Peter Carry in a 1987 cover story commemorating Dr. J's farewell season in the NBA. "That's why he ended up at the University of Massachusetts—you remember the awesome Yankee Conference." Actually Erving had a link to UMass. His high school coach Ray Wilson had played for Matt Zunic and with Jack Leaman at Boston University. There was a soft–spoken eloquence about Wilson that Erving admired and tried to emulate. Erving's dad, Julius Winfield Erving Sr., had left the family when his son was just five years old, and six years later was killed in a car accident. Wilson became a father figure, a man Erving did not want to disappoint. Once Erving missed a bus to a game and arrived late by car. He willingly sat out and cheered on his teammates. In practice the next day he quietly did the extra running for punishment. Only later did Wilson find out that Erving had missed the bus because he had taken the time to help a teacher whose car was stuck on the side of the road. "It was obvious that he was a coach's dream," Wilson said. "I always thought he'd never be a great player because he didn't have that mean streak Matt (Zunic) always used to talk about. Shows you how little I know."

At Wilson's suggestion Erving took a visit to UMass and met with Jack Leaman. A year later he enrolled, joining Wilson's daughter Carmen and singer Natalie Cole in the class of 1972. The following year, with Erving eligible to play varsity, the rest of the Wilson family moved to Amherst, Ray having accepted Leaman's offer to join the staff as assistant coach and chief recruiter.

They arrived at a burgeoning college campus. The student body was growing by almost two thousand a year. Scaffolding and cranes dominated the landscape. A twenty–six–story tower library was under construction. High–rise dormitories sprouted out of pasture land on the southwest part of campus, while bell–bottomed students were huddled in "temporary" triples.

The place swirled with change. Hair was long. Music was loud. Drug use was rampant. The 1971 UMass yearbook devoted a full ten pages to a celebration of alcohol and marijuana, with pictures of kegs and bongs and rolling paper.

The war in Vietnam was a part of every day of campus life. Stories abounded of students who had come home from Southeast Asia in wheelchairs or body bags. On November 17, 1969, just fifteen days before Erving's varsity debut against Providence, eight busloads of UMass students joined a half–million angry idealists at the moratorium march in Washington. Protests abounded that winter when groups like Dow Chemical (makers of napalm), Honeywell (makers of fragmentation bombs) and the Army Material Command (coordinators of chemical and biological warfare research) came to campus to recruit. In February, former vice president Hubert Humphrey was booed off stage at the Cage and pelted with marshmallows and jelly beans when he started talking about the Chicago Seven trial.

Race relations were strained. This was the state university of Massachusetts, a liberal bastion except when it came to skin color. Racially polarized Boston was not viewed as the cradle of liberty by black folks. The Red Sox had a racist reputation, having been the last Major League team to integrate, twelve full years after Jackie Robinson broke the color line in Brooklyn. A tense drama played out on the overwhelmingly white UMass campus in that winter of 1969–70. Black students and white members of the Kappa Sigma fraternity fought viciously one night, resulting in the occupation of the Mills House dormitory and demands for a black cultural center on campus.

Amid all this turmoil, Jack Leaman's basketball team became an oasis. Wanting to assure themselves one of the 4,200 spots in the musty Cage, students started lining up at four o'clock for eight o'clock games. Inside, the atmosphere was electric. Fans chanted and stomped, unleashing all their pent–up steam. In that winter of so much discontent there was something ironic about all this support for a clean–cut basketball team playing for an authoritarian coach, but people needed to believe in something. And they had never seen anything like Julius Erving.

They called him Julie back then, Julie the jumping–jack. He literally brought the game to a new level. Ellerbrook recalls watching Erving stand beneath a basket, a ball smothered in each of his enormous hands. Up he went, tomahawking first one ball and then the other through the cylinder, a wild windmill of power that sent the balls thudding onto the hardwood and the rim rattling while Erving quietly, almost innocently, touched down. An NCAA rule prohibiting dunking during games (mercifully rescinded in 1976–77) denied fans some of the aerial show, but even Erving's rebounding could bring gasps. Sometimes he snatched the ball above the rim with just one hand. "Julius didn't have to box out," Ellerbrook recalls. "He was up where no one could go."

It is difficult perhaps to appreciate just how revolutionary he was. Basketball was still played on the floor, mapped out by blackboard

*Dr. J before he was Dr. J. (Photo courtesy of UMass Media Relations)*

barons like Leaman. It was long before the age of the Air Jordan, when jumping would become that most deified of athletic skills. In a dark and dreary gym in New England, fans were part of a wonderful little secret. There was no ESPN, no *USA Today*. Boston papers never deigned to make the two–hour drive to Amherst to cover the games, once referring in passing to "Julius Irving." But without the eyes of the wide world upon him, Erving was quietly displaying an in–the–air artistry that would transform the game of basketball.

He had a seriousness of purpose, a focus that never wavered. As someone who had known considerable loss—the death of his father, and then, during his freshman year at UMass, the sudden death of his younger brother, Marvin, from lupus—Erving was absolutely determined to make something of himself. The lone black player on the team, he opted not to partake in the political whirlwinds, though he was often approached by campus leaders who hoped he'd lend his name to their cause. Most of all he feared distraction. "By getting too involved in something outside of my primary reasons for being here, my studies and basketball, I might be spreading myself too thin," he said in a *Collegian* profile that winter. "But if I felt strongly enough about that something, I would have to be open about it, taking into consideration its after–effects."

The after–effects of his appearance on a basketball court were stunning. Even as he began attracting defenses designed specifically to stop him, he displayed a night–in and night–out excellence that has rarely, if ever, been duplicated in college basketball. He recorded double–figure points and double–figure rebounds every game that year. During one stretch of ten games he scored more than twenty points and pulled down more than twenty rebounds every single time. Leaman unleashed Erving against his alma mater, and he lit up the Boston University Terriers for twenty–nine points in the first half alone. In the regular–season finale at New Hampshire, Erving capped off the year with thirty–seven points and twenty–five rebounds in a 92–75 win. When the Redmen arrived back on campus in the wee hours of a Tuesday morning, a crowd of students was there to cheer.

The Redmen ended the year with ten straight wins. They set a school record with eighteen victories. They were tops in the Yankee Conference, the Number 1 team in New England. In an article in the *Collegian*, New England's Coach of the Year Jack Leaman saluted his players as "the greatest team UMass has ever had."

Their reward was a bid to the National Invitational Tournament, the second post–season appearance in school history.

Today the NIT is a poor sister to the NCAA, a tournament for second–tier teams that don't make the field of sixty–four. Back then this was not the case. The NCAA field of twenty–five was confined to nine independent teams and one squad apiece from sixteen major conferences. Some top teams even bypassed NCAA bids to play in the NIT at Madison Square Garden. In fact, UMass's first–round opponent, the eighth–ranked Marquette Warriors, had picked the NIT over a first–round NCAA game in Fort Worth, Texas.

To be sure, the NIT was a big deal at UMass. The Redmen were going to play mighty Marquette on the sporting world's grandest stage in a national tournament. The team was the talk of the campus. On Friday the 13th, the day before the game, the front page of the *Collegian* was all but filled with a huge team photo beneath the headline "On to the NIT." After attending morning classes, the Redmen left at one o'clock, sent off by a crowd cheering through snowflakes and a bitter wind. The next day, students followed in a rip–roaring caravan of buses, going first to a party at the Ivy Room at the Statler Hilton and then descending, four thousand strong, upon the Garden.

UMass had never before played a team like Marquette. A national power, the Warriors were coached by the famed Al McGuire. They were seeded first and expected to dominate the field. If the Redmen had the best player in Erving, Marquette had about the next best eight, led by point guard Dean (The Dream) Meminger.

The Redmen played hard, winning over the Garden crowd. They trailed by just three points in the closing minutes, but ultimately fell, 62–55. *The New York Times* account of the game credited UMass for its "surprisingly persistent resistance."

Afterward, the two coaches stood before a horde of media. McGuire shook his head and then spoke: "We were outplayed, we were outhustled and I was thoroughly outcoached. You want to know something about basketball? Talk to this guy." Then he walked away, leaving a wide–eyed Jack Leaman before a small forest of microphones.

UMass, that most innocent of regional basketball programs, was knocking at the door of national acceptance. Truly, there was no finer moment in the school's athletic history. And on this evening, so charged with possibility, Rick Pitino signed on the dotted line.

•

Pitino became an instant darling on campus. Life seemed charged around him. Handsome and confident, he had a way of presenting himself that was at once forceful and sincere. He quickly joined the Lambda Chi fraternity and became its "Social Chairman," charged with getting pretty sorority sisters to the parties. Frankly, who could resist Slick Rick? He was so charming, so cool, such a marvelous dancer.

Off the dance floor, he had some pretty good moves as well. Early in his first semester he took a walk down to a sub shop in Amherst with Peter Trow, a basketball player who would be his longtime roommate. The two of them started playing pool. Trow recalls that Pitino played with zest, but without much success through a couple of games. Sounding innocent, he suggested they play for money. Then he ran the table.

"Rick's a great guy," Trow said more than twenty–five years later, "but he was, and still is, pathologically addicted to competition."

He had to win at pool. He had to win at whist. Most of all, of course, he had to win at basketball.

That first winter Pitino got a mouth–watering taste of what could be. When he arrived at the Curry Hicks Cage on raw winter mid–afternoons, the student line for tickets had already started to form. By the six o'clock tipoff of the freshmen games, the house was jammed. Pitino was, in essence, the warm–up act for Dr. J. A flashy ballhandler, he teamed with future NBA player Al Skinner to spark the freshmen to an 18–1 record. After his games, Pitino took some of the shortest showers in history, threw on his clothes and raced back to the court to watch the wonder of Julius.

Dr. J swooped and soared and swatted the Redmen to a best–ever 23–3 regular season. He averaged 26.9 points and 19.5 rebounds. In the final game at the Cage he led UMass to a fifteen–point victory over the toughest team on its schedule, Syracuse, with a stunning statistical line of thirty–six points and thirty–two rebounds. "Erving simply did everything," wrote a *Collegian* staffer, "and did it to perfection." Afterward, UMass fans cut down the nets as if the team had won the national championship.

Pitino watched with awe. Next year, Erving would be a senior. Next year, Pitino felt sure, he would be the point guard. He would run the show.

First, though, there was another trip to the NIT for Pitino to watch. The Redmen again drew a national power in the opening round. This time it was North Carolina. The Tar Heels were coached by Dean Smith, who had taken over the program in 1961, the same year Jack Leaman had arrived as an assistant at UMass. Finishing first in the mighty Atlantic Coast Conference with a 22–5 record, the Tar Heels lost to South Carolina at the buzzer in the finals of the ACC tournament. That loss cost them a trip to the NCAA tournament, which then invited only one team from any conference, no matter how formidable. Hence, an angry Carolina team arrived in New York for the NIT, determined to mop up.

Deep down, Jack Leaman knew that he was overmatched. Still, with Julius Erving on your roster, who knew? Stranger things have happened.

They didn't happen that night. Carolina's fullcourt pressure hounded UMass from the opening tap. Trying to do it all, Erving picked up four fouls in the first half, which ended with the Redmen hanging by a thread, down by fourteen. He fouled out four minutes into the second half, finishing with thirteen points and nine rebounds—the only time in his collegiate career when he didn't record a "double–double." The final score of 90–49 barely described the humiliation. According to *The New York Times* account of the game, which referred to the UMass coach as Jack Leamons, "Massachusetts didn't belong on the same court as North Carolina."

As Leaman flew out to Houston for the NCAA convention, though, it was hard to avoid feeling optimistic. Next year could put UMass over the top. Four starters were returning. As a senior Erving could be the best player in the country. Some fine talent was coming up from the 18–1 freshman team, people like Skinner and Pitino. Next year there would be no limits. The NCAA tournament beckoned. School administrators might finally get going on that new arena. The bigtime might finally arrive.

Leaman was just digging in at the convention—picking the brains of fellow coaches, taking his usual sheaf of notes, getting ready to watch gentleman John Wooden's UCLA team win its fifth straight NCAA title—when the phone rang. It was Ray Wilson, his assistant coach.

"I've got some bad news for you, Jack," he said.

"What," Leaman said, laughing, "did my wife leave me?"

"Worse," said Wilson. "Julius is leaving."

The American Basketball Association had been in existence for four years. It tried to give the NBA a run for its money with a couple of gimmicks that made purists cringe: a red, white and blue basketball and the equally outrageous idea of a three–point shot. Team owners knew that to really compete, though, it was important to go beyond a few maverick ideas. They needed to break the NBA's hold on quality players. One way to do that was to sign underclassmen before they became eligible for the NBA draft. That winter they went after several talented youngsters, some of whom were classified as "hardship cases" because of their meager financial situations. The policy had staunch critics. Outraged NBA officials said that the upstart league was exploiting kids, tempting them out of their college education.

Erving was offered $500,000 over three years by the Virginia Squires. The temptation was enormous. He had never known money. His family had suffered a great deal. Still, he had promised his mother that he would get his college degree. When she heard his decision to sign, she cried.

Leaman said he had no bitterness toward Erving—he knew that the contract would make him comfortable. "That's what a coach hopes for, I guess, to see his kids become secure," Leaman said in the *Collegian*. "If he's set for life then that's good for him. It's just such a disappointing and disgusting thing to see pro people tempt a 20–year–old like this."

UMass athletic director Warren McGuirk added, "An opportunity for security comes only once in life, and maybe this is his. It sickens me, though, to think of the implications things like this have for college athletics."

•

Julius Erving would keep his promise to his mother and get his college degree (finishing in 1986), but his departure signaled a major change in college basketball. The game was becoming a business. A certain innocence had been lost.

If the modern era of college basketball was hinted at by Erving's departure, it was embodied even more by the arrival of Rick Pitino. He brought flash and fire to the usually controlled UMass game. He was a modern point guard, who loved to dribble the ball through his legs and flip passes behind his back—moves that had not yet made it out to western Massachusetts. A skinny six–footer, he loved nothing more than to take the ball to the hoop against the big boys. The crowd loved him.

He drove Leaman crazy. The coach had cultivated a system, and dammit, it worked. Good fundamental basketball was played in the halfcourt. It involved a well orchestrated series of cuts and picks. The point guard set the offense. He didn't force it. He sacrificed his own game for that of the team.

The clashes were fierce. Pitino would enter the game with instructions to run the offense. He'd stand at the top of the key, directing traffic, calling the play. Then, out of the corner of his eye, he'd see a seam in the defense. Instantly he'd dart like a piranha, knifing, twisting, flicking up some little reverse or whipping the ball across the lane to a cutting teammate. There would be some electrifying baskets, and, too, some ugly turnovers. Glaring, Leaman would take Pitino out; sometimes Pitino would glare right back.

It was a philosophical battle. Pitino believed in a new era of basketball with wide open, athletic spontaneity. Leaman sought structure, choosing substance over style. Sometimes they yelled at each other, a rather comical clash: the gap–toothed coach with the razored r's of Boston talking about the responsibilities of the "point gahd," the pretty–boy slickster with New Yawk in his mouth who seemed to think he was God. To Leaman, there was nothing funny about it. He was not accustomed to such resistance. His coaching staff had learned under Matt Zunic—"Be reasonable: Do it my way." Pitino, they felt, was being unreasonable. "We had been conditioned that the words of the authority were the law," Ray Wilson said years later. "They can't even be questioned. We coached that way."

Sticking hard in Pitino's craw was Leaman's decision to start senior Mike Pagliara at the point. To Pitino, Pagliara was old school, the set–it–up point guard of yesterday. Pitino had never sat before. No one had ever told him he wasn't good enough. He was, he felt, more than good enough.

One day in practice in January, Pitino picked a fight with Pagliara. When the two were finally pulled apart, Pagliara was sidelined with a broken thumb.

"Rick instigated the whole thing," says Peter Trow, a man close enough to Pitino to later attend his wedding. "He was unhappy. He wanted to run the show. He just gave everybody a hard time, and eventually it just exploded into a fight. It was more of a wrestling match. It was pretty funny, actually."

Not so funny, though, was the sentiment expressed by Jack Leaman in the *Collegian* of January 24, 1972. Explaining why Pitino had been suspended from the UMass squad, Leaman said, "He thought too much about himself, and not about the 11 other guys on the team."

The latter part of the 1972 season was supposed to be a glorious time at UMass. It was to be the end of Julius Erving's career, the blossoming of Rick Pitino's. Neither was there. The newly christened Minutemen lost seven of their last ten games, finished 14–12 and tied for second in the Yankee Conference. The season ended not in the NCAA tournament as so many hoped it would, nor at Madison Square Garden in the NIT, but with a long, sullen bus ride home after a loss at Maine.

Pitino had all but decided to transfer. Surely someone else would appreciate his talents. After a long, soothing conversation with Ray Wilson, however, he changed his mind. He decided to bite his tongue. Reasonable or not, he was going to do it Leaman's way.

In later years Pitino would often say that the experience with Leaman, while painful, was pivotal to his own development as a coach. He learned about the need for teamwork, for keeping egos in check. At the time, though, the treatment seemed rough. "The following year Jack treated me below the manager," Pitino said. "For mental toughness, I've never known anything like it."

Pitino never averaged more than 5.2 points per game at UMass, though Kentucky media guides in the nineties claim he averaged twenty–eight points as a senior. Scoring was not something Jack Leaman wanted out of his point guards. He wanted a floor general to run his halfcourt offense. He wanted someone who could put his own interests behind those of the team. Ultimately that's what he got in Rick Pitino.

During Pitino's junior and senior seasons, UMass went 41-12, won a pair of Yankee Conference titles, earned two trips to the NIT, and even won a game there for the first time in school history. His UMass career ended, as it had begun, on the floor of Madison Square Garden, after an overtime loss to Jacksonville in March of 1974. Ray Ellerbrook, who had become the radio voice of the Minutemen for Northampton's WHMP, asked Pitino that night about his future plans. With a jaunty assurance he replied, "I'm going to be a head coach."

# 3: "I Don't Like to Be Compared with Anybody"

1974–1978

y the mid–seventies, the growth of the UMass campus had crested at 25,000 students, an astonishing 250 percent increase since Leaman arrived in 1961. "We went from being a small college," he said, "to a metropolis." What had been a lush green landscape in the fertile Connecticut River Valley had, seemingly overnight, been transformed into a cluttered campus of gray concrete. High–rise dorms created a city–like skyline. The new twenty–six–story library, billed as the world's tallest, was more than the largest phallic symbol in western Massachusetts. It was also the symbol of too much growth too soon. Not long after opening, brick chips began falling from upper stories and slamming into the ground. Things were spinning out of control.

Suddenly, Massachusetts had a huge state university like other states. There was, however, a difference. In places like Virginia or Michigan, State U stood for the best the state had to offer. It was the seat of education. It was something to rally behind. It was the alma mater of many of the state's power elite. Massachusetts, however, had an array of outstanding private colleges that no other state could match: Harvard and MIT, Amherst and Williams, Smith and Mount Holyoke, Tufts and Brandeis, Boston College and Holy Cross. Underfunded and underappreciated, the state university of Massachusetts was not the source of pride that it was in many other states.

What it was was ZooMass. The label, which became fashionable in the seventies, was applied by outsiders with derision, by insiders with a mixture of embarrassment and pride. Several fine academic programs were overshadowed by UMass's growing reputation as a party school. Some 2,700 gallons of beer were served each week in the student center in 1974, according to Food Service Director Phil Amico. It was, Amico maintained, one of the largest on–campus beverage operations in the country.

UMass students did the same things that other college students did—they just did them with a bit more gusto. Panty raids—charges of hormonally–hyped young men into women's dorms—drew hundreds of people. Streaking was embraced with an ardor that would make the state's puritanical forefathers cringe. One night six hundred students pranced naked over campus. Thinking they had set a world record, they arrived at the student center and began chanting, "We're Number 1!"

Racial tension continued to be an ugly part of the mix. An attack of a black woman by five white men after a party led to a protest of police harassment by the Third World Defense League. The firing of the Black Affairs Editor and his assistant by the *Collegian* spurred a tense occupation of the newspaper office. A pair of black UMass students, Robert Earl Brown and Craemen Gethers, were convicted by all–white juries of a robbery at a local McDonald's despite abundant evidence that they could not have committed the crime.

Sports had become an acceptable venue for protest ever since sprinters Tommie Smith and John Carlos raised their fists for Black Power on the victory stand in the 1968 Olympics. Basketball, an arena where black college students were starting to experience a great deal of success, was a natural staging ground. For years black students sat together in a corner of the Cage, refusing to stand for the National Anthem.

The first anthem to be played in the post–Rick Pitino era ushered in the career of a new point guard, the first freshman ever to start for UMass. Next to Julius Erving, Jack Leaman would later say, the guy with the most talent ever to come through his program was Alex Eldridge.

Eldridge had grown up alone with his mother in the South Bronx, where he became a playground legend. He had what were then called "shake–and–bake" moves. In the rugged culture of New York City basketball, played man–to–man because zone defenses were considered almost feminine, Alex Eldridge was a dominant force. He could always take his man.

Eldridge and Butch Lee were considered the two best guards in New York. In the city championship game in 1974, Eldridge's Taft High School team defeated Lee's DeWitt Clinton squad by one point at St. John's Alumni Hall. Lee went off to Marquette, and Eldridge chose UMass, becoming the first high school All–America ever to set foot on campus.

It was a major recruiting coup. "People never expected Alex to go to UMass," said Mike Pyatt, a New York player who also chose UMass that year. "They expected him to go to one of the bigtime schools like UCLA, Indiana, Kentucky or Marquette." The Minutemen had been to the NCAA tournament only once, and that had been thirteen years before. They played in a league that was not highly regarded and never featured on television. And a campus in rural Amherst, Massachusetts, with a checkered reputation for race relations could not have seemed too inviting to a proud young black man who had grown up in a housing project in the South Bronx, attending a high school with just three white students.

In other ways, UMass was an understandable option for Eldridge. Pyatt, a good friend, had already committed to the school. Moreover, UMass also offered a scholarship to Derick Claiborne, Eldridge's backcourt buddy from Taft High School. They had been best friends since age five.

The players were drawn to UMass in large measure by the earnestness of assistant coach Ray Wilson, who would drive down to the city in his Volkswagen Bug, chomping on his favorite chocolate–covered peanuts. Wilson's decency distinguished him from the pack of slimy recruiters who came into the ghetto promising the world. "We loved Ray Wilson," Pyatt recalled years later. "All of our parents believed in him. They were going to trust their sons to go away to Massachusetts with him."

And, of course, they all knew that Wilson had been the high school coach of UMass's greatest player, Julius Erving. Dr. J was then making a name for himself with the New York Nets as the most stylish and dominating player of his day. The fact that Erving had gone to UMass held out a beacon to a whole generation of black kids in New York—magic could happen in Amherst.

The record shows that the four years with Alex Eldridge were successful ones for the University of Massachusetts men's basketball team. The Minutemen had winning seasons every year, triumphing in fully two–thirds of their games. What the record does not show is the tragedy of potential unrealized. It does not show the absolute cult following that Eldridge enjoyed. Nor does it show the way in which this terrifically talented but enigmatic young man systematically took Jack Leaman apart. "Alex Eldridge ruined him," reflected Mark Donoghue, who captained two of those teams. "He broke Jack Leaman down. Everything he had was eroded. He lost what made him a great coach."

The battles started right away. The first team meeting was called for four o'clock on a September afternoon in that fall of 1974. According to Donoghue, Leaman let everyone know that they were expected to be ten minutes early for all practices and meetings. At 3:55 he locked the door of the classroom in the Boyden Building. At 3:58 Alex Eldridge started knocking. Leaman would not open the door.

In preseason conditioning, Leaman took his team down to the track and pushed them to break six–minute miles. This would pay off down the road, he said. In the closing minutes of tight games, conditioning could spell the difference, and no team, he insisted, would be in better shape than UMass. Players strained for the finish line, sometimes doubling over and vomiting. Eldridge would come jogging in last, coolly crossing the line.

It was a battle made for the times: the authoritarian and the rebel just months after the country's top authority had resigned in infamy; the black kid from the South Bronx and the white coach from Cambridge in the same fall when busing began in Boston.

Not that anyone was really looking for a fight. With the basketball season approaching, there was widespread excitement on campus. The team had three top–notch recruits from New York. There was a sense that UMass basketball was about to go bigtime.

Even Leaman was caught up in the excitement. In the basketball preview of the *Collegian*, the usually understated coach talked about this team being potentially the "best ever" at UMass. "We have better material than we've ever had before."

An accompanying article headlined "A reason for optimism? Alex Eldridge," stated, "Many feel Eldridge will be the next UMass basketball star, following in the footsteps of Julius Erving and Al Skinner. But Eldridge regrets any comparison to other players, stating, 'I'm myself. I don't like to be compared with anybody.'"

From the time Eldridge stepped on the floor of the Curry Hicks Cage, the fans loved him. He played the game with flamboyance. Once, when an opponent was shooting free throws, he slipped down to the other end of the court, sat down and started talking with the cheerleaders. As the second free throw went up, he sprang back onto the court, calling for the ball. He was a stylish ballhandler who sometimes beckoned at defenders like a macho prizefighter. Not interested in jump shots, he preferred to drive to the hoop with fearless flash. There was something irresistible about him on the court, an infectious quality. He seemed destined for greatness. And the Cage was his stage.

*Alex Eldridge (Number 24) stands shoulder to shoulder with Jack Leaman.
(Photo courtesy of UMass Special Collections and Archives)*

Away from it, he was inscrutable. His smile was big and warm, but very rare. He was, somehow, a popular loner. There was a mystique about him. He brought New York City cool to campus. He loved his music—Parliament Funkadelic, Kool and the Gang, and all kinds of jazz. He could listen for hours.

Some people found him sullen. Several teammates said he was hard to figure. Ray Wilson reflected that Eldridge was the most misunderstood player he ever met: "He would give you this front of being an angry young man. Some people were turned off by that. But if you just took a half–hour or forty–five minutes to talk with him you would find that he was a warm person. He was honest, sometimes too honest."

Eldridge was not going to go along with something he didn't believe, and he didn't believe in Jack Leaman's system. Practice became a clash of styles and wills. The coach liked the game slow and structured; the freshman liked it fast and spontaneous. Saying that teams would combat his penetration with zones, Leaman wanted Eldridge to work on his jump shot. Eldridge was determined to take the ball to the hole.

They were two point guards from two different eras fighting over what basketball should be. Leaman, the disciple of Matt Zunic, wanted his players to do it his way. To Eldridge, hoops was pure Coltrane, barreling into the lane, improvising, finding some unexpected rhythm and going with it. He was not accustomed to having a rigid conductor like Jack Leaman, barking out plays called "California Reverse Action."

For the first time the team had a strong minority presence. Six black players and one Hispanic made up fully half the roster. The UMass campus was finally gaining some diversity, thanks in part to a recruiting drive by CCEBS, the Committee for the Collegiate Education of Black Students, which had set up shop in the New Africa House. The basketball court was the focal point of the largest minority group ever on campus. It was a place of power and pride. In a corner of the Cage, just behind the spot where former star Ray Ellerbrook did his radio broadcast, black students sat in a unified block. When the season opened with Derick Claiborne on the bench, and Mike Pyatt—a soaring six–five talent—on JV, there were more than a few whispers.

The Minutemen went 18–8 in Eldridge's freshman year of 1974–75, winning their third straight Yankee Conference title. Still, the season was disappointing. UMass had posted better records in four of the previous five years. The "best ever" label was not warranted. The Minutemen were not even invited to the brand new ECAC playoffs, a four–team tournament allegedly matching up New England's finest, with the winner going to the NCAA tournament. Instead, UMass settled for another trip to the NIT, where the Minutemen got thumped in the first round by a mediocre Manhattan squad, 68–51.

•

UMass won its first six games during Eldridge's sophomore year, then lost its next three. The games were free–wheeling affairs decided by scores like 106–101 and 99–87. The defensive focus and pattern–oriented offense that characterized UMass squads in the past were noticeably missing. An analysis of the Minutemen by Milt Cole in the *Daily Hampshire Gazette* ran beneath the headline "Not a Leaman Team."

The battles with Eldridge charged every practice with subtext. "You cannot be a point guard and an individual," Leaman would shout. Eldridge would stare at the floor. Leaman would shake his head. He just couldn't understand the kid.

On the one hand, Eldridge was the ultimate team player. He almost never forced his shot. The favorite part of his game was passing, making other players look good. He would drive into the lane, flash head and shoulder fakes that would get defenders lunging to block a phantom shot just as the ball was dished off to a teammate for an easy hoop. As fans roared and more demonstrative teammates like Pyatt and Claiborne slapped each other five (down low back then), Eldridge would coolly backpedal downcourt as if nothing had happened. "He was so unselfish," Leaman said years later. "He could win games with no points and fifteen assists."

And yet, there were ways that he didn't care about the team at all—at least that's how it seemed to Leaman. Eldridge showed little interest in working on jump shots or free throws, and his conditioning was lax. He was often late for meetings and morning practices. In games, he could be passion or poison. His effort could be visibly intense, the sweat streaming off his burly shoulders, the focus burning in his eyes. The next time downcourt he could be listless, displaying a nonchalance that drove Leaman to distraction, almost as much as his insistence on playing with his shirt untucked.

What bothered Leaman most of all was the cool scowl that Eldridge wore so much of the time. Leaman knew that his point guard loved the game, but he seldom showed it. He seemed to hold his happiness hostage, as if that were part of the power battle. Leaman would often issue the simplest of coaching commands: "Smile." And Eldridge wouldn't.

He was suspended for the tenth game of that 1975–76 season. Wearing street clothes, Eldridge sat just far enough from the UMass bench, quietly watching the Minutemen beat Hawaii, 80–72, at the Springfield Civic Center. Leaman said afterward that backup point guard Mike Stokes had run the offense better than it had been run for two years, since the days of Rick Pitino. As fate would have it, Pitino watched the whole show. Sitting on the Hawaii bench in a loud peach suit, the assistant coach for the Rainbows understood the situation better than anyone. Just three years before, he had been, as Eldridge was now, the sophomore point guard in Leaman's doghouse. After being kicked off the team, he had come back and done it the coach's way.[1]

Would Alex Eldridge come back? Had this most promising talent already run his course at the University of Massachusetts?

Something clicked. The suspension seemed to bring about a cease-fire in the battle of wills. UMass was a house united, and it stood tall. With Eldridge playing the best ball of his life, UMass won fourteen of its last fifteen games, including the final ten in a row. The Min-utemen coasted to their fourth straight Yankee Conference title. They finished the regular season 21–4.

True, the season ended on a down note, with UMass losing both games in the ECAC tournament and failing to make the NCAAs once again. Still, there was an overwhelming feeling of optimism heading into the 1976–77 season. UMass had turned the corner.

The fresh–start feeling came from all over. The NCAA was legaliz-ing the dunk once again, recognizing that the most macho move of the playground had its place in the game. The "alley–oop"—the lobbed pass to a soaring, catching and slamming teammate—became the ul-timate statement play. Few could state it more emphatically than the great leaper Mike Pyatt, and the guy he referred to as "the master of assists," Alex Eldridge.

After twenty–eight years in the Yankee Conference, UMass was also getting a fresh start by joining the brand new Eastern Collegiate Bas-ketball League, a conference that would evolve into the Eastern Eight, and ultimately, the Atlantic 10. Sure, there were some hokey elements to the new league—it had a mascot called the "Hoopster Rooster"—but there were strong teams. Rutgers had gone to the Final Four the year before. West Virginia had a big arena and a great basketball tradi-tion that included Jerry West. Pittsburgh and Penn State were athletic powerhouses. George Washington was returning ten players from a team that had won twenty games. Duquesne had the league's best player in future Los Angeles Laker star Norm Nixon. And Villanova was building a program toward a national championship under Rollie Massimino.

On one level, Jack Leaman was reluctant to give up the regional rivalries. He loved the New England games against the state schools from Vermont, New Hampshire, Maine, Rhode Island and Connecti-cut. He often talked about his goal of being "the best in New England."

Still, he knew that UMass had outgrown the league. The Minute-men had won or shared the conference title in eight of the last nine years, but outside of the region no one cared. It was time to acknowl-edge that college basketball was bigger than New England. The ECBL was unquestionably the strongest league in the Northeast (The Big East was still a twinkle in Providence coach Dave Gavitt's eye). The winner of its postseason tournament would go straight to the NCAAs. That, Leaman knew, had become the only real measure of success.

The team's vision became defined by the glittering ring on the forefinger of Mark Haymore, who had transferred from Indiana after playing sparingly on Bobby Knight's 1976 national championship squad. Leaman knew that UMass had the talent to get to the tournament. All five starters were returning, and all of them had been double–figure scorers a year ago.

Mark Donoghue, a 15.5 points–per–game scorer, was a fundamentally flawless six–eight forward. Mike Pyatt could jump like Julius Erving; he would leave as UMass's all–time leading scorer. Jim Town, a bruising six–seven lefty, would be the last cut by the Denver Nuggets. Derick Claiborne was a pure shooter who would score more than one thousand points in his career.

And at point guard was the guy who ran the show, the player who was voted MVP by his teammates the year before. Alex Eldridge was set to lead UMass into the modern era.

He was suspended for the first two games of the 1976–77 season. Leaman was only allowed to bring twelve players on the road to the Hall of Fame tournament in Springfield. Eldridge was not among them. "He wasn't one of the top twelve in practice is what it comes down to," Leaman said.

Game Three took place at the Cage against Penn State. Eldridge did not start. When he entered the game with six minutes gone, the overflow crowd stood and cheered.

"Sides were taken," recalled Ray Wilson, "and the damage was such that you couldn't repair it. Alex, because of his ability, was one of these people the public would attach themselves to. So it was 'Alex was all right, and Jack was all wrong.'"

Some felt there was a racial element to their conflict. Yes, Leaman's two assistant coaches, Wilson and Ray Ricketts, were black. True, Julius Erving and Al Skinner spoke highly of their former coach. And without a doubt, Mike Pyatt admitted, Leaman would bench any player, white or black, if he didn't go all out in practice or games. Still, there was a perception that Leaman wanted to coach "white basketball." He talked about preferring the layup to the dunk. His brow would furrow at every attempted alley–oop. The coach was extremely unpopular with black fans, who would boo whenever Eldridge was taken out of the game.

The Eldridge/Leaman tension, though, went much deeper than race. It seemed to strike an anti–establishment chord on campus in the post–Watergate era. This was a rough time for authority, and Jack Leaman—with his close–cropped hair and stern temper—embodied the old guard.

"It was pretty funky back then," recalled captain Mark Donoghue. "There were plenty of white kids smoking weed and believing in Alex."

UMass's trademark discipline slowly but palpably eroded. Weekend and intersession practices were no longer held in the morning; this way there was no confrontation with Eldridge about arriving late. Curfew was extended on the road. On the court, the reins were loosened. When conflicts did occur, they were dealt with less by the swift justice of Leaman and more by awkward team meetings. The coach was trying to understand.

"He spent more time babysitting bullshit problems," Donoghue said. "There were more meetings, more counter meetings. He was too caught up in trying to save this kid. It was like having cancer of the wrist and being told you can either cut it off or die. He chose to die."

In January, UMass visited Niagara, a small university just miles from the famous waterfall. Eldridge and Pyatt were benched to start the game after being late for practice the day before. Midway through the first half, Leaman wandered down to the end of the bench, and asked Pyatt if he was ready to play. "Yes," said Pyatt with his customary enthusiasm. Then the coach turned to Eldridge, and asked him the same question. Eldridge just stared ahead at the court and said nothing. It was as tense a moment of silence as they had ever known.

There was a meeting about it, of course, even an impromptu press conference at the Cage. When UMass took the court two nights later against Vermont, Eldridge was playing. The act of insolence, which would have surely resulted in getting kicked off the UMass team a few years before, was now all but ignored. For Jack Leaman, one of the most respected coaches in New England college basketball history, the battle for the soul of the UMass team had been lost.

UMass finished sixth in the eight–team ECBL. The Minutemen did go 20–11, but almost all of the wins came in non–league games against New England foes. For their troubles, the Minutemen earned their sixth trip in eight years to the NIT. By now, the NIT had become permanently entrenched as the second–tier tournament. In the opening round, played conveniently at the Springfield Civic Center, UMass beat Seton Hall by a point. The Minutemen then went down to Madison Square Garden and lost to Villanova, 81–71.

In the NCAA that year, Marquette won it all. The MVP of the Final Four was Butch Lee, Eldridge's old rival from the playgrounds of the South Bronx. The winning coach was the maverick Al McGuire, who rode into Atlanta for the Final Four on his trademark motorcycle. Eight seconds away from the championship over North Carolina, McGuire began sobbing on the bench and left the court. Walking into the locker room, he said, "I want to be alone. I'm not afraid to cry."

At forty–eight, McGuire was three years older than Jack Leaman. He had coached his team for thirteen years, two more than the UMass coach. Now at the very top, he was calling it quits.

•

Coaching had started to take an enormous toll on Leaman. Five years earlier he was still at his playing weight of 175 pounds; now he was well over 200. After home games he went out to a local dive called the McManus Eating Place with the WHMP radio crew of Ray Ellerbrook and Joe Fennessey. Invariably, Leaman pulled out a pen and started diagramming plays on a napkin. Years later, Ellerbrook recalled, "I remember Joe telling me, 'This guy just needs somebody to talk to.' He did. He was pulling his hair out."

At home in Amherst, Leaman's wife Rita certainly noticed the changes. Many a morning she woke up and saw that her husband had never made it to bed. When she went downstairs, she saw him mapping out strategy with a hailstorm of scrunched paper balls lining the floor.

"I'm surprised he lasted in coaching as long as he did, because he got so worked up," said Mike Pyatt. "I always thought he was an old man."

To be sure, he tried to stay young. After the 1976–77 season, Leaman decided to order new uniforms styled like those of Marquette. The Warriors played in long, tight tops that were designed to be worn outside of the short shorts of the era. "Marquette" was emblazoned above the numbers, and down by the exposed shirttails was the name "Warriors." Like almost every piece of seventies fashion, this one would seem ludicrous in retrospect, but at the time Marquette was the hottest team around. For UMass it was a brilliant stroke. Leaman, who seemed helplessly behind the times to his players, could score major points for being hip. Eldridge could be like his old pal Butch Lee, who had just won the national championship. What's more, Leaman was granting his point guard a symbolic victory in the whole tuck–your–

shirts–in crusade. It was the coach's way of saying, "You win, Alex. Now maybe we all can win."

UMass was wearing its road maroon uniforms to open the 1977–78 season at Harvard, a school that had once sought Leaman as its head coach. The word "Massachusetts" hung just above the shirttails outside the pants. No word in his vocabulary meant more to Jack Leaman.

Just before tipoff, Leaman felt a tap on his shoulder. "You're not going to believe this," said assistant coach Ray Wilson, pointing to center court. There was Alex Eldridge about to begin his senior year, with "Massachusetts" tucked into his crotch.

What could you do?

ZooMass was a troubled place that year. Huge budget cuts crippled morale. A cross burning in October set the stage for a year of volatile race relations. White students protested the funding for a Black American Music Festival as the school's only spring concert. On the basketball court, freshman Tom Witkos found himself booed by black students when he checked in to replace Eldridge.

UMass started out 8–2. The next game was set to take place at the Hartford Civic Center against the University of Connecticut. Though they were no longer in the same league, the Huskies were still UMass's arch–rival. A win over UConn still mattered, and more often than not UMass got it. That night, though, the Minutemen played miserably and lost 56–49. Four hours later, the roof of the Civic Center caved in from the weight of recent snowfalls. There was no better symbol for a basketball program about to collapse.

The Minutemen took on the personality not of their coach, but of their point guard. They were sometimes ferocious, sometimes invisible. They pulled a scintillating upset over Villanova when Eldridge sparked a second–half rally. They lost somehow at Maine, and then at home to a 5–19 New Hampshire squad. "I think this was the worst UMass performance I have ever coached," said Leaman, typically taking the blame on himself. "A game played entirely without emotion."

Before the last home game of the year, a worn out and overweight Leaman accompanied Alex Eldridge, Derick Claiborne and Mike Pyatt onto the floor of the Curry Hicks Cage for Senior Night. Pyatt had broken Julius Erving's record as the all–time leading scorer at UMass. Eldridge, the league's assist leader, had scored more than one thousand points in his career, as had his longtime pal Claiborne—the first two guards in school history to reach that milestone. When Eldridge took the microphone from Leaman, the crowd went nuts. "The Cage," said Eldridge, smiling broadly, "is the Joint!"

They won that night, an inspired effort over Pittsburgh, but they finished the year at 15–12, the worst record at UMass in six seasons. There would be no NCAA tournament, no NIT. The senior crew, which had come in with such high hopes and expectations, went out with a whimper.

That night, the New York trio returned to the apartment they shared and cooked up a steak, courtesy of Pyatt's father, a butcher in Harlem. "Damn," Pyatt recalls Eldridge saying, "we're going to miss this."

For Jack Leaman, the season couldn't end soon enough. He was burdened with a heavy feeling of failure. He knew this was the most talented group he would ever coach, and they had gotten worse over time. The coach who was respected for getting the most out of the least had gotten the least out of the most. He had never swallowed a more bitter pill.

All three New Yorkers had been communications majors, but only Pyatt left with a degree. He played one season with the Maine Lumberjacks of the Continental Basketball Association, and convinced team officials to hire Alex Eldridge as the point guard. Eldridge hated it, Pyatt recalls, despising the selfishness of the league. "Everybody was like, 'I want to make the pros [NBA], I want to score my twenty points, I'm not going to pass the ball,'" Pyatt remembers. "He didn't like that."

The next year Pyatt went off to Scotland to begin a successful seven–year career in Europe. After his first season he came home to New York for a few weeks. He was there, in fact, on the day Alex Eldridge died.

Eldridge had been living in Boston. His pro prospects had pretty much dried up. (Leaman tried to convince Red Auerbach to give Eldridge a tryout with the Celtics, a team then desperate for help at point guard; and Julius Erving arranged what proved to be an unsuccessful tryout with the 76ers.) Eldridge was spending lots of time down at the Huntington Avenue YMCA, the very place where his former UMass coach had learned the game. Working with young kids brought a smile to Eldridge's face. He lived for a while with former NBA star point guard and fellow New York playground legend Nate Archibald, then moved in with his girlfriend from UMass. She gave birth to their son, Courtney, in May of 1980.

Two weeks later, one of Eldridge's close friends from the South

Bronx, Tony Price (who had just led the University of Pennsylvania to the Final Four), came up to Boston to visit. They went to the much–ballyhooed prize fight between Sugar Ray Leonard and Roberto Duran at Boston Garden. The next day they drove to New York and spent a few hours at the beach. Eldridge, complaining about fatigue and sore-ness in his leg, went to a doctor, who diagnosed heat exhaustion and told him to rest and drink lots of fluids. They stopped briefly in Harlem and touched base with Mike Pyatt. Then they went home.

Alex Eldridge, twenty–four years young, was curled up like a little boy in his mother's bathtub when the blood clot in his leg traveled to his heart and killed him. The Abyssinian Church in Harlem was over-flowing at the funeral.

•

Eldridge's childhood buddy Derick Claiborne, the UMass captain his senior year, was drafted by the Kansas City–Omaha Kings, but did not make the team. Drifting back to the South Bronx, he became a toll collector for the New York Transit Authority. In 1987 he and Pyatt teamed up on a squad that won the championship of the Over the Hill League, a thirty–and–up organization that attracted former stars from around the city. The next year in the playoff semifinals, Pyatt and Claiborne's team built up a 16–2 lead over a team thought to be their toughest competitor.

"Everything was clicking," Pyatt recalled years later, his voice halt-ing. "We were on a roll. All of a sudden, Derick called time. We were like, 'Why are you calling a timeout—we're blitzing these guys.' He said he was getting shortness of breath."

Claiborne sat on the bench, got some water, then keeled over from a heart attack. "We called 911," recalled Pyatt. "The ambulance took a long time to get there. It was like a major, major mess. We couldn't believe this was happening. It was the same people who were around for Alex. And plus, those two were like the best, the best of friends."

Both were now gone.

•

Mike Pyatt's professional career had ended a couple of years earlier when he tore up his knee while playing for a team in Israel. When he came home to New York, he was not sure what to do with his life. He got in his Jeep and found himself gravitating north to Amherst, Mas-sachusetts. After checking in at the Campus Center Hotel, he limped over to the Curry Hicks Cage to watch the UMass women's team in action. The scene of so much emotion a decade before, the Cage was now a quiet place with a smattering of perhaps one hundred fans. Pyatt climbed up into the bleachers to watch, and was lost in his thoughts when Jack Leaman came to sit down beside him.

Pyatt was struck by how relaxed Leaman seemed. He had stayed on in the athletic department, but the pressurized days of coaching the Minutemen were behind him. They reminisced a little about Alex Eldridge. Leaman said that Eldridge might have been difficult to coach, but felt that he was a warm–hearted person and, without a doubt, one of his greatest players.

The meeting hit Pyatt hard. He was startled by Leaman's compassion, his genuine interest in Pyatt's thoughts about pursuing a Master's Degree. "After I talked to him, I felt really sorry for him," Pyatt later reflected. "I felt really bad that, one, we didn't communicate as a team with him when we were there; and two, he was in an era that was changing. The game was starting to change and move."

# 4: "Really, This Place Can Rock"

1978–1988

Bigtime college basketball was born in the 1978–79 school year. That was the year when Magic Johnson's Michigan State team beat Larry Bird's Indiana State squad for the NCAA championship. The eye–popping 24.1 rating of NBC's broadcast proved that there was a product here, not just a game. Before long, "March Madness" was part of the national sports lexicon. There was a "Road to the Final Four." Secretaries and CEOs furiously filled out their grids in office pools across the land.

It wasn't just Bird and Magic who launched the game. Every revolution involves a confluence of forces, and there were plenty of them at work that year.

In the fall of 1978, a self–proclaimed "little fat dago" named John Paul (Sonny) Vaccaro drove west from his home in Trafford, Pennsylvania, with some sneaker designs, a ton of contacts with college basketball coaches and an idea. He arrived in Beaverton, Oregon, at a fledgling shoe company named Nike, then doing about $7 million of business in basketball shoes. With a fast–talking style and winning sincerity, Vaccaro told the company's chairman Phil Knight how to get a literal foothold on the market then controlled by Converse. College basketball players were basically billboards, Vaccaro explained. If you had contracts with coaches guaranteeing that their players wore only Nikes, kids would take note and sales would soar.

"Picture this," the late Jim Valvano told *Sports Illustrated* in 1988, a year after the sales of Nike basketball shoes hit $300 million. "Two guys named Vaccaro and Valvano meeting at La Guardia Airport. Vaccaro reaches into his briefcase. Puts a check on the table. I look at it and say, 'What's this for?' He pulls a sneaker out and puts it on the table. Like we were putting a contract out on somebody. He says, 'I would like your team to wear this shoe.' I say, 'How much?' He says,

'No, I'll give you the shoes.' You got to remember, I was at Iona. We wore a lot of seconds. They didn't even have labels on them. I say, 'This certainly can't be anything legal.'"

Another meeting at La Guardia Airport that year helped push college basketball into the realm of big business. On May 8, 1979, former Providence College coach Dave Gavitt sequestered a group of athletic directors in a room and hammered out the first made–for–TV basketball conference, The Big East. Choosing teams for the league based on the size of their media market, Gavitt quickly locked up strongholds in New York (St. John's), Washington D.C. (Georgetown) and Boston (Boston College). Before long, Gavitt added teams in Philadelphia and Pittsburgh, securing the first exclusive contract any league signed with a major network, a $14.5 million deal in which CBS paid the schools for the right to give them hours and hours of free exposure.

That landmark 1978–79 year also saw Bill Rasmussen launch ESPN. In the spring of 1978, Rasmussen, then forty–five, was fired from his job as communications director for the New England Whalers of the World Hockey Association. Sensing an appetite in the state for telecasts of University of Connecticut basketball games, he contacted several cable companies. Some of them suggested that he look into a new technology, then hardly utilized, called satellite transmission. On November 17, 1978, an exhibition game between UConn and Athletes in Action hit the air. Fifteen years later ESPN was a billion–dollar industry.

In retrospect, everything seemed to happen at once. College basketball was finding success, losing innocence, going bigtime.

At the University of Massachusetts, the game was headed into the sewer.

When Jack Leaman signed his contract for $27,232.40 in the fall of 1978, he was amazed at the changes that had been wrought in the seventeen years since he arrived as a fresh–scrubbed assistant coach. He had come to work for Matt Zunic, whose credo of "Be reasonable: do it my way" seemed reasonable. At the time John F. Kennedy was just a few months into his presidency. The seven thousand predominantly white students at the state university from Kennedy's commonwealth were mostly proud to submit to authority. Leaman fell in love with UMass and knew almost every professor and plumber on campus.

Vietnam and Watergate and busing had changed the picture. With twenty–five thousand students and a skyline of hideous high–rise apartments, UMass had come to feel far more anonymous. Leaman trudged over to the math office one day to check on the standing of one of his players and couldn't find an instructor he recognized. Academic standards had fallen. For the first time that fall the median SAT score of incoming freshmen dipped below one thousand—and that four–figure benchmark for receiving an athletic scholarship had long since disappeared.

It was a difficult time at the University of Massachusetts. The 1979 yearbook began with the text, "Violent is perhaps the best way to describe the UMass campus from September 1978 to May 1979." In September one student hanged himself, another plunged to his death from the twenty–first floor of a dormitory, and a third—a black woman named Seta Rampersad, who was set to graduate in December with a degree in political science—died under mysterious circumstances in a hotel room in nearby South Deerfield. Before the year was over, there would be two more suicides on campus. A rash of reported sexual assaults led to huge sales of rape–alert whistles. Campus vandalism caused more than a quarter–million dollars of damage. In the spring, several fires were set in the New Africa House, the building that housed what was then called the Afro–American Studies Department.

From this atmosphere of chaos Jack Leaman hoped to harvest a modicum of order during the 1978–79 season. It was still basketball, right? Now that the stormy, disappointing Alex Eldridge days were behind him, perhaps he could find a way to love the game again.

Leaman was not expecting a dramatic turnaround. He knew his talent level had fallen off, and he felt increasing frustration with what he considered to be a meek athletic administration. Basketball scholarships had been cut to ten, well below the NCAA limit of fifteen.[1] Athletic director Frank McInerney and physical education chairman David Bischoff reminded Leaman that it was an era of general belt–tightening on campus, that everyone had to do his part. Besides, they said, he was such a good coach that surely he could make do. Recruiting, however, had changed. It was one thing to compete against Yankee Conference foes like New Hampshire and Vermont, another altogether to go up against West Virginia and Villanova. Recruits at this level had more options. They liked to see flashy programs that played on TV before large crowds. The aging, dingy Curry Hicks Cage, for all its charm, was a recruiting nightmare. Many kids didn't visit campus until after their high school season, by which time the basketball court had been peeled off the dirt floor. Leaman would come in with a recruit and see baseball coach Dick Bergquist rapping ground balls to his infielders. "Really," Leaman would say, "this place can rock."

All energy seemed to fade from the building in the 1978–79 season. There were no lines snaking around campus with freezing students seeking tickets. No revved–up crowds stomping on the bleachers. Basketball was a dreary scene.

UMass split its first two games, then hosted Boston University. The Terriers had gone through hard times of late, finishing 7–19 and 10–15 the previous two years. Desperate to reverse their fortunes, they had hired a new coach for 1978–79, one Rick Pitino. The cocky kid who had come to UMass dribbling a ball between his legs had lived up to his promise. At the tender age of twenty–six, he was already a head coach, ironically enough at Leaman's alma mater.

Pitino could not believe what he saw that night. The discipline had been drained right out of the UMass program. Players weren't playing hard defense. The tightly scripted offenses that he used to chafe against had deteriorated to a laissez–faire, one–on–one play that he hated even worse. Loose balls weren't matters of urgency anymore. Boxing out was an occasional event.

"The Jack Leaman I coached against was not the Jack Leaman I played for," Pitino said years later. "The game had changed. It was like a time warp passing before your eyes. It was not a Jack Leaman–coached team. His [earlier] teams would never get beat for a lack of fundamentals. He was a remarkable man in his threshold for wanting to teach, and in his love for the game, but the times had changed, and he didn't change with them."

When BU beat UMass that night, it was, in many senses, a changing of the guard. Charging up one escalator three steps at a time, Pitino would lead his team to a 17–9 record, establishing himself immediately as a coaching wunderkind. For one nostalgic night he came back to UMass, and saw a burdened Jack Leaman on the other escalator, heading down.

After eleven straight winning seasons, the Minutemen tumbled to 5–22 in 1978–79, 0–10 in the Eastern Eight. They lost their final thirteen games of the year. The Cage, which had in fact rocked since the days of Julie the Jumping Jack Erving, became a hollow place where nobody seemed to care. With modern basketball about to explode, UMass had begun a descent into the depths of the game.

Leaman announced his retirement before the last home game of the year on February 21, 1979. In the *Collegian* account, columnist Steve Zack said that the coach's fire from past seasons had disappeared. "To look at him now, one would see a tired, worn–out, middle–aged man, each loss of a game or a bit of unrespect (sic), taking just that much more out of him." Zack concluded in patronizing fashion: "He is a bit of UM history that should be preserved and not thrown away."

In that Senior Night game against Penn State, the Minutemen took a 4–2 lead when Tom Witkos, who had grown up in nearby Hadley dreaming of playing for Leaman at the Cage, picked off a pass and drove in for a layup. They never led again. At halftime, Leaman spoke to the team for a while, then left the locker room. Witkos stood up and made an impassioned case to his teammates about how important it was to win this game for Leaman. Some of them glared at him. Some stared blankly. One said, "Sit down, white boy."

UMass lost, 54–42, enduring the lowest scoring output in Leaman's thirteen–year coaching career. In the locker room well after the game, Witkos sat alone with team manager Matt Capeless. Witkos would go on to become a very successful high school coach, as well as a corrections officer in the Hampshire County Jail. Capeless would in time make the rare jump from team manager to college head coach (at North Adams State); in the years–long assembly of clinics and camps he needed to visit, he never encountered anyone like Leaman—"the most prepared and focused coach I've ever seen." But on that Senior Night neither young man knew about his future. They sat in a cold locker room in an old building feeling awful. Witkos was crying. Capeless put his arm around him. "Don't worry," he said. "This goddam season will be over soon."

•

Eleven straight winning years were followed by eleven straight losing years. Basketball at the University of Massachusetts in the 1980s was comically bad. The Minutemen earned their name, the joke went, because that's how long they stayed competitive in games. It wasn't far from true. Against West Virginia, they once fell behind, 25–0. Over the course of the decade, the once–proud basketball program at UMass was ranked 259th of 267 Division I teams.

Ray Wilson, the kindly assistant coach, took over for Leaman in 1979–80. His career started with a forty–eight–point loss at Michigan. UMass lost its first sixteen games of the year, extending the school's losing streak to an embarrassing twenty–nine, just short of the national record.[2] The Minutemen finished the year 2–24, the worst mark in the country. Appropriately enough for a plummeting program, the top scorer was named Curtis Phauls (pronounced "falls"). A skinny six–six junior college transfer, Phauls sported a big smile, an all–encompassing philosophy when it came to shot selection, and a distaste for defense. In UMass's home opener against Pittsburgh, Phauls got into a scrap with the Panthers' beefy center Sam Clancy, a man destined for a long career as a lineman in the NFL. Sensing the peril of the situation, Phauls wiggled free and charged into the stands at the Curry Hicks Cage. His girlfriend, though, stormed onto the court in high heels, swinging her pocketbook over her head, trying to get a piece of Clancy. Such was the state of UMass basketball at the time.

After another dreadful season (3–24) in 1980–81, UMass shifted Wilson to intramural director and hired Notre Dame assistant Tom McLaughlin. A former UMass captain, McLaughlin was resourceful. When his wife, Debbie, went into active labor in the wee hours of an April morning while a swirling blizzard made a trip to the emergency room impossible, McLaughlin helped deliver his son Tommy, tying back the umbilical cord with one of the laces from his Converse basketball shoes.

He could not, however, deliver UMass to prominence. He brought in some good players, people like Donald Russell and Horace Neysmith, but his judgment was not always sound. After securing six–nine Tom Emerson from a high school in Tennessee, McLaughlin proclaimed, "At last, our search for a legitimate big man is over." Emerson, eschewing the paint for the perimeter, never averaged more than two points a game. McLaughlin's style was fiery and flamboyant. Swirling his sport jacket over his head, he played to the crowd. It was not long, though, before the fire burned out. "Tom's tumultuous two–year tenure" (as christened by sports information director Howie Davis) came to a close after 7–20 and 9–20 seasons amid widespread team dissension.

Ron Gerlufsen, one of McLaughlin's assistants, was handed the job in 1983. Players generally liked Gerlufsen. Compassionate and non–confrontational, he worked hard and coaxed some modest improvement out of his team. What that meant, though, was that UMass went from pathetic to merely poor in Gerlufsen's five years. The era did have its highlights. The team almost hit .500 in 1984–85, going 13–15. Lorenzo Sutton, a star–crossed guard from Georgia, became the

*Even Bill Cosby couldn't smile as the UMass basketball program took a turn for the worse. (Photo courtesy of the Daily Hampshire Gazette)*

school's all–time leading scorer and just missed making the Detroit Pistons. And the Curry Hicks Cage was given a facelift, made lighter and brighter by the replacement of the dirt floor and temporary stands. The building mostly retained its charm, and—for all the fresh paint— its status as a second–class facility. It seated only 4,058 fans and rarely filled up. Ultimately there was not a lot to see, other than dry, uninspiring teams. Basketball was alternately ignored and ridiculed at UMass. "We were just another team on campus," recalled Ben Grodski, a forward who began playing in 1987, "one with a long his- tory of losing."

Elsewhere, the game was taking off. The NCAA tournament was rapidly earning a place as one of the great sporting events in America, right up there with the World Series and the Super Bowl. Every year, it seemed, the championship game produced gripping drama: Michael Jordan hitting the game–winner for North Carolina as a freshman in 1982; North Carolina State coach Jim Valvano frantically looking for someone to hug after the Wolfpack's buzzer–beating upset of Hous- ton in '83; a couple of guys named Harold helping Villanova stun Georgetown in '85. By 1987 all teams in the field of sixty–four were clearing more than $200,000 from the NCAA, Final Four teams more than $1 million.[3] In 1989, CBS paid $1 billion for the right to televise the tournament for seven years. (By 1994, the network had re–upped for $1.75 billion over eight years.) College basketball was booming.

UMass seemed to play a different sport. Saddened, Jack Leaman watched it all from his vantage point as a teacher in the athletic department. He knew what this place could be. The Cage used to throb with emotion in the days of Julius Erving and Rick Pitino. Leaman had finished his career with a 217–126 record. The three coaches who followed—Wilson, McLaughlin and Gerlufsen—posted a cumulative mark of 76–172. Though all were young men, none would ever coach Division I again. In fact, only Gerlufsen coached at all, latching on at Division II Shepherd College, then moving to the Division III Savannah College of Art and Design, and ultimately leaving the profession altogether.

When Gerlufsen's contract ran out after a 10–17 season in 1988, UMass did not renew it. Administrators said they were going to conduct a national search to bring in a top candidate. Jack Leaman had a hard time keeping his sarcasm at bay. There had been so much lip service from the administration in the past. It didn't really seem that UMass was committed to quality. But then Leaman noticed one thing that made him smile. The search committee included Rick Pitino.

•

The popular image of Pitino is that of a charismatic climber utterly obsessed with winning. After all, in his first job as an assistant coach, he helped land the University of Hawaii on probation; some of the NCAA charges mentioned him by name. He interviewed for his next position at Syracuse on his wedding night, leaving his bride Joanne up in a New York hotel room for hours while he talked with Jim Boeheim in the lobby.

No one had benefited from the college basketball boom more than the former Social Chairman at Lambda Chi. He had become a head coach in that pivotal 1978–79 season. After making beleaguered Boston University a winner—ultimately taking the Terriers to the NCAA tournament for the first time since Jack Leaman was the point guard—he turned a losing Providence College squad into a Final Four team in just two years. Now thirty–five, Pitino was in his first year of what seemed like the ultimate job: head coach of the New York Knicks.

Pitino's alleged obsessiveness suggests that he would have no interest at all in serving on the search committee for a new coach at his alma mater. After all, this was his first year in New York. He had a burning desire to succeed. The last thing he needed was another demand on his time, least of all from UMass, a pathetic basketball program from which, long ago, he had been suspended for selfishness. But when David Bischoff, dean of the School of Physical Education, came down to New York and asked him to serve on the committee, Pitino accepted on the spot.

Committee members say that his commitment was sincere. After the Knicks lost a game in Houston on a Thursday night and flew to New York for a Saturday game with the Celtics, Pitino diverted to Connecticut, where he met with the committee for hours in a conference room between the two terminals at Bradley International Airport. According to committee member Glenn Wong, the head of the UMass Sport Management Program, Pitino made numerous phone calls to people about the UMass job. He suggested several of the people who wound up being candidates. That group included Stu Jackson, Pitino's assistant with the Knicks, Larry Shyatt, a well-regarded assistant at New Mexico, and a fresh-faced young man named John Calipari.

Pitino and Calipari had first met in the summer of 1977 at the Five-Star Basketball Camp in Pittsburgh. Calipari was a fiery teenaged camper, Pitino an impassioned assistant coach at Syracuse. Driven young Italian-Americans, they were sold on the Gospel of Hoop. In subsequent years, Five-Star continued to be the summer center of their basketball universe. Long before Calipari became a head coach, camp director Howard Garfinkel had dubbed him "the next Rick Pitino."

Calipari started his coaching career in 1982 as an unpaid assistant at Kansas, spooning peas and carrots to players at the training table and creating the "Little Jayhawks" halftime ballhandling show. Now, six years later, he was an assistant coach and chief recruiter at Pittsburgh. Focused and aggressive, he was credited with delivering players like Bobby Martin, Sean Miller, Rod Brookin and Brian Shorter—recruits who helped the Panthers become a force in The Big East.

According to Glenn Wong, the UMass committee was taken with Calipari's blend of charisma and preparation. He was the only candidate to bring written materials, immaculately organized three-ring binders that focused on skill development and recruiting strategies. Another committee member, Holyoke Community College president David Bartley, recalls that Calipari had already watched tape of the Minutemen and reviewed the team's academic records. In fact, Calipari had grilled former coach Ron Gerlufsen about the program, not feeling the least bit awkward about pumping the deposed coach for information. Witty and charming, Calipari looked committee members in the eye, convincing them that he was more than a recruiter. His greatest skill, he insisted, was teaching.

Calipari had his share of detractors. As the process of candidate selection heated up, the committee started to receive negative calls from people like Rollie Massimino, head coach at Villanova. Some of Pittsburgh's rivals in The Big East painted a portrait of Calipari's allegedly ruthless, unethical recruiting. According to one story that has never been confirmed, Calipari, trying to steer a young man away from St. John's, lied to a recruit by saying that coach Lou Carnesecca had cancer. The UMass job wasn't exactly a magnet for high–powered résumés. Neither of the finalists—Calipari or Shyatt—had ever been a head coach before. They weren't being wooed by programs with big names. (The other position that Calipari interviewed for at that time was at the less–than–legendary University of Maine.) Still, Calipari pursued the UMass position as if it were the job of a lifetime, displaying an aggressiveness and single–mindedness that would become his trademark.

He lobbied ferociously. UMass sports information director Howie Davis was shocked to get a call from Calipari saying, "I know you're not on the committee, but I just wanted to introduce myself. . . ."

Mike Haverty, a former manager at UMass and a longtime friend of Calipari's pal Bill Bayno, got a call at Belmont Abbey College in North Carolina, where he was working as an assistant coach. Speaking from a restaurant in New York, Calipari explained that he was a candidate for the UMass job, and that some rivals were slinging mud at him. He would appreciate all the support he could get. When Haverty explained that he would love to help, but had already put in a good word with the committee for Belmont Abbey head coach Eddie Payne, he heard an immediate click. "As soon as he realized I couldn't help him, he didn't want to spend another moment of time," Haverty recalls with a laugh. "He was working all the angles."

Some of Calipari's other contacts proved more useful. Kansas head coach Larry Brown placed a call of support from the Final Four just an hour before his Jayhawks took the floor in the national semifinals against Duke. "I was thrilled to do it," Brown said. "John had a lot to do with me being at the Final Four, and our kids being there."

Ultimately, when other committee members explained that they wanted to create a winner at UMass, but not one that would embarrass the school, Rick Pitino objected. He insisted that all of this dissent was just jealousy coming from rivals who had been outcompeted for recruits by Calipari's hard work. The young guy could coach. His rapport with kids and passion for the game were evident at Five-Star. "If we don't hire Calipari," Pitino concluded, "then we're afraid to win."

It went almost unnoticed in the world of college basketball when John Vincent Calipari signed a contract for $63,000 a year. No TV show. No radio show. No sneaker deal. He did, however, negotiate one perk. The membership at Amherst's Hickory Ridge Country Club—necessary to promote his team with some of the town's more influential people—was paid for by a backer of the UMass basketball program.

The check was signed by Rick Pitino.

# 5: "The King of Everything"

1959-1978
Moon Township, PA

t all began where it all began.

The Basketball Hall of Fame in Springfield sits just four miles from the YMCA where Dr. James Naismith invented the game in 1891. Nearly a century later, on April 25, 1988, John Vincent Calipari stood in the Hall, being introduced as the sixteenth coach in the history of the University of Massachusetts basketball program, the fifth in the last decade. Looking right in the eyes of local reporters, the twenty–nine–year–old Calipari said that he was planning to "create a love affair" between his team and western Massachusetts. Who exactly was this guy?

He was the man from Moon, shooting for the stars.

Moon Township, Pennsylvania, is a community of twenty thousand people just west of Pittsburgh. The origin of the town's name is shrouded in some mystery. The reference librarian in the town library suggests that the name stems from the orb–like shape of the original piece of land when the town was incorporated in 1788. Bill Sacco, who has taught history at Moon Area High School for more than thirty years, thinks the name has roots in the French and Indian War. And Donald Maloney, the vice president of the local historical society, admits, "We have no definite information." Maloney offers only that Moon is not far from Mars or Crescent Township. "We're a very celestial area," he says.

John Calipari arrived in Moon by way of the Calabria region of Italy. His grandfather, for whom he is named, emigrated after World War I. Like many Italian immigrants at the time, he went to work in the coal mines of West Virginia. Stricken with polio at a young age, John's grandfather was paralyzed for much of his adult life, and died in 1958, the year before his grandson was born.

John's father, Vince Calipari, was a child of the Depression who went to work in the steel mills as a teenager. Persuaded by friends that there was a better life to be had fueling airplanes, he got a job with Allied Aviation at Pittsburgh International Airport, Moon Township's greatest claim to fame. Here, at age twenty–two, Vince met nineteen–year–old Donna Payne, who was selling flowers in an airport shop. The next year they were married.

Vince and Donna's life became a page out of the American Dream. Neither had gone to college. They never took vacations. Saving every penny, they tried to make life better for their children, Terri, John and Lea. "We didn't want them like us," says Vince.

In 1960, they scraped together enough money for a down payment on a house in Moon. Their home sat next door to the high school, a place with a reputation for dreadful basketball teams.

John's first memory, so long ago that he's not sure if he actually remembers it or just remembers being told about it, is of being hoisted on his father's shoulders to wave to John F. Kennedy. The president was emerging from a speech at the Jones and Laughlin Steel Mill in nearby Aliquippa. "We were real Kennedy people," Vince Calipari recalls. "My kid was the same age as his boy."

Once in a while John would accompany his father to work at the airport. He liked that world: the roar of engines, the smell of petroleum, the hard tarmac of a million takeoffs and landings. There was something exhilarating about all the bustle, the sense of people going places.

Sports was part of the picture from the beginning. Football is the sport of choice in western Pennsylvania, also known as Quarterback Country USA because it has produced players like Johnny Unitas, Joe Namath, Joe Montana, Dan Marino and Jim Kelly. Calipari's hero, however, was not a local product. He worshipped Fran Tarkenton of Richmond, Virginia. A little guy with a big heart, Tarkenton managed to turn the hapless New York Giants into a winner. He seemed to get it done on will alone, bucking the drop–back mold and becoming the original scrambler. "He wasn't afraid to be different," says Calipari.

Determined to play quarterback on his Midget League team, Calipari faced one significant obstacle. Donna Calipari, fearing for the safety of her rail–thin son, refused to sign the permission form. When the night of the first practice arrived, John bolted away from the kitchen table saying, "Mom, Dad signed the papers, and I'm playing!" He hardly even heard her shouted protests as he scrambled out the door. As

Donna tells the story, it was only an hour later that the phone rang. John was in the hospital with a broken collarbone. ("Busted it good," he said with macho satisfaction more than twenty years later.)

He played baseball too, using his father's oversized glove. When he was nine, Calipari made Moon's under–twelve team; he was determined to play with the big boys because they had real uniforms—even though the wool was plenty hot on summer afternoons.

Deep down, however, there was only one sport for John Calipari. He fell in love with basketball when he became the ball boy for the notoriously feeble Moon Tigers, the high school team that played its games next door. "I don't know how he got there, or if anyone invited him," recalls Bill Sacco, the high school teacher who then served as an assistant coach. "He just invited himself and became part of our entourage."

Calipari sat on the bench wearing a polyester sport coat and clip–on tie, staring at the action. "He was really intent," says Sacco. "He'd yell when we'd yell. We'd scream at referees, so I guess he learned all that from us."

By junior high school, he was obsessed with the game. His mother Donna, by then an aide in the school cafeteria, recalls being approached by an attractive but exasperated girl one day at lunch. "Does John have a girlfriend at another school?" she demanded.

"No," Donna said. "Why do you ask?"

"Because a lot of us like him," the girl blurted out, "and we hear he takes a basketball to bed."

In fact, that was his bedfellow for years. Calipari's sisters, Terri and Lea, recall looking in on their brother many a night and seeing him asleep with the family's black mutt Whiskers on one side, and a basketball on the other.

As a teenager Calipari became what Sacco calls "the gym rat of all gym rats." Determined to practice the game he loved, Calipari devised several ways of breaking into the high school gym, all to the consternation of athletic director Rip Scherer. Calipari first found that he could jimmy the door locks with a pocket comb. When Scherer got wise to that plan, he had chains placed around the doors. One step ahead of the law, Calipari had befriended the janitors. Sometimes those chains weren't tied tight. Sometimes there was a window left ajar in the locker room.

Scherer was not always an easy foe to defeat. One night Calipari and his friend Timmy Miller cowered under the bleachers for two hours after hearing police out in the parking lot, apparently tipped off by the athletic director.

Scherer brought his case directly to Vince Calipari. Granted, John wasn't taking anything or causing any damage, Scherer said, but this was a dangerous precedent. He couldn't just allow kids to break into school. Vince Calipari nodded, but he was only able to manage the mildest of reprimands for his son. After all, as he told Scherer, John was just trying to "better himself."

In truth it was hard to be angry with Calipari. His charisma was undeniable. He was a slick talker who always looked you in the eye. "God gave Johnny a gift with the people," his mother says.

Friends marvelled at his ability to handle oral reports, a much dreaded assignment for most students. He'd come jogging over the embankment in his back yard, arriving at school five minutes late with his dark hair sticking out, smile at the teacher and hit the ground talking. "He'd just wing it," teammate Mike Bartels recalls. "That was his natural gift."

Calipari was a superior fundraiser. School groups like the yearbook would enlist his services, because they knew that when he threw his energy behind something, it would get done. All the kids would gather early on a Saturday morning at the K–Mart parking lot near the Calipari home. Soon they'd be scrubbing windshields, while Calipari waved the cars in, luring driver after driver with his charm.

In high school, Calipari was the point guard, the class president and the prom king. "He was," says teammate Bill Mazar, "The King of Everything."

Mostly, he was king of the court. When it came to basketball, his will seemed to be most ferocious. He was a natural leader. His teammates just followed.

"Johnny would suck you into rebounding like a hundred shots in a row," recalls Bartels. "When it was your turn, somehow you only got twenty–five. He was always scamming and scheming on something."

Even rival coaches were entranced by Calipari's spell. They recognized him as much for his gritty play on the court as for his nerve off of it. Without a moment of hesitation, he would call them up to arrange off–season scrimmages. "Yeah, coach, this is John Calipari over at Moon," he'd say to bewildered men three times his age. "Listen, can your guys play on Thursday afternoon at Ambridge?" Just like that it would be done.

During the season he brought his friends along to as many games as possible. Mazar recalls many a winter night spent at a rival's gym checking out the cheerleaders. When he looked over to find his friend, he'd spot Calipari sidled up to some coach in the stands, mapping out a play on a crumpled piece of paper.

Summers meant basketball camps. Calipari's family couldn't afford to send him to Pistol Pete Maravich's camp at $140 a week, so he settled for Elden Price's day camp at Penn State's Beaver Campus. Every morning he waited for Price's old bus at Winky's hamburger joint, then spent the day playing ball. Ultimately, he earned an invitation to Five–Star, the Pittsburgh satellite of Howard Garfinkel's basketball camp empire. It was here that Calipari was first exposed to a whiff of the bigtime. He sat transfixed by the lectures and demonstrations made by dynamic college coaches. They were young assistants on the rise, people like Bob Hill, Mike Krzyzewski and Rick Pitino.

One summer, Calipari even started his own camp for elementary school children at Moon Park. He roped his friends into helping out as counselors. He got high school and local college coaches to come in as guest speakers. He even wrangled some sponsorship from a nearby McDonald's. "He'd say, 'Today, we're playing for a Big Mac and fries!'" recalls Tim Miller. "What a conniver!"

In Moon, Calipari's gravitational pull had no limits. As Mazar says, "He knew what he wanted and how to get it."

What Calipari wanted most of all was to turn the Moon Area High School Tigers into a winner. Moon had not had a winning record since 1961, nor qualified for the playoffs since 1949. Even in Calipari's junior year of 1976–77, the Tigers won just five games for first–year head coach Bill Sacco. People told Calipari that he would never win at Moon. He scoffed.

The summer before his senior year, Calipari went on a crusade. Having convinced his teammates to forgo other sports for basketball, he put them through a schedule of almost military rigor. Night after night he picked them up and drove out to Center Township, where the court was lit and the games were hot. There was sometimes an hour and a half wait to play, and since winners stayed on the court for the next game, a loss meant another ninety minutes to stew. Calipari was not one to wait.

"He was so intense," recalls Mazar, "just going on about winning and keeping the game going. He always put us in those situations where he got the competition going, and the fierceness. He would start it up from the time we got in the car. He'd get us all fired up. The next thing I know we're fighting each other in the car, twisting hands and arms and pulling hair. We actually had to pull off the side of the road a few times to continue the fight."

Thus provoked, the kids from Moon pushed their play further and further into the night at Center Township. When they were done, Calipari invariably drove them to a pizzeria to debrief the action. Chomping on a pepperoni slice, he took out his notebook and dutifully logged the scores and observations about what the team needed to practice.

A few months later, the same crew was back to playing indoors at Moon High's cinder–block–lined gymnasium. This could–be–anywhere facility had been Calipari's stage for years. Here he had sat on the bench with his clip–on tie as a fourth grader, shouting at the referees. Here he had gotten Bartels to rebound shots by the dozens. Here he had cowered behind the bleachers with Timmy Miller when Rip Scherer had called the cops. He had been to almost every game played in this gym for a decade, and he had never really seen a big crowd. "We used to draw flies," said coach Sacco. "And that's only because we played like garbage."

During the winter of 1977–78, a funny thing happened. Led by a skinny point guard with short shorts, high tube socks and a twelve-alarm blaze raging in his gut, the Moon Tigers became the biggest show in town. Suddenly the gym was so jammed that a spillover crowd had to watch the action on closed–circuit TV in the hallway. With Calipari averaging twenty points and seven assists a game, Moon went 17–8 that year, and made the playoffs for the first time in twenty–nine years.

"You talk about something that you take great pride in, one of the accomplishments that make you say, 'Wow!'" Calipari reflected almost two decades later. "That was it."

Calipari had become like his hero, Fran Tarkenton. He had scrambled. He had infused others with his enormous will. Most of all, he had proven that he had the rare ability to turn a losing team into a winner.

# 6: "The Greatest Building Job in College Basketball History"

November 26, 1988

Amherst, Massachusetts

Six minutes into the first game of John Calipari's coaching career, the University of Massachusetts Minutemen were clinging to a four–point lead against Division II patsy Southern Connecticut. Suddenly, a crowd of 1,100 at the 57–year–old Curry Hicks Cage started pointing to the scoreboard hanging above center court. Soon officials and players noticed. Eventually even Calipari looked up from his locked–in focus on the game. What he saw was smoke billowing up to the rafters. The south side of the scoreboard had blown a fuse. While the game was delayed for half an hour, the sizzling contraption was lowered to the floor and removed. Score was kept the rest of the way by flip charts. Welcome to the bigtime, Coach Cal.

John Calipari had been an assistant at Kansas, one of America's legendary college basketball programs, and then at Pittsburgh in the prestigious Big East Conference. He was used to things being run in a first–class way. When he arrived at UMass, he saw no class at all.

The phones in his cramped office were rotary dial. The seats on the bench at the Curry Hicks Cage said "Property of UMass Biology Department." Community interest was meager. Indeed, whole blocks of tickets were actually given away by a local bank during Calipari's first season. The attitude of the students toward the basketball team ranged from indifference to contempt. "Students used to come and hope we'd do badly," recalls guard Cary Herer. "They didn't root for us; they'd root for the other team."

"Unacceptable," Calipari kept saying all season. He was embarrassed when he found out that players were supposed to sleep in the lounge of the foreign students' dorms during intersession in January; at other programs, the kids stayed in hotels. Banned from using buses, UMass players in the old regime traveled to Connecticut's Bradley International Airport in old university vans, the luggage piled on their laps. They used to bring bag lunches provided by the university ("a sandwich, an apple, a cookie and maybe a little juice," recalls forward Ben Grodski); opponents routinely gave their players meal money. Calipari shook his head at the school's unwillingness to pay the Federal Express charges for sending out game films to upcoming foes, even though the opponents routinely provided UMass with that courtesy. It was just unacceptable.

Perhaps most unacceptable of all was the school's insistence that its teams be known as "The University of Massachusetts at Amherst." Were Bobby Knight's teams called the University of Indiana at Bloomington? Was Dean Smith saddled with the University of North Carolina at Chapel Hill? This was the state university, Calipari reasoned, by far the biggest branch of the five–college system. "Massss–a–choooo–setts" (as Calipari liked to say, making his point) was too much of a mouthful. Everyone called the school UMass informally. So the former marketing major commissioned an artist to do some sketches for a new logo. Calipari favored the script "U," followed by the "Mass" in block letters. A new identity was born, one that graced the basketball uniforms, and before long, the outfits and promotional materials of every team on campus. Throughout his UMass career, Calipari proudly kept the original sketches in his desk.

His first players remember him as a kick–ass disciplinarian. When he was hired in April of 1988, he immediately instituted mandatory team breakfasts. If anyone were late or skipped class, the whole team would run at five o'clock the next morning at the football stadium. "Once I was thirty seconds late for breakfast," recalls Matt Anderson. "The next day I was out there running stadium stairs before sunrise."

Once, Calipari was pulled over by a campus cop, who wondered what the ruckus was at the stadium in the wee hours. "I'm the new basketball coach," Calipari said proudly, "and. . ."

To some, the coach's methods seemed harsh, especially in the wake of Ron Gerlufsen's mild–mannered approach. Ranting at referees and hollering at his players, Calipari wore his heart in his mouth. "His show on the sidelines sometimes came at the expense of a player's humility," says Ben Grodski. "He could be very dehumanizing. I felt a tremendous pressure to perform, and to me, basketball is a rhythm game."

Calipari had more than his share of trying moments that first year. Chief among them was the phone call he got from an Amherst police officer at four in the morning on January 3, 1989. Two of his senior starters, captain David (Beetle) Brown and Duane Chase, as well as soon–to–be–eligible junior college transfer George Hardin, had been picked up for burglarizing an Amherst home—on the morning before a game, for good measure. They had been caught in the act, burglary tools and all. A groggy Calipari turned to his wife Ellen and asked, "Have you unpacked all the boxes?" At the time, he later said, he thought he might be fired.

True, the two seniors had not been his recruits. They had been part of a group dubbed "The Jackson Five," after getting wooed by Ron Gerlufsen's assistant, Dennis Jackson. Still, the arrest was an embarrassing reflection on the basketball program. Calipari talked constantly about the importance of "image and perception." This was not exactly the picture he was hoping to paint. The arrested players were dismissed from the team.

Two and a half weeks later, UMass visited a George Washington team that was 0–14, the only Division I team in America without a win. The Colonials would go just 1–27 that year, outdoing even the worst Minuteman teams for futility. The "1," though, was that day, and it came in convincing fashion, 103–77. UMass was up by four at halftime, and then came out with an absolutely disastrous show after intermission: a festival of missed shots, bad fouls and turnovers. As the clock ticked down on a game that had clearly become unwinnable, Calipari lost control. He started screaming at referee Mark DiStaola, trying to get a technical foul. According to UMass administrative assistant Brian Gorman, DiStaola tried to calm Calipari down, telling him, "Sit down, John. The game is over. You're not winning." Calipari took off his jacket and flung it into the crowd. Still, no technical. He ripped off his tie, and heaved it into the stands, where the fans were dizzy with delight. Next, Calipari started unbuttoning his shirt and saying that if DiStaola didn't T him up, he would be naked. Finally, Calipari got his wish. Walking behind the bench after the technical, he started high–fiving GW fans and the Colonial mascot. He left the arena to a loud ovation.

Calipari was passion without polish. He startled students by turning around during games and yelling at them for cynical comments they were making about his players. "You don't do that!" he screamed. "Cheer *for* us." Before long, he won over a number of converts with his flamboyant style. In one game he demonstrated the hustle he wanted by sprinting down the sideline and belly–flopping to the floor, splitting his pants in the process.

He was resourceful, proud of little triumphs. Determined to oust a bird flying through the rafters in the Curry Hicks Cage, he set up a trail of popcorn on the floor one day in practice. The bird ultimately swooped down. Calipari then dropped some popcorn in a trash can. When the bird darted in after it, the coach rammed on the lid with a delighted, "Gotcha," carried the can outside and released his feathered friend.

There were not, however, a lot of big triumphs. For the first time since his junior year at Moon Area High School, Calipari was part of a losing team. When the season was done, UMass was 10–18. It was the Minutemen's eleventh straight losing year under five different coaches. It was, as *Basketball Times* longtime editor Larry Donald would write years later, "as miserable an era as any school had ever endured."

Few observers could hold out much optimism. Calipari's record was actually one loss worse than the previous year under Gerlufsen. UMass had been absolutely pulverized on several occasions, losing ten games by at least nineteen points, six of them by more than twenty–five. The season had been further tainted by the late–night burglary. *This* was the great turnaround?

At the team banquet, held at Season's Restaurant in Amherst, Calipari addressed a small gathering of fans. "He got up there and said, 'We're not planning on getting to the NCAA tournament: we're planning on winning the NCAA tournament,'" Ben Grodski recalled seven years later. "I was thinking, 'You got to be kidding.'"

•

Calipari was confident. Despite appearances, he felt that he had laid the foundation for success. He had demanded, and received, a substantial increase in the basketball budget. His first two recruits, Jim McCoy and Anton Brown, looked like guards he could build the program around. McCoy, a reedy six–three, was the league's freshman of the year, averaging 19.8 points per game; while the six–two Brown was the consummate team player with good shooting touch from long range. The recruiting windfall for the next season included Harper Williams, a tenacious six–seven southpaw from Bridgeport, Connecticut; Tony Barbee, a versatile six–six swingman from Indianapolis; and an intriguing transfer from Richmond, Will Herndon, who played power forward despite being only six–three, thanks to a staggering forty–three–inch vertical leap. What's more, Calipari had surrounded himself with a quality staff. Bill Bayno, who had played two years at UMass during the wretched days of the early eighties, was back with Five–Star Camp connections and a great recruiting touch in the inner city. John Robic, an obsessive student of the game who had worked with Calipari at Kansas, was the restricted–earnings coach.[1] And joining the staff in 1989 from Coppin State was James (Bruiser) Flint, a former Atlantic 10 star at St. Joseph's, who recalled UMass teams so unpopular he once had to go up into the stands to retrieve a ball that had gone out of bounds at the Curry Hicks Cage. All these assistants had been around bigtime basketball. Like Calipari, they were young and aggressive, hungry climbers with a passion for the game. The second season, 1989–90, looked promising.

Calipari was scrambling to establish the "love affair" between his team and the local community that he had discussed on the day he was hired. He held the team's first "Midnight Madness" celebration, drawing a few hundred fans to the Cage for the first practice of the year. In the month leading up to the season opener, he took his team around Western Massachusetts, holding clinics and staging intrasquad scrimmages at high school gyms in Pittsfield, Chicopee and Northampton. Optimism abounded. There was talk about a winning record. Jim McCoy even mentioned his goal of making it to the NIT.

The Minutemen were set to open at home against Lowell, a Division II opponent they had crushed the previous year. The far–from–mighty Chiefs had opened their 1989–90 season a few days before, losing to fellow Division II foe, American International College. A near–capacity crowd of 3,666 turned out to watch the Minutemen launch their breakthrough year with a win.

UMass played miserably and lost, 71–70. Fans filed out shaking their heads. Same old same old.

Glenn Wong, head of the UMass Sport Management Program and a member of the much–ballyhooed committee that had brought Calipari to UMass, visited the locker room that night. Wong saw something he had never witnessed in Calipari before or since: "an edge of doubt." That night the UMass staff stayed at the Curry Hicks Cage until four in the morning, watching the game film and talking. Bruiser Flint, having joined the coaching staff at the strong suggestion of his good friend Bill Bayno, walked out of the building and said with ample sarcasm, "Thanks a lot, Billy."

When the sun came up, UMass basketball started to win. The Minutemen followed up the Lowell fiasco by traveling to Boston University and smashing a pretty good Terrier team, 76–60, behind thirty–two points from McCoy. They opened the Atlantic 10 season with an almost unthinkable six straight victories. Fans started flocking back to the Cage. Cary Herer, an athletically limited but fiercely competitive senior who became the starting point guard that year when Anton Brown went down with an injury, was approached for autographs for the first time in his life. When the Minutemen gathered for post–game meals at Chequers Restaurant in Amherst, they were greeted on several occasions with a standing ovation.

On January 30, 1990, a 10–7 UMass team faced old rival Connecticut, then emerging as a national power. The Huskies were 17–3, ranked Number 13 in the nation. They had just knocked off three teams ranked in the AP Top 25, including a convincing win over Number 15 St. John's a few nights earlier, christening the Huskies' impressive arena, Gampel Pavilion. UMass and UConn had played almost every year since the series was launched in 1904. The Huskies won sixty of the ninety–seven games, dominating except during the coaching heyday of Jack Leaman, when Julius Erving, Al Skinner and Rick Pitino owned the UMass campus. Now the Huskies were stepping into the national glow, while the Minutemen, after years of darkness, were just beginning to see the light. Just back from UMass's long intersession, students seeking tickets lined up for more than three hours outside the Curry Hicks Cage.

Starting a six–seven center (Williams), a six–three power forward (Herndon), and a slow–moving point guard with no jump shot (Herer), UMass did not have the horses to compete. Playing hard, though, the Minutemen found themselves just eight points down with under four minutes to go. Then the game got away, with UConn winning, 94–75. It was to be the last meeting between the schools for many years.

"We are bigger than Massachusetts," UConn coach Jim Calhoun told the *Daily Hampshire Gazette*, "and probably a little quicker, and deeper than they are. They are making great strides, and they are catching up."

"We've come a long way," said Calipari. "But we still have a way to go."

Less than two weeks after the UConn game, UMass hosted Temple. The Owls had established themselves as the premier team in the Atlantic 10 for the last several years. In 1987–88, they helped the A–10 escape the considerable shadow of The Big East by becoming the Number 1 team in the AP poll for much of the season. Working with limited resources and a home gym (McGonigle Hall) that was nearly as minor league as the Curry Hicks Cage, coach John Chaney had built a nationally acclaimed program. His tools were simple: an immensely disciplined style, centered on the best matchup zone defense in college basketball; a raging competitive fire that he instilled in his players; and a fearless scheduling plan, taking on any national–caliber non–conference foe he could. Calipari often said that he admired Chaney. Deep down, the Temple coach was something of a role model. If he could take his team to the top in the A–10, Calipari reasoned, so can I.

Temple had dominated UMass the way few Division I schools had ever dominated anyone. It was not really a rivalry, simply because Temple always won. The two schools started playing in 1982, when Temple joined the league. Since then, they had played sixteen times, with the Owls winning every game. Only one of those contests had been decided by fewer than ten points.

That night proved to be an epic struggle. Emotions ran hot almost from the opening tip. At one point, late in the second half, a UMass defensive flurry denied Temple a shot until Mark Macon forced up a leaner just as, or just after, the shot clock expired. Initially the basket was ruled good, and Calipari exploded at referee Art McDonald. With the UMass coach screaming, the referees huddled and decided that indeed the shot should be disallowed. John Chaney, his tie knot plunging southward, his face concentrated with rage, stormed to the center of the sideline, demanding a conference with the officials. Calipari, determined to hear every word, charged into the fray. Words were exchanged. Chaney reached out, his hands briefly rising to Calipari's neck, before McDonald pulled him away.

The game went to three overtimes before Temple emerged with an 83–82 win. It was a bitterly disappointing loss, but for the dreary UMass basketball program, tunnel light was filtering through.

The Minutemen closed the year with three straight wins, then posted two more to start the Atlantic 10 tournament, advancing to the title game for the first time in their fourteen–year history in the league. "Each win was one of those games where we jumped on each other at the end," recalled Herer. "Each win was bigger than the last."

In an effort to guarantee a good crowd—and in a tacit admission of its far from elite status—the A–10 still granted the homecourt for the championship game to its highest remaining seed, in this case Temple. At stake for UMass was a first–ever A–10 title and an automatic bid to the NCAA tournament. The Minutemen played hard, but lost, 53–51.

Calipari knew his team was not headed into the NCAAs, but he fervently hoped for an NIT bid. Sure, the NIT was firmly established as a second–tier tournament at this point, an afterthought of almosts, but it represented postseason play, something UMass hadn't tasted in years. It represented a rung on the ladder, the beginning of national respect.

Through the first rounds of selections, Calipari heard nothing. Finally, at 11:30, he perked up when the phone rang. Jack Powers of the NIT offered his congratulations. UMass was in, slated to play against Maryland at Cole Field House in College Park. Euphoric, Calipari instantly called his captain, Cary Herer.

Beating a school from the Atlantic Coast Conference was still unthinkable, but the Minutemen played well in a 91–81 loss.

It had been a landmark season. UMass went 17–14, posting its first winning mark in twelve years. At the team banquet in April a notable alum gushed with pride, saying he wouldn't be surprised to see UMass in the NCAA tournament next year. "And when that happens, let me tell you," he said, "I'll be there with the maroon sweatshirt that says 'UMass,' cheering for the team."

Slick Rick Pitino was back on campus. His protégé had created a winner.

It wasn't just the record, though. Under John Calipari, the Minutemen had established a way of playing that would come to define them. There was a certain urgency to their effort, a fury that allowed them to win despite having a significantly undersized team. There was no label for this style quite yet—in later years Calipari would talk about "UMass Basketball" as if it were a separate species of the game. There was no slogan to define it—"Refuse to Lose" was still a few years away. There was just a sense that UMass was going to play the game as if it mattered in some absolutely fundamental way, because the coach accepted nothing less. As center Harper Williams said about Calipari, "Hard ain't hard enough for him."

Players weren't the only ones who found him demanding. Calipari's assistant coaches grew accustomed to his occasional calls in the middle of the night. If he were thinking about basketball at two o'clock, he reasoned, they should be doing the same. Referees knew they were earning every penny when they got set to call a UMass game. Calipari defined the modern school of coaching where "working the ref" was considered part of the territory. He would push to the limit almost every night out. Sometimes his commentary was vulgar; sometimes amusing. Once, after losing two consecutive road games where Murph Shapiro had officiated, Calipari reacted with a sardonic bite when he saw Shapiro on the court yet again for UMass's next contest. "Hey Murph," Calipari said, "you know that saying that association breeds assimilation?" Shapiro stared quizzically at Calipari, who then added, "Now we suck, too."

Calipari wasn't in this business to make friends. Asked to name his favorite book in a published questionnaire for *Hampshire Life* magazine, he responded with Allen Neuharth's *Confessions of an S.O.B.*[2]

•

In 1990–91, UMass improved to 20–13. Two landmark events marked the year.

In January, bulldozers tore up part of the western end of campus that had, until very recently, housed sheep barns for UMass's animal husbandry program. Almost thirty years after the promise of a new basketball arena had lured Johnny Orr as coach, the project was underway. As charming and character–filled as the Curry Hicks Cage was, John Calipari knew that a new arena was a critical factor for success in modern college basketball. It helped with recruiting, with television, with the whole "image and perception" that the coach talked about all the time. If they built it, the bigtime might come.

Then in February, UMass played its first scheduled game on ESPN. The Minutemen had appeared on the all–sports cable station the year before in the A–10 title loss at Temple, but they had never been part of the preseason lineup—a status that was starting to separate the hoop haves from the hoop have–nots. Calipari had befriended Tom Odjakjian, the station's scheduling chief for college basketball. UMass would play anybody, Calipari said, anywhere, anytime. Odjakjian finally tossed him a bone, a midnight game against Boston University. This was not exactly a ratings blockbuster, but it seemed special at UMass. Students lined up early with painted faces and deflated basketballs for caps. Calipari, well on his way to folk hero status, ordered one hundred Domino's pizzas for the fans. By the time the game tipped off, the Cage was rocking, and UMass rolled to an 82–65 win.

Alas, hopes for an NCAA tournament berth crashed to earth in the opening round of the Atlantic 10 tournament, when UMass was picked off in overtime by George Washington University and its first–year head coach, Mike Jarvis.

Back in the NIT, UMass won its first two games over La Salle and Fordham, then set its sights on Siena. The Minutemen were 19–11 when they traveled to the Knickerbocker Arena in Albany, N.Y. At stake was not only the first twenty–win season since 1977; a victory would also mean a trip to the NIT Final Four. Granted, this was not the "real" Final Four. It was still the NIT. But the semifinals and finals would be played at Madison Square Garden, the most famous arena in the country. It was a trip the players desperately wanted to take.

Down three points with 2.9 seconds to go and inbounding the ball from under the Siena basket, UMass seemed to be finished. In fact, Siena PA announcer Bob Lawson told the 14,084 fans assembled during the timeout that a ticket and bus package was available to watch the Saints at Madison Square Garden for $45. He even gave a phone number. Calipari later admitted that he caught himself thinking, "Well, 19–12, that's not bad. That's a step."

Tony Barbee fired a baseball pass to halfcourt that seemed to be tailing out of bounds when Anton Brown jumped high to snare it, calling another timeout with 2.3 seconds left. On the ensuing inbounds pass from Brown, the first option was to go to Jim McCoy, who was tightly covered. Option two called for three–point specialist Rafer Giles, who was similarly locked up. In desperation, Brown finally flipped the ball to Barbee, who was racing back toward the sideline, far beyond the three–point arc. The sophomore from Indianapolis had hit only two of thirteen shots that night, missing his last eight. Careening to the floor just after releasing the ball, Barbee never saw it sail through the hoop.

"It was the shot of maybe the century for the University of Massachusetts," exclaimed an exultant Calipari after the Minutemen had won in overtime.

"It just seemed like we just kept winning that game, winning that game," said a despondent Siena coach Mike Deane. "And UMass would not go away."

For many UMass fans, this would be the night when the team's defining spirit was born. Even when the Minutemen went on to lose both games at Madison Square Garden, there was a clear sense that the bad days were gone forever.

•

The anticipation for the 1991–92 season was greater than UMass had known since the days of Dr. J. Calipari's first recruits, Jim McCoy and

Anton Brown, formed an experienced senior backcourt. McCoy was well on his way to becoming the school's all–time leading scorer, and Brown had become a steady point guard. Electrifying senior Will Herndon and versatile junior Tony Barbee provided an inside–outside combination of experienced forwards. And junior center Harper Williams had grown into the definitive Calipari player—relentlessness on both ends of the court. Plus, the promising new wave of recruits was led by the highest–profile prep player Calipari had landed at UMass, a forward from Atlantic City named Lou Roe.

The Minutemen opened their season at home against Siena, another midnight bone from ESPN, and rolled to a thirty–five–point win. After a forty–nine–point blowout over Keene State, the Minutemen traveled to their first nationally recognized in–season tournament, the Great Alaska Shootout. Three victories later, UMass was 5–0, boarding a plane for Cincinnati, en route to Lexington, Kentucky.

Rick Pitino was now in his third year as head coach of the Wildcats. At thirty–nine, he had enjoyed a peripatetic and hugely successful career already. After staging dramatic turnarounds at Boston University and Providence, he jumped to the NBA with the New York Knicks in 1987. Returning to his New York home, a seeming dream job for Pitino, he quickly worked his magic at the professional level. The Knicks, 24–58 the year before, improved to 38–44 in his first year—the same season in which Pitino played an integral role in getting Calipari hired at UMass. His second year in New York, the Knicks were 52–30. Pitino was hailed as a coaching genius, a man at the very top of his game. But he wasn't happy. The next season he shocked people in New York by leaving for Kentucky, a place he liked to call "The Roman Empire of College Basketball."

The Empire was in ruins. Winners of five national titles, the Wildcats were coming off a humiliating 13–19 season in 1988–89. Worse, they had just been hit with NCAA probation after an embarrassing string of misdeeds was brought to light. The once regal reputation of the basketball program had unraveled, along with an infamous Emery Air Freight envelope with twenty $50 bills sent to the father of a recruit. The *Sports Illustrated* cover said simply, "Kentucky Shame."

Pitino blasted into the bluegrass, launching another turnaround. Banned from television and postseason play and restricted in recruiting by the NCAA, Kentucky went 14–14 in 1989–90, then 22–6 in 1990–91. Now, eligible once again for the postseason, Pitino was determined to take Kentucky to the top. Coming into the UMass game, his team was ranked fourteenth in the country.

Playing before a crowd of 23,000 at Rupp Arena, the largest ever to see a UMass game, the Minutemen hung tough for a half. In the second half, though, the Wildcats surged for an easy 90–69 win. Afterward, Pitino visited the UMass locker room to talk with Calipari and the players. He told the Minutemen that they were the best UMass team he had ever seen. As a UMass graduate, he said, he was proud. He expected the Minutemen to do some damage in the NCAA tournament.

UMass had clearly taken some big strides in three–plus years under John Calipari. The Minutemen had traveled the road from awful to average to pretty good, but they were still a long way from the Road to the Final Four. They had yet to play in the NCAA tournament, nor had they beaten a team that was ranked in the AP Top 25. Their status was evidenced by the contract Calipari signed with Oklahoma for the Sooners to play at the Springfield Civic Center on the night of January 4, 1992. "Sure," Oklahoma coach Billy Tubbs said, "I'll come to Massachusetts to play you a game, Johnny, just as long as you come back to Oklahoma to play in each of the next two years." Without hesitation, Calipari signed.

The Oklahoma game held the lure of national acceptance. UMass, 10–2, faced a 10–0 team then ranked Number 14 in the AP poll. The game was televised by ESPN right in primetime, eight o'clock on a Saturday night. Some 8,400 fans packed the Civic Center—the largest home crowd that had ever been to a UMass game.

They went home just south of delirious. Calipari whipped his players into a defensive ferocity that forced the Sooners to work mightily for everything. When it was over, the Minutemen had a convincing 86–73 victory. "They'll probably never play as good as they did today," said Oklahoma center Bryan Sallier.

On Monday, January 6, UMass found out that it was ranked twenty–fifth in the nation. The Minutemen had cracked the AP poll for the first time in school history.

It was a marvelous year. The players didn't look like much in the layup lines, but the wins kept piling up. Calipari proudly talked about UMass embodying New England, by doing more with less.

On February 16, a Sunday afternoon, the Minutemen played host to the Temple Owls at the Curry Hicks Cage. Though not a great Temple team, the Owls were still 12–8. In Philadelphia, they had manhandled the Minutemen, 83–61. No team in the nation enjoyed a larger win streak over another than Temple's mind–boggling 21–0 lifetime mark against UMass.

Toward the end of the Minutemen's emphatic 67–52 victory that day, a funny thing happened at the hot and humid Cage, crammed with 4,058 fans. Swirls of paint from the ceiling became dislodged from all the moisture and cascaded down to the floor. The game had to be stopped on a couple of occasions as the accidental confetti was cleared from the court.

Afterward, nearly the whole crowd stuck around as Calipari reported to the press table for his postgame show on local radio station WHMP. Just three years ago he was chastising fans for their sarcastic remarks about the Minutemen; now many were bowing to him with reverential salaams.

He owned the place. Even as the UMass athletic program reeled that winter from the sudden resignation of popular football coach Jim Reid (who claimed that he was forced by the administration to renege on scholarship commitments he had already made), Calipari stayed above it all. He was seemingly immune to the morass of budget cuts and low morale afflicting much of the campus. The Mullins Center was going up. So was UMass basketball.

The Minutemen won their first–ever Atlantic 10 title in that 1991–92 season, followed by their first–ever A–10 tournament championship.

The hallowed NCAA tournament, an age–old quest for UMass, had finally been attained. The Minutemen entered as the third seed in the East with a 28–4 record. No team in America had more wins.

The Minutemen crushed fourteenth–seeded Fordham in the opener in nearby Worcester, and faced sixth–seeded Syracuse two days later. To defeat a Big East foe and make it to the Sweet Sixteen would top off the greatest season in UMass history.

It was a tight game throughout regulation, which ended in a 64–64 tie. In overtime, clinging to a 72–71 lead with thirty–eight seconds left, UMass inbounded from under its own basket. Not noticing the shot clock ticking down, Will Herndon dribbled away from the basket where he heard Harper Williams screaming for the ball beyond the three–point arc. Williams had had a tremendous year, winning the Atlantic 10 Player of the Year Award, but he was the author of precisely one three–pointer in his career. "I *am* a three–point shooter," he insisted after his shot sealed a 77–71 victory.

*Anton Brown and Lou Roe celebrate UMass's first Atlantic 10 championship in 1992. (Photo courtesy of the Daily Hampshire Gazette)*

Earlier in the day at the same arena, second–seeded Kentucky won a free–wheeling 106–98 decision over Iowa State. Johnny Orr, the Iowa State coach late in a successful career that had started at UMass in 1963, was not in a gracious mood. In the postgame press conference he repeatedly and bitterly complained about the antics of Kentucky coach Rick Pitino, who, Orr claimed, constantly stepped outside of the designated "coaching box" in violation of the rules. The rule was not often enforced, he admitted, but rules are rules.

The next weekend of college basketball will always be remembered for the 103–102 victory posted by Duke over Kentucky in the East Regional finals at the Spectrum in Philadelphia. Commonly referred to as the greatest college basketball game ever played, it ended with Christian Laettner gathering in Grant Hill's length–of–the–court pass, spinning and burying a jump shot at the buzzer. The shot sent Duke to the Final Four, and ultimately, to the national championship.

First, though, both teams had to advance to the regional final. Duke did it with a relatively easy victory over Seton Hall. Kentucky did it against UMass.

The media built up the Sweet Sixteen game as the story of Rick Pitino coaching against his clone, John Calipari. The UMass coach did little to discourage that line, showing up at a press conference in a Pitino mask that had been used in a Kentucky promotion. Asked to contrast his style with Pitino's, Calipari said, "He wears Gucci shoes. I wear itchy shoes."

UMass could not handle Kentucky star forward Jamal Mashburn that night. The Wildcats built up a seemingly insurmountable twenty–one–point lead in the first half. Frothing with his usual intensity, Calipari exhorted his players to work harder. Anything was possible.

In the second half, the Minutemen stormed back, drawing within two points at 70–68 with 5:47 remaining. After Kentucky grabbed an offensive rebound, the whistle blew. It was a sound heard all over New England. Referee Lenny Wirtz, pointing diagonally across the court at Calipari, signaled a technical foul for straying out of the coaching box. It was, even Pitino admitted, "the turning point of the game." While contending that Calipari didn't deserve the technical, Pitino speculated that the UMass coach had been whistled because of his game–long badgering of the referees. In any event, UMass was never able to regain momentum and lost, 87–77.

Calipari never lashed out at Lenny Wirtz. In the postgame press conference he bit his tongue, saying that officials have a right to make that call. There was still plenty of time left, Calipari pointed out. The Minutemen still had ample chance to win. They just didn't get it done.

Others around the UMass program were not as charitable. "Lenny Wirtz" would become synonymous in certain circles with "getting screwed." Veteran sportswriter Milt Cole of the *Daily Hampshire Gazette* couldn't resist a shot. The five–six, sixty–four–year–old Cole referred to Wirtz as "aging and diminutive."

For Calipari, the fight wasn't worth it. Life was good. His team had gone 30–5. He had led UMass to the NCAA tournament for the first time in thirty years. He had orchestrated what Rick Pitino would soon call "the greatest building job in college basketball history."

# 7: "REFUSE TO LOSE"

January 12, 1993
Piscataway, N.J.

ohn Calipari struck gold with "Refuse to Lose." Mike Williams was the miner.

The 1992–93 Minutemen suffered a major setback on December 26 when senior Harper Williams (no relation to Mike) broke his right hand in practice. As a junior, Harper had been the first Minuteman ever to receive the Atlantic 10 Player of the Year award. A gangly six–seven forward forced to play center, he had become Calipari's prototypical player: small of stature, huge of heart. It wasn't that other players weren't trying their hardest—under Calipari, they had no choice but to give their all. Still, Williams's hardest was harder; his all was more. He seemed to have a special gift for effort. Calipari christened him "The Warrior."

Without him for weeks, UMass survived against some of the softer teams on the schedule. In January, though, the Minutemen lost consecutive games to Cincinnati and Temple for their first back–to–back losses in almost two years. They went into Rutgers for a game at "The Rack" (Rutgers Athletic Center) where UMass had won just once in sixteen tries. Sensing a season headed south, Calipari worked himself into an emotional frenzy in the locker room. Administrative assistant Brian Gorman recalls him saying, "You've got to dive after every ball. Stick your nose in their chests on defense. Contest everything. You've got to refuse to get boxed out. Refuse it! You've got to refuse to lose!"

With the score tied at seventy–eight and the clock ticking down, sophomore guard Mike Williams steamed upcourt. He had three–point specialist Jerome Malloy wide open on the right wing, but Williams didn't even look at him. From far beyond the three–point line he let fly. The ball sailed through the cylinder with 1.7 seconds remaining. Calipari said it was UMass's biggest victory in his five years at the school.

"Refuse to Lose" became the UMass battle cry. Before long it was affixed to the team's warmup suits. It was shouted from T-shirts. The UMass summer basketball camp became "John Calipari's Refuse to Lose Basketball School." A few years later, Calipari filed paperwork to trademark the phrase. But long before it became a cash cow for the coach, "Refuse to Lose" simply defined the way the University of Massachusetts basketball team played under John Calipari. It was the perfect slogan.

And it might never have been adopted if Mike Williams hadn't hit that shot, his first of many game–winners at UMass.

Williams's shot launched a twelve–game winning streak that occurred at a landmark time in UMass history. One of those wins was the last game ever played at the Curry Hicks Cage. The farewell party was a midnight contest between UMass and Southwestern Louisiana, billed as "Rage in the Cage vs. the Ragin' Cajuns." It was a made–for–ESPN event, a cutesy matchup based on a pun.

In some ways the real finale at the Cage had been the previous game when the Minutemen hosted Temple. As it was so often, the steamy, sticky Cage was a vat of emotion that Thursday night. Sitting on top of the action, the fans shared the experience in a way that was only possible in the old gyms of a bygone day.

During its sixty–two–year history, the Cage had been, at various times, both an embarrassment and an absolute haven for college basketball. The Cage had seen squirrels and paint chips, a dirt floor and Dr. J. This was where Jack Leaman coached. This was where Rick Pitino broke Mike Pagliara's thumb. Here Alex Eldridge had closed his controversial career by saying, "The Cage is the Joint." UMass teams had sparkled and suffered in the old building. At the Cage John Calipari began his coaching career by trapping birds in trash cans and watching the scoreboard smolder.

Sporting a huge splint on his right hand, Harper Williams returned from a nine–game absence to keep the Minutemen afloat in an otherwise woeful first half against Temple. After intermission, the team surged. The crowd pulsed. At one point, pep band director Tom Hannum went jaw to jaw with one of the officials.

UMass almost choked the game away, then found new breath. At the buzzer Tony Barbee scored for a 52–50 win.

Amid the bedlam, Jay Neugeboren—UMass professor of English, writer–in–residence and basketball junkie—took a moment to soak up the joy with his son, Eli, who would head to college the next fall.

The two had been coming to games at the Cage for ten years, since Eli was eight.

On the way home Jay turned to Eli and said, "When one day you fall in love, I hope you'll be as happy as you were tonight."

"I better be," said Eli.

"Well," replied Jay, "that'll be the test."

The $51 million Mullins Center opened on February 4, 1993. John Calipari, architect of the UMass basketball program, hailed it as "the nicest building in New England." To be sure, it was testimony to the bigtime. As the clothes make the man, the building makes the college basketball program. The Mullins Center was, for Calipari and the university, all about improving image and perception. It would boost recruiting and generate revenue. There were 9,493 seats, more than twice the capacity of the Cage. The Minutemen christened it that night with a sloppy, but characteristically scrappy 64–59 overtime win against West Virginia.

In 1993, the Minutemen again won the Atlantic 10 regular season title, and again played host to the A–10 tournament championship game. After beating Temple, 69–61, they received the trophy on the floor of the Mullins Center, and Temple coach John Chaney made his team watch the awards ceremony. "Normally losers run off the floor," Chaney explained. "But I wanted my team to sit there so they know what it means to be a champion. We may have learned something from that."

Third–seeded in the NCAA East Regional, UMass barely edged fourteenth–seeded Penn, 54–50, at the Carrier Dome in Syracuse. In the second round the Minutemen were manhandled by beefy Virginia, a middle–of–the–pack team from the mighty Atlantic Coast Conference. Late in a 71–56 loss, a worn–down and bitterly disappointed Harper Williams made a lackluster semi–dive after a loose ball. Instantly, Calipari took him out of the game. The Warrior finished his college career on the bench for not hustling.

The UMass coach later said that he regretted his decision. It was just a reaction. Anything less than all out, after all, was unacceptable. This was the way Calipari coached. This was the way he expected his players to play. They were supposed to refuse to lose.

A 24–7 season was over.

•

The 1993–94 team looked young and inexperienced. Tony Barbee and Harper Williams, two of the five leading scorers in school history, were gone. There was only one senior, seldom–used walk–on Craig Berry.

Just about everyone felt that the team was one year away from any chance at greatness.

There was a talented freshmen class with guards Edgar Padilla and Carmelo Travieso joining a silky center named Marcus Camby. A pair of rugged sophomore forwards, Donta Bright and Dana Dingle, looked promising. The heart of the team consisted of three juniors. Lou Roe was the marquee player, a six–seven forward with tenacity and an expanding game in the low post. Derek Kellogg, a local kid from Springfield, was emerging as a steady point guard. And then there was Mike Williams.

Calipari referred to Williams as his one "breakdown player," a term he used without irony to describe the guard's capacity for beating back any defensive challenge. His teammates called him "Uzi" because of his willingness to fire up large numbers of shots. He was Mike Williams, sometimes exasperating, sometimes exhilarating.

The youngest of Al and Sarah Williams's two sons, Mike grew up in Hartford. He was an inner–city kid, but a relatively comfortable one. His parents were together. They both had good jobs. Mike was their baby. "Mike's a good kid," Lou Roe said after their playing careers were over at UMass. "But he was always a little bit spoiled."

After only one official college visit, Williams chose UMass and its brash young coach. He liked Calipari's competitive fire because he knew that underneath layers of distance, the same flame burned in his own gut.

He arrived as a freshman in 1991–92 as a backup for Jim McCoy, the senior guard who was already the school's all–time leading scorer. Almost immediately, Williams and trouble began running together. The breakthrough win that year came against Oklahoma, the magical night at the Springfield Civic Center when UMass posted its first victory over a ranked team and vaulted into the AP Top 25 for the first time. The sweet aftermath of the win was soured somewhat when Mike's parents, angered at the lack of playing time for their son, began screaming at UMass assistant coach Bruiser Flint.

As a sophomore Williams disagreed with Calipari's decision to use him as the sixth man, but he established himself as a gamebreaker. He hit that three–pointer in the closing seconds at Rutgers to launch "Refuse to Lose." Later in the season UMass played George Washington at the Smith Center, the scene of Calipari's partial striptease a few years back. All game long, the Minutemen endured a barrage of abuse from the GW fans, as well as some fierce effort from the Colonials. With the score tied and the clock ticking, Mike Williams nailed another game–winning three–pointer, this one with 0.4 seconds left. After the ball sailed through the hoop, Williams took a triumphant victory lap, taunting the GW fans. John Calipari smiled and winced at the same time.

There was a gentle side to Williams. He was nice with children. After his sophomore year, Williams's girlfriend gave birth to adorable twin sons, Michael and Mishawn. They became regulars at UMass games at the Mullins Center. After the games, Mike would hoist them in his thickly muscled arms and gently coo in their ears. He spoke about them with enormous pride.

There was also an angry side. One year he responded to a sports information questionnaire about his goals by writing, "To get the fuck out of UMass." On a number of occasions he came out for warmups wearing a black shirt with big white lettering that read, "In Your Face."

Mostly there was a mysterious side. Mike Williams was as inscrutable as any player Calipari had ever coached. In some ways he was unbelievably candid—sometimes to his detriment. In other ways he was maddeningly aloof, walling out the world with his Walkman.

Returning for his junior year, Williams was poised to step into a starting role for the first time. This, he felt, would be his breakthrough year. In fact, the 1993–94 season would prove to be a roller coaster of Space Mountain proportions.

Sparked by twenty–three points from Williams, UMass opened the season at home with a victory over Cleveland State in the Preseason NIT. "Mike Williams is our strongest player," John Calipari said that night. "He's our quickest player. He's our best defender. He's got more courage and ability to create shots in a tough time than anyone on our team. If he comes out with this kind of effort, he's first–team All Conference, and maybe Player of the Year in our league."

After routing Towson State, UMass advanced to the NIT semifinals, held the night before Thanksgiving at Madison Square Garden. The opponent that night was North Carolina. Twenty–two years earlier they had met on the same stage in the final college game of Julius Erving's career. North Carolina had won that night, 90–49.

No college basketball team is invincible, but the 1993–94 Tar Heels looked to be one of the mightiest teams in many years. Four starters were returning from a team that won the national championship the year before. What's more, the Tar Heels added the best freshman class in the nation, headed by Jerry Stackhouse and Rasheed Wallace, players destined to be picked in the top–four of the NBA draft just two years later. Carolina was atop every poll, capable, it seemed, of going undefeated. This very night the legendary Dean Smith was going to be coaching the thousandth game of his career. A Tar Heel loss was unthinkable.

Three minutes and forty–one seconds into the game, UMass was trailing, 11–0, when an irate John Calipari called timeout. His face was flush with fury. Sure, no one expected UMass to win, but this was humiliating. The Minutemen were being embarrassed on the grandest basketball stage of them all while millions watched on ESPN. Dick Vitale's pregame forecast seemed dead on target. No chance, baby.

Perhaps Calipari's best strategy would have been dispatching manager Matt Komer to the hallway to yank a fire alarm. Instead, Calipari got right in the face of his players, and screamed, "I'm not letting this happen!"

The words were completely uncalculated: pure reaction, pure rage. They were at once arrogant and preposterous. They were wildly egocentric. *He* wasn't going to let this happen?

Yet this was the way it had always been for John Vincent Calipari. His iron will was so ferocious. His greatest gift as a coach was his ability to infuse others with this will, to get inside their hearts and make them grow. He wasn't going to let this happen.

It didn't. Led by a positively relentless Lou Roe, UMass stormed back. Roe scored twenty–eight points, grabbed fourteen rebounds and practically heated the building with his effort. As the game progressed, wild things started happening. Gawky junior reserve center Jeff Meyer dunked in the face of Carolina's All–American center, Eric Montross. Freshman Edgar Padilla came off the bench to score the first two buckets of his career.

With twenty seconds left and UMass down three, Mike Williams launched a rainbow just over the outstretched hand of Jerry Stackhouse. It sailed cleanly through the hoop, and somehow UMass was going to overtime.

"We've got five minutes to go," Calipari thundered in the huddle. "I need every ounce you have!"

UMass surged ahead. Carolina fought back. With forty–five seconds left, Stackhouse dropped in a pair of free throws to cut the UMass lead to 85–84. The Minutemen fought through Carolina's tenacious trap and got the ball to Mike Williams on the right wing with the shot clock ticking under five. Roe came out to set a screen on his left, but Williams dribbled right and elevated. With thirteen seconds remaining, the ball dropped in for three.

Calipari was surprisingly subdued after the 91–86 win. In part, he was concerned about Camby, who had hurt his knee in the overtime.[1] In part, Calipari's reserve stemmed from respect for Dean Smith, a man he called "an icon." And too, there was always an element of letdown in the immediate aftermath of any game for Calipari—his joy was in competing.

In the wee hours of Thanksgiving morning, though, the scope of the achievement hit him. Watching the game tape with staff and friends in his suite at the Marriott Marquis, Calipari was astonished: UMass beating North Carolina! The remarkable rise of UMass basketball had seen its finest hour. Suddenly, anything was possible.

At three o'clock, Calipari invited friends to go out for a bite to eat. Walking the streets of Times Square, surrounded by the neon flash of theater marquees, the larger–than–life billboards, the site where delirious crowds gather each December 31 to cheer the wild optimism of something new, Calipari glowed.

"He was as excited as I've ever seen anyone be," recalled Duffy Burns, a former Five–Star Camp crony then coaching the women's team at Central Connecticut.

"It was," Calipari would later admit, "one of the greatest nights of my life."

In truth, Calipari probably would not have been basking on Broadway that night were it not for Mike Williams, who had hit the two biggest shots of the game. "With courage, game on the line, who wants the ball?" Calipari said in the postgame press conference. "Mike Williams."

•

After losing the finals of the Preseason NIT two nights later to sixth–ranked Kansas, UMass immediately flew to Norman, Oklahoma. This was the third and final game of the "two–for–one" pact Calipari had signed a couple of years ago to help give the Minutemen some national exposure. The landmark win in Springfield in 1991–92 had been followed by a close loss in Norman a year later. Now a tired Minuteman team returned to the great dust basin to face a Sooner squad that was playing its first game of the year. With UMass trailing, 83–82, in the closing seconds, Williams knifed through the lane in heavy traffic and flipped up what looked like a ridiculous scoop shot from his right hip, too high off the glass. His touch, though, was uncanny. The ball caromed gently off the front rim and dropped through the hoop with 1.4 seconds left. UMass 84, Oklahoma 83.

When the AP poll was released the next day, UMass had reached the Top 10 for the first time in school history. Suddenly, the team that was a year away had arrived in spades.

Praising Williams's courage for taking and hitting last–second shots, Calipari said, "He has testicles the size of a hippopotamus." Of course, Mike Williams had another side, too. Later in the year, Calipari would tell a reporter that Williams was "taking his asshole pills again."

In December, Williams fit in a season's worth of drama. Suspended for a game for missing a morning practice, Williams publicly threatened to transfer after he didn't get his starting spot back the following game. He infuriated Calipari by telling a reporter that he was misused by the coaching staff, and resentful of their showcasing of Lou Roe ("I could dominate just as much as he can.") By the end of the month, though, Williams was back in Calipari's good graces. He apologized in front of the entire team, then went out and won the MVP at UMass's Christmas tournament in Springfield with a couple of superb performances against Hartford (twenty–one points, seven of nine from the field) and Maryland (twenty–five points, seven rebounds, a career–high ten assists).

Williams sputtered in January with some awful shooting nights: five of fifteen, three of fourteen. Against DePaul he hit just six of twenty–one, but still felt stung when Calipari designed the final play for Roe with UMass trailing by two. Roe's three–point bid at the buzzer rimmed out and UMass's ten–game winning streak was over.

The Minutemen lost another two–point game the following week at Cincinnati with Williams shooting just four of fourteen, but it wasn't his statistics that made this game memorable.

It was a furiously paced game in an overheated arena under the glaring lights of ESPN. In the first half UMass looked overmatched, trailing by twenty–two points. After intermission, though, the Minutemen surged. Williams made a great pass to Roe for a basket that closed the gap to three, then started running back upcourt. Suddenly, he collapsed, losing consciousness without even being touched.

Calipari raced onto the court, the first one on the scene, and reached frantically for Williams's chest, trying to find a heartbeat. A raucous Cincinnati crowd turned silent. Awful echoes filled the air. Exactly six months ago, Celtic captain Reggie Lewis had collapsed and died while shooting hoops at Brandeis University. Back in 1990, Loyola Marymount had lost superstar Hank Gathers from cardiac arrest in the middle of a playoff game against Portland.

Williams quickly regained consciousness and was taken off the court by stretcher. From the ambulance he tried to phone a message back to Calipari that he felt fine and wanted to play. (There was no last–second three–pointer that night, and UMass lost, 76–74.)

Initial tests in Cincinnati were inconclusive, and Williams flew back a day later for exhaustive testing at the UMass Medical Center in Worcester. These were tiring and unpleasant days for Williams. Forced to eat a hospital diet and subjected to a battery of neurological and cardiac assessments, he fought a fear that his career could be over. Or worse.

The tests showed nothing. Doctors speculated that Williams had been felled by nothing worse than dehydration. The Nyquil he took before the game for a head cold could have dried him out.

Williams missed three games—wins against Rhode Island and Florida State, and a tight three–point loss at the Meadowlands to Rick Pitino's Kentucky Wildcats. Sitting on the bench in street clothes, he was more openly supportive of his teammates than he had ever been in a UMass uniform, cheering especially for his freshman replacement, Edgar Padilla. Eventually cleared to practice with a "loop monitor" on his heart, Williams proceeded cautiously at first, then let loose. One day he broke up his teammates with a fake fainting spell that had Calipari reaching for the Maalox.

Williams returned to action on the road against Rhode Island, and Calipari used him with the utmost restraint. His first playing stint lasted all of fifty–four seconds, his second thirty–five. He wound up scoring nine points in twenty–one minutes, during which, he insisted, he wasn't concerned about his heart. "I have to put it behind me," he said. "I don't even think about it at all on the court. The only thing I was thinking about was coming out of the game and having Coach Cal yell at me."

UMass returned home on February 13 to take on Temple.

In some ways, the two schools have little in common. Temple is a commuter school plunked down in a rough neighborhood of North Philadelphia. UMass is a state school that sits astride apple orchards in Amherst. They basically share two things: Bill Cosby (who earned his undergraduate degree from Temple and his doctorate from UMass) and a burning rivalry on the basketball court.

For many years Temple had been the mentor and tormentor of the Atlantic 10. The Owls always beat UMass, taking the first twenty–one games of the series. That included the first eight games under John Calipari, though as the Minutemen climbed the college basketball ladder two rungs at a time, the games had gotten closer and closer. In the 1990 game in which John Chaney's hands almost extracted a piece of Calipari's neck, Temple needed three overtimes to turn back UMass.

They were, in a sense, birds of a feather. Impassioned coaches with a lifelong love for the game, Calipari and Chaney were both enormously colorful characters. Calipari was a walking sound bite, Chaney a pugnacious poet who often waxed eloquently about the sociology of the sport. Both preached defense, Calipari a relentless man–to–man, Chaney the most flustering zone in the country. They shared a demanding and animated sideline style, a monomaniacal need to rule, and the initials J.C.

Still, their contrasts were sharp. Even sweating buckets at the end of a game, Calipari seemed poised for a GQ shoot, perfectly tailored, perfectly coiffed. Chaney was a rumpled blanket before games even tipped off. As the action unfolded, his shrapnel voice croaking, his baggy eyes fixed in a glower, he dispatched his sport coat, and his tie knot drooped lower and lower. Set to meet again, Calipari was thirty–five, white, on the rise. Chaney was sixty–two, black, burning to get back on top.

UMass had finally beaten Temple two years ago at the Cage on the day when the paint–chip confetti swirled to the floor. In March of 1993, the Minutemen won their second straight A–10 tournament title by beating the Owls in a bitter battle at the Mullins Center, 69–61. That was the night when Chaney kept his players on the floor for the awards ceremony in the hopes that they would learn "what it means to be a champion."

The Owls entered the 1993–94 season as the prohibitive league favorites. They featured an outstanding senior tandem of Eddie Jones and Aaron McKie, both of whom would become first–round NBA draft choices a few months later. The Owls arrived at the Mullins Center as the eighth–ranked team in the nation with a 17–3 record, while UMass was thirteenth at 18–4. In the league, UMass had the edge, 9–0, to Temple's 10–2.

A capacity crowd and ABC viewers across the country saw a marvelous game—indeed, college basketball at its best. Two defensive-minded teams made each other work for everything. Every possession mattered. Every pass was contested. Every rebound became the most important thing in the world.

McKie and Jones hit all manner of outrageous shots with defenders draped all over them, scoring twenty and nineteen points, respectively. The Owls' renowned zone gave UMass fits. Temple did a particularly good job of bottling up top scorer Lou Roe in the paint, holding him to just six shots from the field and nine points.

The one guy they couldn't stop was Mike Williams, the Minutemen's lone double–figure scorer with seventeen points. When the game came down to one possession, with Temple leading, 55–54, there was absolutely no question who was getting the ball.

With 10.2 seconds left, Calipari called a timeout to design a play. Dana Dingle inbounded to Williams, who had cut hard behind Roe's pick to get open. Williams dribbled left and backed in on Rick Brunson, just left of the free–throw line. When Brunson made a swipe at the ball, Williams took a diagonal step back into the lane, ducking past the defender, floating up toward the hoop, and releasing the ball eight feet from the basket. It sailed cleanly through with three seconds left.

When McKie's desperation heave at the buzzer clanged off the rim, UMass emerged with a 56–55 win.

An exhausted and bitterly disappointed John Chaney summoned the utmost graciousness during Temple's portion of the postgame press conference in the Green Room of the Mullins Center. "A great ball game, wasn't it?" he croaked out for openers. He talked about his daughter and grandchildren being in attendance. He said all the right things about UMass: "First of all, this is a championship ball club. This club should perhaps be the Number 1 team in the country in my opinion." His competitiveness got the best of him only once, when he was asked about the strong likelihood of losing the A–10 title to UMass for a third straight year. "We don't play games on the block," he said. "We don't play community games. The biggest thing for Temple is to get to the NCAAs. So you're the biggest bully on the block—so what?"

While Chaney spoke to the media, Calipari stood out in the hallway talking with Atlantic 10 Commissioner Ron Bertovich. At one point, one of the three referees—Gerry Donaghy, Joe Mingle or Larry Lembo—

emerged from the officials' locker room. What was said has never been clear, though two days later Bertovich released a statement in commissionerese meek–speak: "Approximately 10–15 minutes after the game, Coach Calipari and myself were in the hallway having a private conversation when one of the game officials exited the officials' locker room, located just a few feet away. Coach Calipari made one comment to the official and the official responded. The entire conversation lasted less than one minute and voices were never raised. I reminded both parties that situations such as this should be handled in accordance with conference policies."

Calipari seemed drained when he walked to the lectern. Derek Kellogg, Mike Williams and Donta Bright were seated to his left. The coach looked at the stat sheet. He talked about "a terrific basketball game" and "two teams [that] really fought like heck." Asked about Mike Williams, he said, "The kid's got all the courage in the world."

Then, in a move decidedly not in accordance with conference policies, John Chaney returned to the room. "You've got a good ball club," he said, "but what you did with the officials out there is wrong. I won't be a party to that!"[2]

Calipari pointed his left index finger at Chaney and said, "You weren't out there, Coach. You don't have any idea."

"You don't say shit to officials without me being involved in it," Chaney shot back. "You got a game that was given to you by the officials right here with GW on three bad calls, okay? And you send your guys out there pushing and shoving. The guys did a hell of a job. You had the best officiating you could ever get here. And for you to ride them, I won't be a party to that. I just got my ass blasted for giving them hell down in West Virginia. And here you did a hell of a job riding them today. Good job! Three class guys, and you pick on them out here and single them out—"

"Hey Coach, Coach, I'm going to tell you something—"

"Shut up, goddammit!" Chaney said, starting to charge toward Calipari at the front of the room before being physically restrained.

"You weren't there, Coach," Calipari said.

"I'll kill you," Chaney shouted as he was led away. "You remember that, I'll kick your ass. Kick your ass! You've got a good team and you don't need that edge! That's why I told my kid to knock your fucking kid in the mouth!"

The incident topped sports broadcasts across the country. It was

*When John Chaney ran at John Calipari, Mike Williams was there to take the charge. (Photo by Emily Kozodoy)*

rare for the cameras to be rolling in the heat of such genuine rage. There were juicy, if frightening, elements to the whole thing. The threat of violence. Racial overtones. Passion absolutely exploding out of one of the most respected coaches in the business.

Scarcely noticed in all the commotion was this fact: the player who leaped to his feet to protect Calipari, absorbing Chaney's open hand to his face, was none other than Mike Williams.

•

There are people who swear by John Calipari. In Western Pennsylvania, people say that he has never forgotten his roots. He is still good friends with his high school coach, Bill Sacco. He still gets together with high–school buddies. His college coach, Joe DeGregorio, remembers that Calipari is the only player he ever coached who sent a thank–you note to his wife after a team dinner. At ESPN, Tom Odjakjian says, Calipari always remembered the names of the interns. The vast majority of his former players speak about him with genuine warmth.

And there are people who swear at him. Calipari is too brash, they say, too crass, too image–conscious. Some feel that he is obsessed with winning, that his "Refuse to Lose" bespeaks an arrogance, that he will do anything to win. When he talks about playing as if a loss means a trip to the electric chair, some infer that basketball is life or death to him. Calipari's commitment to his job creates some comical moments. Once he tried to convince the local NBC station to televise a Thursday night game, only to be told that they couldn't interrupt network programming. "I understand, " Calipari said, "you can't preempt Cosby." The Bill Cosby Show had been off the air for more than a year.

His commitment can also be poignant. Once, he admitted, he overheard his daughter speaking with a friend. The friend said that Erin was lucky to have such a famous father. "Why am I lucky?" Erin demanded. "He's never here."

He sees himself as a family man and as an educator, but he also knows he is the fiercest of competitors. In the aftermath of the Chaney incident, some people derided his "aggressive counseling" of players and "working the refs," but he wasn't about to change. He certainly wasn't the only emotional coach out there.

Besides, he had not been the one who had exploded in front of the cameras. He chafed mightily at the media descriptions of the incident between him and Chaney. "There was no between," he said emphatically. He likened himself to figure skater Nancy Kerrigan, who had recently been clubbed by Tonya Harding's henchman Shane Stant.

On Monday, February 14, Chaney was suspended for one game by Temple president Peter Liacouras, a punishment UMass officials privately ridiculed for its leniency. That same day, before UMass flew off for its game at St. Joseph's, Erin Calipari turned to her father with a doleful expression and asked, "Are you going to get hurt in Philadelphia?"

In a manner of speaking, he was. On Tuesday night, the Minutemen lost their first league game of the year to the last–place Hawks, suddenly reopening the A–10 race. UMass had one loss in the league and faced tough road games coming up at Temple and George Washington. Two losses, and Temple would be tied with the Minutemen.

On Wednesday, a teary–eyed John Chaney apologized to Calipari through the Philadelphia media, saying that neither his wife nor his daughter was talking to him. The next day the two men spoke on the phone and apparently cleared the air.

Still, the atmosphere was supercharged the next week when UMass returned to the City of Brotherly Love to battle Temple at McGonigle Hall. Outside, on the frigid corner of Norris and Broad Streets, a large mural spelled out, "To err is human, to forgive divine. We love Coach Chaney." Inside, the student section was packed and rocking two and a half hours before game time. The students had come out for Senior Night, the last home game for star players Eddie Jones and Aaron McKie. They were there for Chaney. They were there to avenge the stinging loss in Amherst eleven days before, and to make sure the home streak continued: UMass had never won in twelve tries at the McGonigle Hall of Horrors.

When Chaney arrived at courtside shortly before the 9:30 tipoff, he was treated like a head of state, ringed by cameras and escorted by a large entourage. Calipari did not receive quite the same welcome. He was booed upon arrival and shadowed all night by two beefy security guards. Before the game Chaney walked over to Calipari, and in a made–for–ESPN moment, stiffly hugged the UMass coach.

The two men coached with their usual fervor. Calipari squatted courtside, one hand on the sideline, lasering his brown eyes on the action. Chaney glowered and glowed, exacting every shred of effort from his players.

Mike Williams took apart the Temple zone in the first half, hitting four three–pointers while UMass opened up a 30–21 lead. In the second half, the Owls rallied behind Eddie Jones and some suffocating defensive pressure to take a 50–48 lead in the final minute.

After calling their final timeout with twenty seconds to go, the Minutemen inbounded from halfcourt. The Owls had four fouls to give before hitting the one–and–one penalty, and their strategy seemed clear when Rick Brunson fouled Derek Kellogg forty feet from the hoop with seventeen seconds remaining. By fouling every couple of seconds, Temple could eat the clock without giving UMass a chance.

As the Minutemen again inbounded, though, Jones neglected to come after Williams, who was way out on the right wing. ("Eddie just completely forgot," Chaney later said.) Williams thought about penetrating, but changed his mind when he saw some room. The six–two guard launched a three–pointer from at least five feet behind the arc, just over the outstretched fingertips of the six–six Jones.

It was an awful looking shot. Way too high. Way too hard.

It banged off the backboard and rattled through the rim with eight seconds left.

When UMass survived a furious Temple charge at the finish, the Minutemen escaped with a 51–50 victory, clinching the league's regular–season title for the third consecutive year. As an incredulous John Chaney shook Calipari's hand, Mike Williams shot his fist in the air and shouted at the Temple fans.

It was the most riveting moment of a staggeringly dramatic season. Needing some time to decompress, the Minutemen bused down to the nation's capital that very night, arriving at four in the morning. They had a couple of days before the GW game on Sunday and they took full advantage. On Saturday, they got a tour of the White House, courtesy of National Security Advisor Anthony Lake, a longtime resident of western Massachusetts. Calipari, the scrappy kid from Moon who had once been hoisted on his father's shoulders to see John F. Kennedy, sat briefly at Bill Clinton's desk. The Minutemen were on top of the world.

Sunday's game against the 15–9 George Washington Colonials had little meaning for the eleventh–ranked Minutemen. Still, it irked Calipari when UMass was manhandled by a physical GW club that desperately needed a win to get into the NCAA tournament. Calipari stalked the sidelines, railing at the referees for, in his view, swallowing their whistles and playing to the home crowd.

For all the recent hullabaloo with John Chaney, it was really GW coach Mike Jarvis who felt most like a porcupine in Calipari's socks. Early in the year when UMass defeated the Colonials at the buzzer after trailing all game, Jarvis smiled at reporters and said, "Tell Calipari he's a lucky son of a bitch." After Chaney's Green Room eruption, Jarvis told a Boston reporter that the Temple coach "had a point." Now, with the Colonials up by fourteen points with forty seconds remaining, Jarvis called a timeout and then, staring at the UMass bench, returned his starters to the floor. Calipari was outraged. He instructed his players to walk out on the court and call a timeout of their own, even though UMass didn't have any timeouts remaining. The technical foul would be worth it to show up Jarvis.

"Don't do that," Calipari heard from the huddle. "Show some class." He looked up and saw Mike Williams talking. Calipari could only shake his head. The kid was right.

The long season spilled into March. In the regular–season finale at home against Duquesne, Williams was pulled from the game after some sloppy play down the stretch, and became involved in a screaming match with assistant coach Bill Bayno. When Bayno turned his back, Williams flung a towel at his head. Once again, storm clouds gathered.

After meeting with Williams and Bayno, Calipari decided to take no action. It was a "heat–of–the–battle" kind of outburst, he said, and Calipari of all people knew about fire. Besides, it was time for the postseason.

The opening rounds of the Atlantic 10 tournament took place at Philadelphia's fabled Palestra. Top–seeded UMass blitzed past St. Joseph's and Duquesne. Second–seeded Temple beat Rutgers and then smothered GW, holding the Colonials to just ten second–half points in a 54–34 win—the 500th of John Chaney's distinguished coaching career.

Chaney knew that number 501 was going to be tough, especially because of the A–10 policy of staging the championship game at the homecourt of the highest remaining seed. Few fans at the Mullins Center were in a forgiving spirit. Even Chaney's daughter Pamela, who works for a Massachusetts pharmaceutical company, had a hard time letting go of her anger. "She's still ashamed of me," Chaney said. "In fact, she's already bought herself a Massachusetts sweater, and she's going to be sitting on their side. She'll probably be throwing things at me, too."

In the ninety–eight–year history of Temple basketball, no team had ever defeated the Owls three times in one season. Both twelfth–ranked Temple (22–6) and ninth–ranked UMass (26–6) were a bit banged up and tired after playing exhausting schedules, but neither wanted any excuses. "If you're not excited and you can't get up for this time of year, so be it: your ass should be out of here," said Chaney. "Pack your bags and go home, and look at the TV at the guys who don't get tired when it's time to win."

The six–seven Lou Roe soared over the six–eleven William Cunningham to win the opening tap, and seconds later Mike Williams buried a three–pointer from deep on the left wing. It was the beginning of an avalanche. Six minutes and fourteen seconds into the game, John Chaney, who generally refuses as a point of honor to call a timeout to cool off an opponent, swallowed hard and stopped the clock with UMass leading, 15–2. Moments later, the lead ballooned to 24–3. For UMass, the game was Fantasy Island; for Temple, Murphy's Law.

It couldn't last. Behind an acrobatic assortment of leaning, twisting jumpers by Aaron McKie, the Owls closed to 35–21 at halftime. With McKie and Eddie Jones doing all the scoring, Temple began the second half with an 11–0 run that cut the gap to three. That sweetest of candy that had been dangled in front of the Mullins crowd was now cruelly snatched away.

Until Mike Williams yanked it back. On successive possessions he knocked down a pair of three–pointers. UMass won, 70–59.

McKie had been majestic, scoring a Mullins–record thirty–three points. Williams, though, had answered every challenge. He led UMass with twenty–one points, and when the tournament's Most Valuable Player was announced, there were no surprises. As the crowd thundered, Williams walked out to center court to accept the trophy, carrying son Mishawn on his shoulders.

Temple met first with the media in the Green Room, and Chaney lauded the champions: "It's up to them, but I think they have the capability of being the very best team in this country. I haven't seen anybody better."

Long after UMass finished its portion of the press conference, Mike Williams remained in the locker room. Slowly, he dressed while answering questions from reporters. Asked about Calipari, Williams said, "I have to give Coach Cal so much credit for keeping me here and having confidence in me. It's time to give something back, and that's what I'm trying to do, trying to give something back to him. He gave me a chance, something to live for. My dream's still alive because of him."

As it turned out, Calipari was standing in a corridor outside the locker room at the time, talking about Williams to a cluster of local media: "Does he have some screw–ups every once in a while? Yeah. But he's got money in the bank now. And it has nothing to do with basketball. He's grown."

It was well past midnight when Williams emerged, spotting Calipari inside the semicircle of TV cameras and tape recorders. The junior guard walked by with a quiet, "All right, Coach."

Calipari looked up. "All right, Michael."

•

The state of Kansas has a grand basketball tradition. Just seven years after inventing the sport in western Massachusetts, Dr. James Naismith—the original Dr. J—was hired as a professor and inaugural basketball coach at the University of Kansas. In time, the Jayhawks became synonymous with bigtime college hoops. The great Phog Allen won more than five hundred games. Two of his players, Dean Smith and Adolph Rupp, became legendary coaches at North Carolina and Kentucky, the two winningest programs ever. Wilt Chamberlain played at Kansas. National championships were won. Kansas was also where twenty–three–year–old John Calipari began his meteoric rise in college coaching as an unpaid graduate assistant.

But that basketball tradition was all up the road in Lawrence. In Wichita, where UMass was plunked down as the second seed in the Midwest Regional, there was not much history with the game—just a couple of decent teams at Wichita State. At the sixteen–year–old Kansas Coliseum, there was no hoop tradition at all. The Harlem Globetrotters had wheeled out their tired act a few years ago, but there had never been a competitive basketball game in the building until this set of opening–round NCAA games in 1994. Sitting astride corn fields and a dog track on the periphery of the city, the coliseum had served as the home of moderately popular indoor soccer and minor league hockey teams, and as the host of star–studded events like the Kansas Beef Expo. Just three days earlier, the Western Trails Rodeo had pulled out of town. In the exhibition hall next to the arena, the place where postgame interviews were conducted, the strong scent of manure was still pervasive.

The 1993–94 season had already been an all–consuming ride for UMass, a truly landmark season. The Minutemen cracked the AP Top 10 for the first time, landing in Kansas at Number 8. They knocked off Number 1 North Carolina. They defeated their old nemesis Temple three times. They won twenty–seven games, as many as any team in the country. They won the Atlantic 10 regular season and tournament titles for an unprecedented third straight year.

Still, John Calipari knew that John Chaney had a point: community games didn't really matter in the big scheme of things. So you're the biggest bully on the block—so what? The proving ground of college basketball was the NCAA tournament. There the really elite teams navigate through the sport's maze of alliterations: the Sweet Sixteen, the Elite Eight, the Final Four. "We've had a great year," Calipari said, "but we're going to be judged on what we do in this tournament. We know it. We accept it."

The Minutemen opened against fifteenth–seeded Southwest Texas State. It was a pairing most intriguing for its matchup of Roe v. Wade, UMass's Lou vs. STSU's Lynwood. UMass looked reasonably good in the 78–60 victory. Mike Williams scored seventeen points in the first half while the Minutemen opened a fourteen–point lead. More significantly, late in the second half Williams was five steps ahead of the field on a breakaway when he fed back to Roe for a dunk. All of a sudden he had become the definitive team player: more Cousy than Uzi.

"He gave up a little bit of himself for our team," said Calipari. "He's grown a ton."

"Right now," said Williams, "it's all about finding a way to win."

UMass seemed loose before its second–round matchup with Maryland. Surrounded by a patchwork of national media in the lobby of the Wichita Sheraton, Calipari coolly answered a series of unconnected questions. One television reporter from Chicago, working on a story about coaching superstitions, asked Calipari if he had any. Was he, for instance, wearing the same jockstrap during the team's recent win streak? Calipari stared right into the camera and said calmly, "To tell you the truth, I haven't worn underwear for weeks."

In round two, the Minutemen faced Maryland, a 17–12 team that had lost by twelve to UMass in December. Granted, the Terrapins had girded themselves for postseason play by competing all year in the mighty ACC. Admittedly, they had a superstar freshman named Joe Smith who would be the NBA's top draft pick a little over one year later. Still, UMass was the strong favorite to advance to the Sweet Sixteen.

The Minutemen seemed to be in control with a ten–point lead early in the second half. Then, shockingly, the starry season crashed to earth. Maryland played the half of its dreams, shooting seventy percent, including eight of ten from three–point land. Smith and Mario Lucas, each of whom had hit exactly one three–pointer all year, tossed in one more apiece. The vaunted Minutemen defense disappeared. The fierce will that Calipari had a knack for instilling in his team melted. The Minutemen seemed to be trapped in a basketball quicksand: the harder they tried to escape, the deeper they plunged. Lou Roe, who had risen in big games so often, was neutralized. Mike Williams, Mr. Clutch, scored only four of his thirteen points in the second half. Only the breakthrough performance by freshman Marcus Camby (thirty–two points, ten rebounds) even kept the game close. UMass lost, 95–87.

It was an underachieving finish to an overachieving season. The expectations that flowered in Madison Square Garden wilted in Wichita. A somber Roe stood in the manure–scented hallway, stinging from the loss and its awful abruptness. He liked to talk about the NCAA tournament with the usual clichés—it's one and done, go hard or go home—but now that it was done and time to go home, he couldn't really believe it. Shaking his head slowly he said, "I thought we could do things with this team."

Roe's fellow captain, Derek Kellogg, bawled like a hungry baby in the locker room, a rare show indeed from the usually unflappable point guard who liked to sing Elvis songs on the bus and study the stock listings. Out in the hallway, he admitted, "I don't know when I'm going to be able to touch a basketball again—there's a lot of pain inside me. This outweighs any loss that I've had since I began playing basketball."

Mike Williams, head down and lost in the music on his Walkman, walked slowly to the bus.

John Calipari, his hard brown eyes looking suddenly vulnerable, lingered for a moment in that hallway, talking to UMass president Michael Hooker. A man who had earned his PhD in philosophy from UMass, Hooker was something of an unlikely sports fan. Nonetheless, he and his wife Carmen Buell, a state representative from Greenfield, were fixtures at UMass games. They even had their wedding reception at the Mullins Center. Now, in the anguished abruptness of this second–round NCAA exit, Hooker just wanted to let Calipari know that he had had a great year, that he was, as Hooker often said, "our greatest asset."

Later that day, Calipari, his wife Ellen and their two young daughters Erin and Megan drove to his in–laws' house in Osceola, Missouri, a little town where the press couldn't bother him. During the four–hour drive Calipari didn't say a word.

The coverage of Maryland's upset in Sunday's *Washington Post* included a column by Michael Wilbon, which read in part:

"While we're on the subject of Calipari, let's set something straight.

"John Chaney was right.

"Every single whistle against Calipari's team is greeted with screaming and ranting and raving and violent shaking like you wouldn't believe. No player of his has ever committed a foul or a traveling violation or missed a shot that shouldn't have been called a foul. He's a very good coach who still hasn't won anything, and because of his absurd behavior it was easier than ever to root like hell for the underdog."

When Calipari returned to Amherst four days later he reflected on the year during his weekly radio show. "I think we had an outstanding year," he said. "The players overachieved: I really believe that. [But] I was very disappointed the way it ended. I was very humbled the way it ended. I'm not so sure this was our year anyway. But at the time I'm too much of a fighter, too much of a competitor to say, 'Next year.'"

Next year, of course, was supposed to be *the* year at the University of Massachusetts.

# 8: "IF WE FALL, WE'RE DONE"

1994–95

Jack Leaman returned for the 1994–95 season. In one sense, the school's winningest coach had never left. After finishing up his 217–126 career with thirteen straight losses at the end of a nightmarish 1978–79 season, Leaman stayed on at UMass. Teaching in the athletic department, he watched the basketball program tumble through the eighties. Attending virtually every home game, he generally sat by himself, offering whatever support he could. He didn't feel bitter as much as sad, very sad.

UMass asked Leaman to coach the basketball team for the Stockbridge School of Agriculture, a branch of the university that offered two–year Associate's Degrees and remained one of the last vestiges of the university's "Mass Aggie" roots. At first, Leaman balked. He had coached Julius Erving, dammit. He had been acknowledged as one of the finest coaches in New England. Now they wanted him to coach a bunch of farmers against community colleges?

Through Stockbridge, though, Leaman regained his love for the game. There was something wonderfully unpretentious about basketball at this level. He never had to worry about recruiting. Games were played before crowds of a few dozen fans. The kids had limited skills, but they listened. And year after year, while the Minutemen were losing games in record numbers, Stockbridge was posting records like 10–2 and 11–1. In 1986–87, the UMass women's team, which had suffered through five straight losing years, needed a one–year interim coach. Leaman jumped on board and coached the team to a 14–12 record. It would be eight more years before the Minutewomen broke .500.

Leaman was a regular guy. He often wore suspenders to work. Almost every morning he had coffee at the Atkins Fruit Bowl, and he liked to have lunch at a local diner called The Stables. For a couple of years he helped broadcast local high school basketball games on WHMP with George Miller, bringing his wisdom and his accent to a small but appreciative audience.

Now sixty–one, Leaman was the new color analyst for the Minutemen's radio crew, working alongside the twenty–nine–year–old Miller. After fifteen years away, through fall and rise, Jack Leaman was back home. He was set to watch the most anticipated basketball season in UMass history.

•

The excitement was hard to contain. Everyone was back from a Top 10 team. Senior Lou Roe and sophomore Marcus Camby both appeared to be locks for the NBA—this at a school that had not sent anyone to The League since Al Skinner more than twenty years before. Junior forwards Donta Bright and Dana Dingle were piranhas in the paint. The senior backcourt of Derek Kellogg and Mike Williams presented complementary talents: the coach–on–the–floor point guard and the gamebreaking shooter with ice in his veins. Little known sophomore backups Edgar Padilla and Carmelo Travieso looked terrific in the preseason.

College basketball magazines consistently placed UMass among the best five teams in the country. Some had the Minutemen rated as high as second. The only team consistently ahead of them was defending national champion Arkansas. As fate would have it, UMass was set to open up against the Razorbacks on November 25. There was something to shoot for.

Coach John Calipari, entering his seventh year, was poised for something special. "We know what's out there for us," Calipari said. "We just need to stay on course."

The first inkling of trouble came on October 4, eleven days before formal practices began. While Calipari was in Houston attending a coaching conference, UMass issued a release stating that the coach had suspended Mike Williams for both exhibition games and the opener against Arkansas because of unspecified "academic reasons."

"Let me emphasize that Mike is not academically ineligible by NCAA or institutional guidelines," Calipari said in the statement. "But the standards we have for the team are higher than those required by the school and the NCAA, and it is important for the players in our program to understand that."

Williams was stunned. Sure, he'd been caught up in UMass's wild ride of basketball the previous spring like everyone else. Yeah, he'd fallen behind in his studies. But he wasn't the only one—he knew that. What happened to all of Calipari's comments about "having money in the bank that had nothing to do with basketball," about having "grown a ton"? To Williams, this wasn't fair: Arkansas was the most eagerly awaited game of his college career. "I don't know how he arrives at his decisions," Williams groused to The *Hartford Courant.*

By the opening practice a week and a half later, they had made their peace. Just before Midnight Madness festivities began at the Mullins Center, Williams told reporters that he and Calipari were on the same page. Calipari emphasized that Williams was now doing well in school, and that he had been tremendous in preseason conditioning workouts. "He's going to have an unbelievably strong senior season," Calipari predicted. Upon being introduced over the public address system a few minutes later, Williams blew kisses to the cheering crowd.

At the team's "Media Day" on October 18, optimism reigned supreme. Fifth–year senior reserve Jeff Meyer, the only holdover from the pre–NCAA days, explained that the team concluded each practice by joining hands and shouting in unison, "Seattle!"—the site of the 1995 Final Four. "That's where we want to go," said Meyer. "I don't think anybody will be satisfied with the season unless we go there."

The next day was one of the darkest in UMass basketball history. "High rank, low grades" read the front–page headline in *The Boston Globe.* Citing "sources and student transcripts made available to the *Globe,*" writer Dan Golden detailed a litany of academic problems for the Minutemen. Most damning of all was a chart of grade–point averages. The reported GPAs of four players—Camby, Williams, Bright and Tyrone Weeks—ranged from 1.80 to 1.96. Because these GPAs were under a 2.0 (C average), those players were placed on "academic probation." None of them was prohibited from playing ball, however, because all were still deemed to be in "good academic standing." A couple of other players, Lou Roe and Dana Dingle, were given warnings because of a semester under a 2.0. The article went on to detail some of the courses taken by the players, classes with titles like "Sex, Drugs and AIDS," and "Sociology of Sport and Physical Activity." Reaction ranged from embarrassment to snickering to rage.

Calipari was furious. He felt a deep sense of betrayal from within his own ranks; somebody had stolen this information, and leaked it to the press.[1] Most of his anger was directed at *The Boston Globe.* Through six years of coaching, Calipari had been the darling of the local press; now here he was, about to enter the most important season of his life, and he had been slapped in the face. Hard. In his mind the *Globe* had taken illegally obtained documents—ones the players' own parents couldn't access—and paraded them before public view. Several times in the succeeding months he talked about the way his players had been "raped" by the press. Deep down, he felt that the paper was humiliating his players to get to him. The Minutemen were being portrayed as mercenary morons who were just in college to play ball. And Calipari felt that he was being portrayed as a fraud, someone who only talked the talk. So often that talk had been about the importance of "image and perception." He knew how bad this whole thing looked.

In Calipari's view, UMass had done an excellent job of walking the student–athlete tightrope. He defended his program in the *Globe* story by citing a graduation rate of seventy–five percent, higher than that of the university as a whole. Where was the *Globe* in the eighties when the team stunk and its academics were even worse? How come nobody mentioned the contributions he had made to the school library for the last four years? Where was the comparison to the grades of players at other schools? Screaming at beat writer Joe Burris, who had nothing to do with the story, Calipari referred over and over to "the fucking *Boston Globe.*"

Others picked up on the story. One California columnist referred to UMass as "Team Thick as a Brick." In Worcester, a columnist referred to Donta Bright as "misnomered." Most damning of all was the *Sports Illustrated* "Scorecard" account headlined "UMess." Referring to Calipari as "the apotheosis of the ambitious, Armani–wrapped basketball coach" and his players as "academic snorkelers," *SI* implied that UMass was selling its soul for a winner. The article called Calipari to task for the seventy–five percent graduation rate, pointing out that the figure was based on "a decidedly small–time recruiting class that came to UMass as freshmen in 1987, before Calipari arrived on campus." Further, the *SI* story chided UMass for accepting a verbal commitment from high school senior Mark Blount who "has drifted through six high schools, encountered discipline problems and failed to meet his required test score under Prop 48."[2] Finally, the magazine cited details of Calipari's contract first published in Springfield's *Union–News*: a total package of more than $500,000. It was not a pretty picture.

Was it fair?

Calipari quibbled to a degree with the accuracy of the reported grades, but he admitted in the initial *Globe* piece that the team's academic performance had fallen during the 1993–94 season. "Part of the problem has been me," he said. "I got a little soft on the disciplinary side. I didn't suspend a guy when maybe I should have." Still, Calipari and school officials maintained that basketball players were not being treated differently from other students. School records show that more than five hundred non–athletes were on academic probation at the time with GPAs under 2.0. None of these people were prohibited from participating in extracurricular activities.

Grades are impossible to compare from one institution to the next because they are generally not public information. The leak at UMass was exceedingly rare. It's hard to imagine, though, that several other teams in the country did not have players competing with GPAs in the 1.80–1.96 range. Consider, for instance, that high–profile players like Joe Smith of Maryland, the first pick in the NBA draft come June, and Bryant (Big Country) Reeves of Oklahoma State were withdrawn from consideration for the John Wooden Award because of academic reasons. Given annually as one of the most prestigious national player of the year honors, the Wooden Award requires recipients to hold a minimum GPA of 2.0.

Graduation rates are easier to compare, although they certainly do not provide the ultimate barometer of a program's academic success. The NCAA has been monitoring graduation rates on an annual basis since 1984, evaluating how many athletes graduate within six years from the institutions that offered them athletic aid as freshmen. Sample sizes for basketball teams are necessarily small. The "seventy–five percent" Calipari reported, for instance, meant that three of four 1987 recruits graduated within six years. The "fifty percent" that came out the following year, meant that one of Calipari's two recruits in 1988 donned a cap and gown by 1994. Obviously, these numbers only gain significance over time.

The most recent NCAA records show UMass graduation rates as follows:

| Incoming class | Graduation rate |
|---|---|
| 1984–85 | 0 |
| 1985–86 | 0 |
| 1986–87 | 50 |
| 1987–88 | 75 |
| 1988–89 (Calipari's first class) | 50 |
| 1989–90 | 100 |

Four–year averages of graduation rates compiled by the NCAA for incoming freshmen show that basketball players do not earn degrees as often as typical college students. Data in the *1994 NCAA Division I Graduation–Rates Report* (covering the graduation years 1985–1988— the most recent available at the time of the *Globe* story) reveal that the average graduation rate for basketball players in the 301 Division I programs was forty–two percent. For all students, the average rate was fifty–five percent. Among teams in the AP Preseason Top 25, only one (Villanova) had basketball players graduating at a higher rate than the school's student body.

Reasons abound for the poor graduation numbers. Basketball players often come from backgrounds where the quality of their academic preparation has been less than that of the typical college student. Further, they are taken out of class far more often than most students because of the basketball schedule. Even those players with excellent motivation are often at a competitive disadvantage in school. And, to be sure, there is a darker side. Some student–athletes lack the skills and/or the desire to complete a college program. Some coaches care far more for the athlete than for the student.

UMass basketball's graduation rate during that 1985–1988 period was twenty–seven percent (four out of fifteen), compared with sixty–five percent for the student body as a whole. The twenty–seven percent figure was equal to that of Kentucky, and better than that of seven teams in the 1994–95 Preseason Top 25. Still, the number is low and looks damning of Calipari on first glance. That conclusion, however, does not hold up under greater scrutiny.

The statistic was compiled using data from the incoming freshmen classes in the falls of 1984–87, all recruited by Calipari's predecessor, Ron Gerlufsen. Granted, that was all the NCAA data available at the time, but closer inspection by the *Globe, Sports Illustrated* or any media outlet would have revealed that Calipari's recruits were graduating, or on course to graduate, in relatively successful fashion. (The most recent NCAA graduation report, published in July of 1996, shows that seventy–five percent of UMass basketball players entering school from 1987–90 graduated within six years. That report includes Calipari's first two recruiting classes. Of six players he brought in, five have earned degrees. *USA Today* compared the four–year averages of the twenty–five teams that were ranked in the final 1996 *USA Today/* coaches poll. UMass placed third, behind only North Carolina, at eighty–five percent, and Villanova, at seventy–nine.)

Standardized test scores provide another reference for comparison, although these again are limited. SAT scores for basketball players tend to be low. Of the twenty–five teams ranked in the 1994–95 preseason poll, twenty–one had four–year average combined SAT scores (for incoming classes in the falls of 1990–93) listed in the 1994 NCAA graduation report. Those averages ranged from 730 (Cincinnati) to 898 (Indiana). These scores were all significantly lower than those of their respective student bodies. At UMass the average basketball SAT score was 790 in that period, compared with a student body average of 1005. Disparities of that proportion are the rule, not the exception. Often the disparities are more pronounced. Cincinnati's basketball/student body average SAT scores were 730/985. At Georgia Tech they were 856/1193.[3]

Again, there are plenty of reasons for such a disparity. Many claim the tests are culturally biased against the largely minority populations that compose the bulk of most basketball rosters. Time spent honing basketball skills represents time away from academics. Further, great talent in basketball is viewed by colleges across the country as one of the special skills (like talent in music or theater) that influence decisions around admissions.

UMass's lower–end SAT average was influenced in significant measure by its willingness to accept Proposition 48 players.[4] When the *Globe* story came out, UMass had accepted three Prop 48 players: Kennard Robinson in 1989, Donta Bright in 1992 and Tyrone Weeks in 1993. Bright and Weeks, both education majors, were still in school, both mentioned in the *Globe* story. Robinson graduated on time with a degree in real–estate management.

Calipari liked to point out that UMass was a state school, whose "mission was to educate the commonwealth." This school promoted opportunity, he argued, not exclusion. It attracted all types of students.

Scholarship athletes on his team also included Derek Kellogg, a senior who would earn a place on the five–man Atlantic 10 All–Academic team for the third consecutive year; Jeff Meyer, a fifth–year senior who was already in graduate school; junior Dana Dingle, who would start from his freshman year on and graduate in four years; and sophomore Carmelo Travieso, who was pursuing a demanding major in economics.

Yes, there were players enrolled in courses entitled "Sex, Drugs and AIDS" and "The Psychology of Sport and Physical Activity." Then again, at neighboring institutions Amherst and Williams, course titles included "Sport and Society" and "Witchcraft, Sorcery and Magic." At Princeton, students were enrolled in something called "Earthquakes, Volcanos and Other Hazards." Were these books to be judged solely by their covers?

If far from ideal, the academic situation at UMass was also far from uncommon. Nevertheless, with the 1994–95 season approaching, John Calipari's program became the poster child for college sports out of control.

Rival coaches didn't lash out at Calipari—perhaps fearing the scrutiny would then fall on them—but few exactly leaped to his defense. The perception that UMass's path to the top had been filled with corner–cutting was one lots of people liked to embrace. A sports editor in upstate New York admitted receiving what he termed "sperm–stained faxes" of the *Globe* story from Calipari detractors. To the UMass coach, this was all about jealousy. He had come to believe that Americans have an ambivalent relationship with achievement. "We love success," Calipari was fond of saying, "but we hate successful people."

UMass players were infuriated. Some perceived an undercurrent of racism.[5] Donta Bright later talked about his anger at "the dumb black jock stereotype." The perception of racism was bolstered when *Union–News* reporter Brad Smith, speaking at a journalism class, distributed the grades of every African–American athlete on campus. While expressing outrage at the violation of privacy, UMass chancellor David Scott pointed out that the school was required to keep such a list by the NCAA.[6]

Players were sealed off from the media in the weeks following the grades story, a stark contrast to Calipari's former policy of open practices. They later admitted that the story provided more than a source of anger; it provided a bond.

"That really pulled us together more than anything," said Lou Roe. "Everybody was trying to go after us."

"There was anger," Jeff Meyer said, "but also the hint of challenge. Someone had laid something out in front of us, and we were going to see how this team would handle it."

•

Arkansas was the first defending national champion in twenty–seven years to return its entire starting five. Renowned for their "Forty Minutes of Hell," the Razorbacks were an imposing squad cut from the same cloth as their intensely proud coach, Nolan Richardson. Their marquee player, a six–seven block of granite named Corliss Williamson, was nicknamed "The Big Nasty." During the preseason, he had stated his belief that Arkansas' second team could beat UMass's first team.

On Thanksgiving night, November 24, the teams sat together eating turkey in a sterile banquet room at the Springfield Sheraton. The next night, down the street at the Civic Center, the season began. The nine thousand tickets had been sold out for months. Press row was jammed with reporters from *Sports Illustrated, The New York Times* and *The Boston Globe.* Dick Vitale was spewing exclamation points on ESPN, a few chairs down from Jack Leaman, who couldn't help referring to "we" during his college broadcasting debut on WHMP. In the moments before the game, John Calipari, resplendent in a new suit, sat alone on the end of the UMass bench, furiously chewing some gum and studying an index card scrawled with strategy.

Four seconds into the game, Lou Roe dunked home two points and a message: this team was for real. Two hours later, the dismantling was complete. UMass 104, Arkansas 80.

One would think that Jack Leaman, who had watched this team through good times and bad, would float back to Amherst that night. One would think that John Calipari, the Man from Moon, would be on top of the world. But both were brought back to earth by the postgame show of Mike Williams, who stormed into the locker room, hurled his uniform onto the floor and took off with some friends from Hartford. Several school officials, congratulating the team on its landmark win, witnessed the outburst. It was embarrassing. Leaman said in later months that he thought Calipari was "trying to save the kid" by keeping him on the team. Calipari later said that Williams's actions "spoiled the night." To Mike Williams, though, the outburst was merely a protest against injustice. Maybe he had had the worst academic semester of anyone on the team the previous spring, but not by much. He felt singled out for special treatment, not unlike Calipari's reaction to the whole grades story. Perhaps it wasn't the most mature way to make his feelings known, but he felt some sort of statement had to be made. On Monday evening, November 28, 1994, the new AP poll came out. The University of Massachusetts, ranked 259th of 267 teams for the decade of the 1980s, was now Number 1.

In Tuesday's *Boston Globe*, a red numeral "1" ran the entire length of the page in the front of the sports section, detailing the first time in the forty–five years of the the AP poll that a New England team had made it to the top.

The season was one game old.

•

Calipari tried to downplay the ranking. He told his players and the press that Number 1 in November didn't mean a whole lot. It was a long season. The important thing was to be there in March. "Things are never quite as good as they seem," he preached. "Things are never quite as bad as they seem. In between falls reality." But at home he often turned to his wife Ellen and said, "Can you believe it? We're Number 1!"

On December 1, the Minutemen bused down to Bradley International Airport for the first trip of the season, bound for Anaheim and the inaugural John Wooden Classic. Taxiing onto the runway, Captain Robert Everley greeted passengers, extending "a special welcome to the top–ranked college basketball team in America, the University of Massachusetts." There was applause up and down the aisles. The team's new academic coordinator, Dave Glover, distributed diskettes and portable computers to team members. Assistant coach Bill Bayno paid $4 for a headset to watch "Forrest Gump." The USAir flight soared across the continent.

The field for the Wooden Classic consisted of three true giants of college basketball: Kentucky, Kansas and UCLA. UMass, the brash interloper, completed the foursome. The day before the games, Calipari had a hard time wiping the smile off his face while he shared a press conference podium with the three other coaches, and the great John Wooden himself, eighty–four years young. Reflecting on UMass's perch at the top of the polls, Kentucky coach Rick Pitino said, "I never felt in my wildest dreams that that would be a possibility."

A few hours later, the coaches mugged with Mickey Mouse in front of Sleeping Beauty's Castle at Disneyland, the self–proclaimed "Happiest Place on Earth." Given a half–hour to enjoy themselves, the Minutemen let loose. Marcus Camby bombed down the Matterhorn, his knees to his chin. Mike Williams, emerging from a spinning "Teacup" with Lou Roe, beamed, "That was fun. What's next?"

A loss to seventh–ranked Kansas. The 81–75 defeat dropped UMass from the top after just one week. It had been a quick stay, but the Minutemen were given a taste of what could be.

During December, the UMass house seemed to be in order. The fall semester concluded with six team members—including Marcus Camby, Donta Bright and Tyrone Weeks—proudly listed on the Athletic Director's Honor Roll with GPAs over 3.0. Recruit Mark Blount, the one lampooned in *Sports Illustrated* for being the first player ever to choose a college before a high school, was quietly released from his commitment to come to UMass.[7] When UMass played Princeton, it was the Tigers' legendary coach Pete Carril—not John Calipari—who got tossed from the game for arguing a call with official Rich Sortino. "I don't like the son of a bitch," Carril said in the postgame press conference. "The worse I condemn him, the worse I look. But I'll tell you what, I don't think he's a good ref. I at least think I have the right to say that."

Mike Williams left controversy behind him. Inviting team leader Lou Roe to his home in Hartford on a couple of occasions, he seemed to cement his standing on the roster. In practice he worked hard. In games, he worked harder, never grousing about coming off the bench. The NBA was his goal, he maintained, but right now UMass came first.

Against Western Kentucky in the final game of the semester, he got his first start of the year and responded with a team–high twenty–one points. "This is his senior year; he wants an opportunity to play at the next level," Calipari said in the postgame press conference. "It's not about made shots. It's about, is he a player that can make us a better team? Can he defend? Is he a team guy? Does he have a good attitude? You know what the [NBA scouts'] answers are right now? 'Yes, yes, yes, yes.' So what I'm saying to him is, 'Sustain. Every day.'"

The Minutemen were 5–1, ranked Number 4 in the nation, on course for Seattle.

Over Christmas they headed in the other direction, flying to France to participate in an exhibition tournament with five professional teams from Europe. The tournament's sponsor, a beverage manufacturer named Buckler, picked up the bill, and UMass traveled in style aboard the Concorde. Upon arrival in Paris, Team Gourmand went right to McDonald's for dinner.

Games were played in Strasbourg at Hall Rhenus, a converted theater with stage lights and curtains. French fans pounded drums and blew airhorns. UMass players were introduced as "Mar–coose Camby" and "Jeff Mee–her." The Minutemen bombed.

Losing a pair of close twenty–minute games to French teams the first night and a tight forty–minute affair to an Italian squad the second night, UMass finished sixth in the six–team field. The players did not respond well to the more physical, more wide–open style of European ball. Calipari certainly did not respond well to what he considered a major home job by the officials. Convinced that the referees were doing anything in their power to prevent the ignominy of a French pro team losing to a bunch of American college kids, Calipari refused to sit back and take it, exhibition games or not. At one point against Pau–Orthez, he earned a technical by striding out onto the court. He berated someone at the scorer's table, even yelled at one of the French coaches after Tyrone Weeks was knocked cold by an elbow to the chin. After the first night of games he sat with some of his assistant coaches and athletic director Bob Marcum at the hotel restaurant, trying to convince them to give the officials a sardonic standing ovation when they finished their meal.

The headline of the French sports daily *L'Equipe* read, "Massachusetts au Tapis" (on the carpet). The story began, "John Calipari is a winner. It's sufficient to see him gesture like a madman (*'comme un fou'*) along the sideline, howl at one of his players for losing the ball, or put pressure on one of the officials, to convince yourself. You can easily imagine that last place in the tournament at Strasbourg didn't give him pleasure."

During the short stay in France, Calipari's ferocity rubbed even his staff the wrong way. "If we're going to have practice all the time, it's not really worth coming over here," grumbled his hard–working assistant Bruiser Flint.

To Calipari, though, this was a business trip. It was about getting better. This, after all, was *the* season. He had his most talented team, his most experienced team. Three senior starters would be gone next year. Sophomore standout Marcus Camby, the most talented player he had ever coached, might well leave for the NBA. No one was saying, "Now or never," but deep down Calipari knew this might be the only real chance he would ever have to make a run for the national title.

In Paris the night before the team flew home, the UMass coach finally relaxed. Recovering his charm, he took the team out to a trendy Left Bank restaurant called La Coupole and tried to convince his reluctant players to try the escargots. In line a few hours later to go up the Eiffel Tower, he had Italian tourists laughing with stories of his family's heritage.

High above Paris, looking out over the colorful Ferris Wheels that dot the city at Christmas time, Calipari smiled. Life was good. Next to him, a slightly acrophobic Donta Bright uttered words that hovered over the team all season: "If we fall, we're done."

•

As the calendar turned to 1995, UMass didn't fall at all. Wins piled on top of wins. Blowouts and buzzer games, love–fests at home and minefields on the road—the Minutemen won them all. They blocked twenty shots against West Virginia in Springfield, survived a one–point game against Temple (the UMass games will always be close, said John Chaney, "because of the unwritten contract between us"), rocked twenty–first–ranked Pennsylvania by thirty–three, outlasted St. Bonaventure in overtime while Bonnie fans chanted "Hooked on Phonics!" and "You Fix Grades!"

Amid the neon backdrop of casinos, the kitschy bustle of the boardwalk and predatory pawn shops promising "cash for gold," UMass played La Salle in Atlantic City, a homecoming game for Lou Roe. The six–seven forward had become UMass's unquestioned leader. He was the top scorer, the top rebounder, the man destined to be the first player from UMass to make it to the NBA in more than twenty years.

It hadn't always looked that way. Growing up amid the glitter and green, the not–so–quiet desperation of this city by the sea with its casinos offering their poisonous promise of something for nothing, Roe was not a portrait of motivation. There was a rough–edged quality to him, a taste for trouble. Sometimes he hung out at the Atlantic City Convention Center, home to heavyweight championship fights, Miss America pageants and a lot of false hopes. In high school, he said, "I was a lazy sack of stones."

Calipari had been the perfect coach for him. He had challenged Roe, ignited his competitive fires, galvanized him with possibility. The fan favorite introduced by UMass PA Announcer Jack O'Neill as "Looooooooo Rohhhhhhhhhh" had learned the value of hard work.

He was a conditioning maven, a monster in the weight room. In big games, he seemed biggest, mustering what Calipari often referred to as his huge "work capacity." Sometimes in the heat of competition the coach and the star would yell at each other, but it was always rooted in a common desire to win. Calipari, Roe sometimes said, had become a father figure to him. The coach reserved the highest praise for Roe— he, like Harper Williams before him, was a warrior.

Back in Atlantic City, Roe had perhaps his worst collegiate game, scoring only two points, but UMass still coasted to an 87–64 win. Afterward, the Minutemen regained the Number 1 ranking.

The news was heralded in the upper left–hand corner of the front page of U*SA Today*, where a photo of Derek Kellogg appeared beneath the headline "UMass Tops N. Carolina in Hoop Poll Shake–up." On the bus to the airport in Philadelphia, assistant coach John Robic turned to Kellogg and said, "Hey Derek, how'd you get two pictures on the cover?" Kellogg looked up and saw Robic pointing to the upper–right hand corner of the page where a picture of Barney sat atop the caption, "Dinosaur's profits enviously eyed." The Minutemen had clearly reached the bigtime. The game was pure fun.

Being Number 1 this time was different. Calipari exhorted his team to make the most of the experience. One day in practice he commended his players on their willingness to stay in an Amherst pizzeria the night before, signing autographs and talking to kids. "You've been put in a position where you can make a difference," he said. "Who knows why? You're role models. People look up to you. You want the country walking around like this?" He tucked his chin to his chest. "You guys were great last night. In ten years you might only be able to influence your families. But now—what an opportunity!"

In Pittsburgh on January 24, Kellogg limped into the team's afternoon shootaround sucking on a pretzel rod. Team trainer Ron Laham told reporters that Kellogg had to sit out of that night's game against Duquesne because of a "groin/hip flexor problem near his pubic bone." Jeff Meyer quickly piped in, "Point guard plagued by pubic problems."

After the laughter subsided, Calipari turned to Mike Williams and nodded. He would start his first game ever at point guard, running the UMass offense. "Do you understand the challenge?" Calipari asked.

UMass ran wild and free that night. Everything seemed to click. Williams set the table beautifully. Camby was dominant. Sophomore Carmelo Travieso came off the bench to have the most productive game

*From the beginning, John Calipari felt that he had to keep a close eye on Mike Williams. (Photo by Richard Carpenter)*

of his career. Even Meyer looked menacing; late in the game, the seven–two center dunked with such authority that former Minuteman John Tate, sitting behind the UMass bench, stood and shouted, "The Lord can take me now. I've seen it all." Final score: UMass 103, Duquesne 53.

With a sizable contingent of fans from his childhood days in Moon Township looking on—everyone from his high school coach Bill Sacco on down—Calipari basked in the moment. He was back home with the Number 1 team in America. "We played above ourselves tonight," he said. "I thought the difference in the game was Mike Williams playing point guard. He only got seven points, but he was unbelievable." To celebrate, Calipari invited his coaching staff over to visit his grandmother ("Nunny") in Coraopolis. "My grandmother makes an unbelievable sauce," Calipari crowed. "When you're an Italian, it's not the pasta, it's the sauce. She'll come out with Mancini bread. I told her six people: she'll cook for twenty–seven."

•

That week, *Sports Illustrated* ran a story about UMass and UConn. Truly, this was a landmark time in New England. The seat of power in college basketball, residing in recent years along the nine–mile stretch of road between Duke and the University of North Carolina, had now found a new "tobacco road," a forty–mile stretch of western New England that is, in fact, dotted with leaf–tobacco barns. The two schools, which used to play out an obscure, if intense, rivalry on tiny stages known as "The Cage" and "The Torture Chamber," were now ranked Number 1 and Number 2 in America.

After ninety–eight games, the series had been terminated in 1990 at the behest of UConn coach Jim Calhoun. Though unplayed since, it was a rivalry with an edge. Calhoun bristled at a T–shirt then in vogue in western Massachusetts. The shirt depicted UMass with its motto "Refuse to Lose," and UConn as "UScared" with a motto of "Refuse to Play." To Calhoun, there were lots of good reasons for keeping UMass off the schedule. The Big East Conference slate promised plenty of tough league games. He said that non–conference contests against Connecticut teams like Yale and Fairfield were good for the state. And in a column in the school's own sports magazine, the *Husky Blue & White*, Calhoun said that he preferred tough non–league opponents like Virginia and Kansas: "schools we have more in common with. . . . We recruit the same kids and we have respect for them. I'm not sure if that's the case with UMass."

Calhoun, an Irish Catholic from Boston's South Shore, also chafed at John Calipari's occasional description of UMass as embodying the spirit of New England. Calhoun, after all, was the native New Englander. After playing his college ball in Springfield, he rose through the high school and collegiate coaching ranks, always working in Massachusetts or Connecticut. New England was in his accent, in his blood, in his crust. He had turned the Huskies from a loser into a top–flight national program, and he didn't need any Johnny Come Lately from someplace called Moon telling him about New England basketball.

Sure, Calhoun's team wasn't exactly peppered with New England talent. The closest any of his starters lived to the region was Ray Allen, who hailed from South Carolina. Granted, UMass had five scholarship players from New England, including three starters, two of whom—Marcus Camby and Mike Williams—had been plucked from the playgrounds of Hartford. But Calhoun told *Sports Illustrated*'s Gerry Callahan that Camby could not have gotten into UConn because of academics. (Remembering just how aggressively Calhoun and assistant Howie Dickenman had pursued him, Camby—an in–state, minority, non–Proposition 48 megatalent—could only shake his head.)

Heading into the last weekend in January, Calhoun felt that his 12–0 Huskies deserved to be ranked Number 1 in the country, instead of the 11–1 Minutemen. He said just that on a nationally syndicated radio talk show. Asked who should be ranked Number 2, Calhoun said, "UCLA."

In fact, most college basketball analysts agreed, UConn would leapfrog UMass in the polls if both teams won their games over the weekend. UMass was busing down from Pittsburgh to Morgantown, West Virginia, to play a mediocre Mountaineer team. UConn was traveling to Kansas for its first legitimate non–league showdown. The Jayhawks had given UMass its only loss of the season. Should UConn beat them at Kansas, that should be enough, most people figured, to propel the Huskies to the top.

On Thursday, January 26, the day before the West Virginia game, John Calipari put UMass through a particularly rigorous practice. "Force yourself to be uncomfortable," he shouted during a grueling defensive lunging drill. "Challenge yourself. Make your legs hurt. Challenge yourselves to be your best. Don't cut corners. You're Number 1 in the country.

"You know how to demoralize guys? When you come out, you don't walk. You run. They'll be thinking, 'These sons of bitches never stop.'

"We've got to get better, you understand? This may not be for West Virginia, this workout. This may be for Seattle."

Sucking wind, the Minutemen pushed through the comfort zone. The next day at the shootaround Calipari continued his diatribe while his team stretched out: "There are only twelve games left. I don't care if you're tired, sick, pissed off, pissed on. You gotta work. All we've got to do is stay on the path."

That night the student section of the West Virginia Coliseum was packed more than three hours before game time. The biggest crowd of the year, 13,862, filled the place with noise. A variety of beverages were consumed in souvenir plastic cups that commemorated the West Virginia NCAA champion runners–up team from 1959. Sparked by Jerry West, that team had narrowly defeated a Boston University squad led by Jack Leaman to get to the Final Four.

For the longest time, those cups were held aloft in joyous toasts. The Mountaineers dominated: a step faster to every loose ball, a hand higher on every rebound. UMass looked awful, committing fifteen turnovers in the first half alone. In the second half, it got worse. With 4:48 left, UMass was down, 80–62. More than just the loss of a game and the Number 1 ranking, this was pure humiliation.

Then, with staggering speed, the game turned. Camby scored, then Travieso, then Roe, then Dingle, then Bright. It was an eight–point game. Mike Williams hit the team's first three–pointer of the night, then Edgar Padilla hit one. UMass put a major scare in the Mountaineers, but the game still seemed to be over when West Virginia's Cyrus Jones hit a layup for an 86–82 lead with 14.1 seconds left.

Mike Williams steamed downcourt and forced up a ridiculous–looking three–point shot from the left wing, which missed with 9.1 seconds remaining, but he drew a foul from Jones. He hit the first two shots. Everyone expected him to try to miss the third on the off chance UMass could grab the offensive rebound. The ball caromed high off the back rim. Dana Dingle leaped into West Virginia's burly Damien Owens, who had inside position. Deflecting high off Owens' hands, the ball dropped cleanly into the net.

As the teams prepared for overtime, the crowd sat in disbelief.

A few minutes later, with the score tied at ninety–four, the game clock ticking under twenty, the shot clock ticking under ten, the ball—not surprisingly—was in the hands of Mike Williams. He let fly from behind the arc on the left–hand side, twenty–two feet from the basket. There was no doubt about it. As the Minutemen ran for the locker room, 97–94 winners, the court was showered with souvenir cups commemorating college basketball greatness from 1959.

Jack Leaman practically shouted into the microphone. It was the greatest comeback he had ever seen. Never had the team's indomitable spirit known a greater moment. And in the end, of course, there had been Mike Williams.

"In the history of college basketball," Calipari said to Leaman on the postgame show, "no one has hit more clutch shots than Mike Williams."

UMass flew home on Saturday and moved back into the dorms for the first time since before the trip to France. They had lived in hotels for thirty–three straight days, a period that spanned six states and one foreign country.[8] Now they were back, winners of fourteen straight games, 15–1, Number 1 in the country. While unpacking, some of the players watched the national telecast of the UConn–Kansas game, a contest that included an appalling sight for Husky fans, halftime commentary from John Calipari. There was no need for postgame commentary. Kansas won, 88–59.

•

If the road to March Madness was paved with January Jubilation, it was also pot–holed with a February Funk.

On February 1, in the midst of a school record sixteenth straight victory, some troubling signs began to show up. Williams started displaying a curious docility on the court, a tentativeness that had never been part of his makeup before. "Shoot, or sit!" Calipari yelled at the player often known as Uzi. He was held scoreless that night, and spent much of it on the bench. Far more disturbing was the moment in the first half when Marcus Camby dropped with a thud at center court, gripping the back of his leg in anguish. Three minutes of near total silence at the Mullins Center was interrupted only by the one–word prayer of a little boy: "Marcus!" Camby had pulled a hamstring, and would be lost for two weeks.

Taking their act on the road to George Washington, the Minutemen were met at the Smith Center by metal detectors and sniffing dogs. The nation's Number 1 Fan had decided to check out the nation's Number 1 team. Sitting with daughter Chelsea and eating some pizza, Bill Clinton took in the scene: the fan sitting behind Calipari with a sign reading "U–Mass–Hole" and heckling the UMass coach as "a poor man's Pitino"; the Minutemen debuting some sleek black road uniforms;

Marcus Camby sitting on the bench next to two of the tallest crutches in America; Calipari ranting at official Art McDonald; and the joyous jig done by GW coach Mike Jarvis—bypassing a handshake with Calipari—after the Colonials' 78–75 victory.

The handshake would come from Clinton himself, who visited the UMass locker room, congratulating the Minutemen on their fine season, and Calipari on building such a successful program. Hours later, Calipari confessed, he didn't even know where Clinton had been sitting during the contest; alone among the five thousand people sardine–packed into the little Smith Center, Calipari had not even sneaked a peek. He was so locked in on the game, the season, the chance of a lifetime.

That night the Minutemen were snowed–in by a blizzard in the Northeast. Sitting in the lobby of Washington's Embassy Suites Hotel, Derek Kellogg, Edgar Padilla, Carmelo Travieso and Rigo Nuñez confessed to being tired, worn down by the grind of a long season.

In practice two days later on February 6, Calipari took out the proverbial whip. "We've got to get back to what makes us good," he said, patrolling the Mullins Center floor with a scowl. During a defensive "shell drill," he erupted, "Too much switching! Play your fucking man! Everyone's looking to switch. You know why? Guys are cutting every corner. Everyone's looking to do the easy thing. Look to do the hardest thing!"

That night they bused down to New Jersey, leaving Camby behind.[9] The following night the Minutemen took the floor against Rutgers. Through a half, the funk continued with UMass trailing a weak Scarlet Knight team, 31–29. Mike Williams continued to slump. Lou Roe was unable to take over. UMass was being outplayed by a team that would get nowhere near postseason play. Returning to the floor, the Minutemen were determined to beat back the first hints of doubt creeping into a special season.

They never had a chance. Just before play was set to resume, a predominantly black group of Rutgers students staged a sit–in on the court, silently protesting comments by school president Francis L. Lawrence that had come to light early in the week. In a meeting of the school's faculty senate, Lawrence had said that disadvantaged populations don't score well on some standardized tests because of their "genetic, hereditary background." A man regarded by many minorities as a champion of their causes in the past, Lawrence was now being tagged as a racist. A basketball game against a high–profile team seemed to be the perfect venue for bringing the issue into the public eye. After thirty–five minutes of peaceful but unbending protest, the game was suspended.

Though peripheral to the controversy, the Minutemen nevertheless connected with the issue. Players knew what it was like to have their intelligence questioned. They had heard the taunts of "Hooked on Phonics," felt the sting of "Team Thick as a Brick," absorbed the indignity of having every African–American athlete's transcript distributed as a lecture tool. It was a hassle to have the game suspended, especially in this year of already grinding travel, but busing back into New England in the wee hours of a winter morning, they understood. "I'm going to support my black folks whatever the situation is if I think they're right," said Lou Roe. "I think the president of Rutgers University was wrong."

Their more pressing concern was basketball. From the outside, things didn't seem so bad. UMass was 17–2, ranked Number 4 in the nation. From the inside, though, the fraying was evident. They held an emotional players–only meeting the next day, convened by Derek Kellogg. Everyone spoke. Personal issues abounded. They even summoned the courage to tell Calipari that they didn't like the way he subbed them so quickly after making mistakes; it made them feel too tentative on the court, too afraid to fail. Flying down to Louisiana, they felt that some air had been cleared. They bused from Baton Rouge to Lafayette, traveling over swamps with names like "Atchafalaya," quietly taking in the strange landscape. And on Saturday they absolutely walloped Southwestern Louisiana, 94–63. Other than Williams, who continued to struggle, the team seemed to reclaim its former ferocity. It looked like a step in the right direction.

That night Calipari ate a classic Cajun meal in Prejean's, a restaurant that featured a centerpiece of stuffed gator named "Big Al," which had been fourteen–feet long, eight hundred pounds and sixty–five years old when it was caught by Wilton (Boo Boo) Quibodeaux. Later, back in Baton Rouge, Calipari called the team together in his hotel suite, and began an impassioned talk: *It's been a long season, filled with distractions. You guys have been tested, and you've responded. You overcame every piece of adversity that people threw at you. Yeah, we hit a bump in the last ten days, but now we've turned the corner. Marcus will be back soon. It's time to dig in. We've got to recommit, refocus, realize just how much is at stake. We can do it if we really want it. We can get to Seattle. We can win this whole fucking thing. Do you understand how rare this is, how precious? The dream is right there for you. Just stick together. Take care of your bodies. Get your sleep. Let's pull together once and for all, and go after this with everything we've got.*

Calipari went to bed feeling good. There was a commitment to the common goal. It could happen.

The next morning, Sunday, February 12, UMass's flight was scheduled to leave at 6:50, and Calipari was blazing with rage in the hotel lobby at 5:30. He had just seen Mike Williams and Baton Rouge native Andre Burks (a freshman out for the year with a knee injury) returning from a night out on the town. As the players filed groggily out to the bus, Calipari huddled with assistant coaches Bill Bayno and Bruiser Flint. "I don't even want him in the fucking stands," Calipari said. "Should I do it now, Bru, just so I feel better?"

His anger smoldered from Baton Rouge to Atlanta, where UMass had a layover before flying back to New England. At the airport in Atlanta, the team was initially directed to gate A1, but found passengers there waiting instead for a flight to Seattle. This was not the Minutemen's destination—not yet, anyway. Redirected down the Delta terminal, they met for several minutes with a still steaming Calipari.

That day UConn beat Syracuse and became the Number 1 team for the first time in school history.

Two nights later, on February 14, Mike Jarvis and the George Washington Colonials came calling at the Mullins Center. It was a night of loss for the University of Massachusetts Minutemen.

They lost a game, 80–78. They lost an on–campus winning streak of forty–one games, including all twenty–seven ever played at Mullins. They lost their cool, picking up three technical fouls.[10] And on Valentine's Day, they seemed to lose a little bit of their heart, too.

"We had guys who didn't understand the pride factor," said Calipari. "My fear is that the losses don't hurt as badly as they used to. A loss has got to tear you from the inside out."

It all seemed to be unraveling. UMass's trademark relentlessness seemed to be gone. The easy confidence was missing. Fun had disappeared. Just two weeks earlier, the Minutemen had been on top of the college basketball world. Now they were plummeting, 1–2 in their last three games (not counting the losing half at Rutgers), losers at home for the first time in more than three years, sinking in the polls. A year of big dreams was crashing to earth. Just one month before the NCAA tournament, UMass was playing its worst basketball of the year. Going to sleep late that night, John Calipari had a sense of something precious slipping away.

At the team breakfast the next morning at the Hampshire Dining Commons, players filed in wearing sweat pants and baseball caps, putting four and five glasses of juice on their trays. There was almost no conversation. There was also no sign of Mike Williams.

Something snapped. Calipari told his assistant coaches to deliver the message: Mike would not be welcomed at practice that afternoon.

As tension swirled around the team, the public was kept in the dark. Neither the Louisiana episode nor the missed breakfast made the papers; Calipari would forever keep these pieces of dirty laundry out of the public eye. Wednesday's Williams–free practice was also kept under wraps in a week where media members were unwelcome on the practice floor. Thus, it came as a surprise, when, ten minutes before Thursday night's home game against Duquesne, a terse press release was issued, informing the media that Williams had been suspended indefinitely for violating unspecified team rules. Rumors abounded on press row. *There was something monstrous. Drugs were involved. Crime. Mayhem. This was, after all, his third suspension in the past two seasons, and in February of his senior year it had to be something outrageous. Right?*

After the game, an emphatic 73–56 victory that featured the return of Marcus Camby, Calipari was tight–lipped. "He's been suspended," Calipari stated flatly. "I'll evaluate it after the weekend."

In the hallway outside the Green Room, Derek Kellogg looked down at the floor when asked about the Williams situation. "Mike's a good kid," Kellogg said. "At times he might lose focus. But all in all, he's one of the nicest kids I've been around since I've been here."

Six more days of tense drama played out. On Friday night, February 18, Williams left campus for his home in Hartford, telling the *Union–News,* "People have to know what's happening. I want to clear my name." Discussing the night out in Louisiana, he insisted that Calipari had not established any curfew. He also said that he tried to notify team personnel that he would miss breakfast because he was sick. "Other people have been late and missed breakfast. . . .There's this cloud over my head. I want the truth to come out and show I'm not a bad guy."

On Saturday, Williams's mother Sarah said, "Why this is all happening is beyond my wildest dreams. I just don't understand. It comes out like my son is a bad, bad, bad guy."

Sunday saw UMass look impressive in a 91–76 rout of Louisville at the Worcester Centrum. "This was a terrific effort," said Calipari. "We can't play much better." About Williams, he said only, "He's suspended indefinitely. That's all I'm going to say."

On Monday, with Williams back on campus, his parents called a press conference in Manchester, Connecticut. Fighting back tears, Al and Sarah Williams made an impassioned plea for their son's return to the team. "Let's get on with what we're all there for," said Al. "Let's recognize the players and their dreams and desires, and give them every opportunity possible that they may achieve as they dream."

•

The setting for the Williams's press conference, the Clarion Suites Hotel, was suffused with irony. "Clarion," after all, had special significance for John Calipari.

Years before, as a sophomore point guard at the University of North Carolina at Wilmington, Calipari had run into major conflict with his head coach, Mel Gibson. Stuck on the bench behind a junior college transfer, Calipari felt that Gibson had lied to him during the recruiting process. In a move that defined the loss of Calipari's basketball innocence, he left UNC–W—his first taste of Division I basketball—and transferred home to a Division II program in western Pennsylvania, Clarion State.

"I learned a lot about college athletics at that point," Calipari admitted years later. "It's a business. If you're there, fine. If you're not there, that's fine, too. In high school it was more personal, more about you. That was a little bit lost when I went to college. It was a stunning kind of thing for me."

When he decided to go into coaching, Calipari got a message from his father Vince: "You remember what happened at UNC–W? Don't ever treat a boy like that."

•

Calipari, usually as rash as Romeo, suddenly seemed as hesitant as Hamlet. What to do? There were so many conflicting images. There was Mike Williams cooing into his little boys' ears, and Mike Williams keeping the world at bay behind his Walkman and "In Your Face" T-shirt. There was Mike Williams cracking up the team with his fake fainting spell, and Mike Williams undercutting the team discipline with his knock–kneed nonchalance. He seemed like the quintessential team guy. He seemed unbelievably selfish. After launching "Refuse to Lose," Williams embodied it like no one else. He also defied it like no one else. Testicles the size of a hippopotamus. Asshole pills. Do what's best for the team. Don't ever treat a boy like that.

Behind the scenes, there were arguments among the staff. Assistant coaches had advocated getting rid of Williams in the past; Calipari had balked. The debates continued.

Could they win without him? In the NCAA tournament, the true proving ground of college basketball, guard play always became more important. UMass didn't have anyone like Williams—no one who could penetrate like him, no one who could create his own shot. And when the game got tight down at the end, as it inevitably would at some critical juncture, wouldn't they need him? Hadn't he hit more game–winning shots than anyone in the history of college basketball? Wasn't it practically destined that this team would need a last–second three–pointer to achieve its dream of checking in at the gate for Seattle? Wasn't there only one guy who would hit that shot?

And yet, could they win with him? Hadn't the team responded with two excellent performances since he was suspended? Hadn't they throttled Arkansas without him? Maybe they gained in chemistry what they lost in penetration, guts and last–second heroics. Maybe they could punch that ticket to Seattle without him.

Calipari talked it over with his players. He wasn't putting this to a vote, mind you—this was no democracy—he just wanted to see how they felt. It was hard, they said. They liked Mike. They wanted to win. Williams's recent offenses were not exactly felonies, but they knew it was important to be together. They supported Calipari in doing what he felt was best.[11]

On Tuesday, Williams, his parents and a lawyer met with the UMass coaching staff on the third floor of the Mullins Center. They talked for a couple of hours behind closed doors. When the meeting broke up, the Williams family went down the elevator, and then Mike popped up and encountered Calipari by himself. "Coach, can I talk to you for a second?" he asked.

•

That night, five nights after the suspension had been handed out, Calipari did his weekly WHMP radio show with George Miller from Bertucci's Restaurant in Amherst.

"Late last week, John," Miller said, "you told us that early next week, meaning Monday or Tuesday, you would have some sort of decision, some sort of resolution, on the Mike Williams situation. Well, it's almost Wednesday. What can you tell us, the latest, about the Mike Williams situation?"

"We've discussed it as a staff," Calipari said. "We've done some things. A decision is forthcoming."

"What was so important about waiting until early this week to come to this decision?"

"We had too many games back–to–back–to–back. I had to worry about my basketball team, the guys that were there."

"Was it just that difficult of a decision that it took a few extra days?"

"It is. You've got to understand. I'm trying to be fair. I'm trying to make sure that I'm looking at the big picture. Bottom line, whatever decision we make as a staff, and whatever decision I make—the final comment from me—will be what's best for this basketball team."

"What kind of reaction did you come away with from the Williams family press conference yesterday?"

"I did not see it. Did anybody see it? Honestly, I did not see the press conference."

"Have you heard about it? Have you heard about some of the comments that were made?"

"Yeah, but that's fine. See, you have to understand, whatever happens here, and you people know how I am, I'm not going to get into any kind of dialogue trying to make anybody look bad. I don't want Mike Williams to look bad. I want Mike Williams to look good. If me looking bad makes him look good, that's fine with me. . . .I've got to make a decision that's best for my basketball team, and that's what I'll do."

"So you are sensitive to some of the concerns that the Williams family raised yesterday?"

"I didn't hear them, so how can I be sensitive to them?"

"Did you not hear them by choice, or by circumstance?"

"I was out of town. . . .I was out of commission last night, so I wasn't around. But I think everybody knows that I am fair, that I've been fair since I've been the coach here, and that I'm going to make a decision that's the best thing for our basketball team. Now, now, let's move on and talk about our basketball team."

"I can't let you get off that easily, John." (Calipari tried to interrupt.) "I cannot do it." (Interruption.) "Why do we do this radio show?" (Interruption.) "Why does this show exist?"

"It doesn't matter why it exists."

"Oh absolutely it does."

"Let me tell you this. This is my show. It's not your show. It's my show. I've already made some comments about it. We're not going to spend an hour—"

"We don't have to spend an hour—"

"We're not going to spend time trying to make anybody look bad. I'm not going to do it. I just told you what's going to happen. It's forthcoming. I've looked at it. We've talked about it as a staff. What else do you want me to say?"

"With all due respect, John, all I'm giving you the opportunity to do is put the cards on the table—just as the Williams family has already done."

"No, George, I'm not going to lay out there what we're doing. All right, go to a commercial. Go."

It was the testiest public exchange with the media that Calipari had ever had.

The next day, Wednesday, February 22, a press release was on the computers of the UMass media relations office by noon. It was not faxed to media outlets, however, until three o'clock—at which time the Minutemen were en route to the airport in Hartford for a flight to Philadelphia. The release did not say that Williams had been thrown off the team, stating instead that his suspension was "extended" for the rest of the season. "This is one of the hardest things I've had to do as a coach," Calipari said in the release. "Coaching is about teaching life skills, not just basketball. Mike will retain his scholarship and have the opportunity to finish his education here at UMass. We wish him the best."

While the news got out, UMass prepared for Thursday night's nationally televised game against Temple. The Temple game, of course, had become Williams's grand stage. In each of the last four nerve-wracking wins against the Owls, including a one-point victory at home earlier in the year, he had been the key performer. Twice he'd come through with the winning shot in the closing seconds. But those days were over. Ten minutes into what proved to be an embarrassing loss to the Owls, already trailing 25–10, Calipari called a timeout, while the Temple fans taunted over and over, "Where's Mike Williams? Where's Mike Williams?"

He was nowhere to be found.

•

The Minutemen started winning again, closing the season with three straight victories. Touched with the surreal, the finale was the resumption of the Rutgers game, played out on a Friday afternoon at the Philadelphia Spectrum. It was Calipari's first return to the Spectrum in three years since the NCAA loss to Kentucky when he had been whistled for the infamous "out of the box" technical by Lenny Wirtz. This time, before acres of empty seats, the Minutemen came out of the locker room while a tape of the first half against Rutgers was being played for the 445 fans. Just as UMass arrived on the court, the action showed Mike Williams making a strong move to the hoop and getting fouled. The national anthem was played for the second time. Marcus Camby, who had been recuperating in New England when the first half was played in New Jersey, was the star of the second half in Philadelphia. At one point, with UMass up seventeen points and 4:02 remaining, Tyrone Weeks was shooting a one–and–one free throw opportunity. As the first shot went up, Lou Roe, in the second position on the lane, spun hard around a Rutgers player to get inside position—hardly necessary with the game in hand, and all the more unnecessary with the shot going in. Still, it was the kind of play that seemed to define UMass at its hungriest. From the bench, Rigo Nuñez' shouts were audible to everyone in attendance: "I see your work, Lou! I see your work!"

John Calipari had his team full of focus and fire once again. He told a quizzical media corps that the Minutemen had "good synergy" and "positive physiology." Asked to explain, he said, "We had a couple of guys who wanted to mope. [I tell them,] 'You got the world by the gazones, man! Don't be sad. You've got to be happy! You've got to walk in: breakfast—hey, man! I'm up against the world, we're in the Top 10, you know what I'm saying?' It's just a frame of mind I'm trying to get them in so that they can be relaxed and play."

It was all paying off. In Philadelphia at the Atlantic 10 tournament, the Minutemen got hugs from Dr. J, advice from Bill Cosby, "aggressive counseling" from Calipari and a pair of impressive victories. Then they came home and throttled Temple in the championship game, 63–44. "This team has always built their basketball on pride," Roe said. "Tonight wasn't just a championship. It was a pride thing."

They were 26–4, winners of six straight, ranked Number 8 in the country. They had dominated the Atlantic 10 as it had never been dominated before, winning four straight regular–season and tournament titles. They didn't, however, cut down any nets. They had larger goals in mind.

The year before, Calipari had acknowledged that the Minutemen would ultimately be judged by their performance in the NCAA tournament. "We know it," he said. "We accept it." The greatest team Calipari had ever coached was now four wins away from its season–long dream of getting to Seattle.

While the Minutemen geared for that challenge, there were other battles to fight. Around the edges of the team, a public relations war was being fought. The need for a positive "image and perception" was never greater.

UMass knew that Dan Golden, writer of the initial *Globe* piece on grades back in October, was working on another large story about Minuteman basketball and academics.[12] Further, ABC Television's Armen Keteyian, the co–author of *Raw Recruits* (a book that analyzed the seedier elements of college basketball recruiting), had been on campus researching a segment for "The American Agenda."

In the days leading up to the *Globe* story, which appeared on March 14, UMass took a couple of preemptive public relations strikes. On March 7, the school issued a media advisory entitled "UMass Library Scores Big With Coach Calipari." While Calipari had been donating to the library for four years, he had always done so quietly. This time a ceremony was planned for his $20,000 donation. "The entire UMass community has been terrific in supporting the men's basketball team," Calipari said in the release. "As I've always said, UMass fans are the greatest fans around. The feeling is mutual. I want to support this campus. And the best way to do that is by supporting the heart of this great teaching and learning university, the library."

The same twenty–six story library that had earned national infamy for falling pieces of brick years ago would soon have an instruction room named after John Calipari.

On March 13, the UMass Media Relations Office issued a six–page "fact sheet" that underscored all the positive impact that Calipari and the basketball program had had on the university. Sections ranged from "The Student–Athlete at UMass" to "Quotes on John Calipari and UMass Basketball."

The story in the *Globe* the next day proved to be almost shockingly tame. Headlined "Basketball glory may have academic cost," Dan Golden's lengthy front–page piece offered nothing particularly incriminating. Privately, members of the athletic administration admitted their relief.

•

Drawing the Number 2 seed in the East, the Minutemen bused to the Knickerbocker Arena in Albany, New York. Four years before, almost to the day, UMass had last played there, stunning Siena when Tony Barbee's desperation three–pointer forced overtime. After the Minutemen prevailed, they earned a trip to Manhattan and an appearance in the Final Four of the NIT. At the time it seemed like a huge deal, perhaps the biggest win in school history. Now that lofty moment seemed almost quaint by comparison. The goal now was the real Final Four.

"There's no pressure to win," insisted Calipari. "No one has told us we have to win. It's not like we have to win or we're done. What this is about is, let's just do our best, let's prepare, and let's see what happens. We call it letting it fly. Just let it fly."

For twenty–nine minutes of the Minutemen's opening game against fifteenth–seeded St. Peter's, the pressure seemed to be tugging hard around their necks. The little–known Peacocks, sparked by ponytailed point guard Mike Frensley, were giving UMass all it could handle, leading 49–48. Then Marcus Camby took over the game and the Minutemen rolled to a 68–51 win. In a withering defensive display, UMass held St. Peter's without a field goal in the final eleven minutes. "Guys just felt we had worked too hard too long to have this season end," Camby said. "We didn't come this far to go home so quick."

In each of the last two years, UMass's season had come to an abrupt halt in the second round of the NCAA tournament with the Minutemen getting upset by lower–seeded teams. This time they got set to take on tenth–seeded Stanford. Not surprisingly, this matchup dredged up old academic questions as media seeking a spicy angle portrayed the game as a showdown between one team hitting the books versus another one hitting the boards. The pregame press conference was peppered with questions about academics. Camby politely pointed out that Stanford was not the only team with scholastic pressures; he had two papers due the following week. Even Stanford coach Mike Montgomery tried to defuse the story by saying, "I was a PE major at Long Beach State—you're probably asking the wrong guy," and then excusing himself from the interview podium by saying,

"We're going to study now. I've got a badminton paper I've got to write."

On the court the next day, UMass left no doubts. Playing the best NCAA tournament game in school history, the Minutemen raced out to a twenty–point halftime lead and coasted to a 75–53 victory. They seemed fresh and energized all afternoon, supercharged with defensive intensity, above–the–rim rebounding, and a ravenous hunger for loose balls. It was UMass at its best, infused with every ounce of Calipari's ferocious will.

"It's disheartening to play against them," said Stanford forward Darren Allaway. "They're very focused. Roe is the hardest playing guy I've played against this year. Him and (UCLA's Ed) O'Bannon share an inner drive that permeates through the team. Just that will to win, that desire to win—that was probably the most powerful thing."

For the first time in three years, and just the second time in school history, UMass had advanced to the Sweet Sixteen.

On Monday night, March 20, the "American Agenda" piece was broadcast on ABC's *World News Tonight* with Peter Jennings. The segment called into question UMass's institutional priorities. Had the school compromised its academic mission in a quest for the prestige and profits of bigtime basketball? Calipari's financial package, estimated at $600,000,[13] was juxtaposed with the school's more than two–year freeze on professor's salaries and a recent report on more than $300 million of overdue maintenance. And yet, the report proved far less damning than many people in the athletic department had feared. It acknowledged that the school's basketball success had generated enormous interest in UMass, as well as a profit of almost $800,000 a year ago—money that had helped to fund scholarships in sports like women's soccer. Calipari's appeal on campus was summarized in the statement by senior Arthur Stapleton: "He's been God."

The next day before practice Calipari seemed unusually relaxed, his arms folded in a sleek maroon and white Nike warmup suit, a smile on his face. He looked out at the Mullins Center, the house that he had built, and at his players who had come through a simply astonishing season.

They had reached Number 1 after the first game, earning applause from strangers on airplanes. They had been taunted and lampooned. They had watched the world from the Eiffel Tower, from Disneyland, from the Atlantic City boardwalk. In backroads America, they had been the biggest show in years to come to Olean, New York, and Morgantown, West Virginia. They had witnessed a halftime sit–in, and mustered a crunchtime comeback for the ages. They had endured the wrenching Mike Williams miniseries. They had met everyone from Bill Clinton to Bill Cosby to Mickey Mouse.

Through it all, they had more than survived: they had prospered. UMass was now one of only sixteen teams left with a chance at college basketball's biggest prize. The Minutemen were playing great ball. Just two more wins and they would be flying to Seattle for the Final Four—the sport's ultimate stamp of legitimacy, its proof of having arrived. John Calipari could only smile.

"We're one of those teams that have been talking about it all year," Calipari said. "We never backed down from it. We talked about Seattle. You may say that's added pressure, but we haven't been afraid to dream. That's something we've always told our kids: 'Dream big dreams, don't be afraid to dream.' The big picture has always been Seattle. And it's always been not just getting to Seattle, it's winning the whole thing. You can't be afraid to dream."

•

In a sense, the Meadowlands represented the many sides of UMass basketball. The arena beside a swamp sits astride the New Jersey Turnpike, exit 16W. It is also right next to a service area named for coaching legend Vince Lombardi. Looking east as the sun goes down, you see the silver skyline of Manhattan beckoning. There is both muck and glitter.

UMass had played at the Meadowlands just once, losing a thriller the year before to Kentucky, 67–64. It was after that game that Wildcat coach Rick Pitino called Calipari's work at UMass "the greatest building job in college basketball history." Now it was time for the next step.

On Friday, March 24, UMass absolutely overwhelmed Tulsa, 76–51. It was another full–throttle defensive effort, holding Tulsa to anemic twenty–seven percent shooting. Camby was unstoppable at both ends: twenty points, nine rebounds, five blocks. After the first few minutes, the game was never close.

In the Elite Eight for the first time in school history, the Minutemen could now taste their dream.

"This is what we've been working for all season," said Dana Dingle. "This is what it's all for—all the preseason, all the extra hard work— it's all for this."

"Our job is not done yet," added Camby. "Our goal was not to get to the Final Eight. It was to get to the Final Four."

The opponent was little–known Oklahoma State, a school that had once tried to lure Jack Leaman away from UMass. Ranked fourteenth in the final AP poll, the Cowboys had finished the season very hot. Their strong play continued into the NCAA tournament, culminating with an upset over top–seeded Wake Forest in the East Regional semifinals. Though not regarded as a team with a significant chance of winning the national title, the Cowboys presented some big problems for UMass. Prime among these was the enormous seven–foot center, Bryant (Big Country) Reeves. His low–post power would confront the reedy agility of Camby in a matchup of two vastly different big men. Shooting guard Randy Rutherford had as quick a release and as deep a range as any player UMass had encountered all year. And the suffocating defensive style of veteran coach Eddie Sutton had flustered opponents throughout the tournament.

On Sunday morning, John Calipari tried to conceal his nervousness over breakfast. He saw Edgar Padilla hopping around on crutches, almost certainly unable to play after severely inflaming tendons in his left ankle during the Tulsa game. That meant UMass would be down to two guards: Derek Kellogg and Carmelo Travieso. Further, Calipari saw Lou Roe hobbling noticeably, ice on his right hamstring. Roe would play, of course, but his mobility had seemed limited during practice the day before. Calipari stared at his food, talked urgently with his assistant coaches, then summoned team manager Lou Castellano. Nodding, Castellano went up to the hotel's gym and guarded one of the treadmills. Calipari needed some time to work off the tension.

Padilla tried to warm up at the Meadowlands, grimacing with every step. He couldn't do it. UMass went through its pregame routine, looking focused, serious. Roe sat out by halfcourt, stretching for several minutes. As the clock ticked down, the team gathered at the foul line, placing all hands up toward the middle, where the long right arm of seven–two senior center Jeff Meyer held a ball aloft. With one word, they broke camp: "Seattle."

It was a fiercely physical battle. At one point Kellogg was led off with a badly gashed elbow. Oklahoma State's Scott Pierce had to pick one of his teeth off the court.

In the first half, Camby struggled, raising his fist for a sub before the game was two minutes old. Roe lacked his usual explosiveness. Kellogg and Travieso, though, helped spark UMass to a five–point lead at the break. The Minutemen had not played well at all. They still led. They were twenty minutes away.

The second half had an inexorable quality to it, the same maddening quicksand that had swallowed UMass up a year ago against

Maryland. No one was able to stop Reeves. Camby seemed frail and winded. Roe, giving up five inches and seventy pounds, leaned nobly on Reeves, but couldn't contain him. Meyer came off the bench to block one shot, but couldn't match Reeves's power. Nor could Tyrone Weeks.

When Rutherford started heating up from outside, Oklahoma State's lead ballooned to double digits. Timeout after timeout could not stem the tide. With 6:22 left, the season seemed over at 58–43.

UMass reached in and summoned its Refuse to Lose spirit, scoring the next eight points. Ultimately, though, the Minutemen could not sustain the offensive rhythm. They couldn't grab the rebounds they needed. They couldn't contain Oklahoma State when they needed the stops most desperately. With a sunken expression, Calipari was left to hug Camby, after he fouled out, and then Roe and Kellogg as they came out in the closing moments of a 68–54 loss.

The Oklahoma State Cowboys were going to the Final Four.

In the cramped, cinder–block–lined UMass locker room, the atmosphere was somber. Camby, a blue towel over his head, blamed himself for the loss. Padilla, looking at the floor, limped slowly off with crutches. After an impassioned plea to the underclassmen to remember this pain—to use it to get better—Kellogg walked out to the bus. Roe, who would drive home to Atlantic City that night and have to be helped out of the car, groped for words: "I know it's been a great run for us, but we're just like anybody else. If you don't win it all—especially for us—the dreams we had coming into the season. . ."

Calipari answered questions for a long time in the corner of the locker room. Asked about his feelings in the game's closing minutes, his voice softened: "You get to the reality of it. It's over. It's finished. The season's done. It's the final game. It's been a great season. It's been a great ride. You don't want it to end. But you say it's over. This is over. And then you say it's over with. . . ."

Of course, there were other teams that fell short of their goals in the 1994–95 season. The players from North Carolina, Kentucky and Kansas also yearned to cut down the nets in Seattle. At UMass, though, there was a special sense of urgency that extended beyond the current roster. Those other schools would certainly be back in Final Fours and probably win national championships. They were storied programs with staying power. For UMass, though, this looked like the only shot.

In seven years under Calipari, the Minutemen had soared from one of the worst to one of the best, but it seemed almost certain that they had reached their peak. Seniors Roe and Kellogg—and, of course, Mike Williams—were gone. It appeared quite possible that Camby, the most gifted player at UMass since Julius Erving, might join a parade of top underclass talent declaring their eligibility for the NBA draft. Recruiting classes did not seem to be replenishing the talent pool. This year's freshman class had been weak, and the recruiting for the next year also looked subpar. Administrative support appeared in jeopardy when UMass president Michael Hooker, a near constant presence at Minuteman games, abruptly broke his contract to take over the chancellor's position at the University of North Carolina at Chapel Hill. The coaching staff also seemed poised for a shakeup. Top assistant Bill Bayno, the key recruiter for players like Roe and Camby, accepted a job a week after the season ended to become the new head coach at UNLV.

And even Calipari, the miracle worker himself, would speak to three NBA teams about their coaching vacancies in the coming weeks.

UMass coaches, players and fans had come so close to something they wanted so much, and they just didn't get there. They had climbed the mountain, but just hadn't reached the summit. Now they seemed ready to tumble.

It had been a great ride.

# 9: "THIS IS A GREAT COUNTRY, THIS AMERICA"

November 28, 1995
Auburn Hills, Michigan

They had gone bigtime. The rise of UMass from one of the worst teams in the country to one of the best had been, in many respects, a bonanza for the university.

John Calipari and his basketball team had created a true sense of excitement. The days when the Minutemen couldn't give away enough tickets to fill the 4,058–seat Curry Hicks Cage had been replaced by sellout after sellout at the 9,493–seat Mullins Center. Games were now events. The student section stood the entire night, bowing to Calipari, hiding behind newspapers when the opponent's lineup was introduced, "whooshing" with every made free throw by the Minutemen. Bankers wore deflated basketballs on their heads. Tom Hannum's pep band pumped up even the most sedate fans. When PA announcer Jack O'Neill introduced the final starter as "Marcussssss Cam–beeeeeee," cheerleaders thrust their arms to the sky and glowed with pride as if the very name had conferred greatness upon them. Outside of the Mullins Center, alumni gathered in sports bars. Children pleaded with parents for bedtime extensions when the Minutemen tipped off with Temple at 9:30. The "love affair" that John Calipari had boldly promised back in 1988 was hot and heavy.

For UMass, the success was much more than excitement. Bigtime basketball was good for business. School officials said the success of the team was in large part responsible for the sharp increase in applications: up 26.6 percent from 1992–1995, 58.6 percent for out–of–state applicants. Coaches of other sports heaped credit on Calipari for putting the school on the map, and said that their own recruiting had benefited immensely. The overall athletic program had never known greater success or prosperity.

Private financial support for the university soared from $8.4 million in Fiscal Year 1988 to $14.0 million in FY 1995. The UMass Athletic

Fund, a separate branch of university development devoted to sports, raised more than $1 million in FY 1995, only its fourth year of existence.

UMass merchandise was everywhere. Just a few years back, local kids in western Massachusetts never wore T–shirts and hats from the State U. Now you couldn't walk by a school recess without seeing the maroon and white facsimile Marcus Camby or Lou Roe jerseys. Basketball apparel filled the shelves of Calipari's own store in Amherst, Coach Cal's Closet. The merchandise also sold nationally, courtesy of Champion Products and J.C. Penney. The UMass logo—original sketches still sitting in Calipari's desk—was making big bucks for the university.

Wins on the court and money in the bank helped boost pride in oft–maligned UMass. There were many things to crow about that had nothing to do with basketball, things that in the final analysis were far more important. A business school and an engineering school that were nationally ranked. An English department with two Pulitzer Prize winners. Alumni who had won every award from the Emmy to the Nobel. But without question it was the exploits of a small group of young men and their ferocious coach that helped lift UMass from the doldrums.

The coach had become the most important employee of the university—"our greatest asset" according to outgoing president Michael Hooker. The only faculty member to address the state legislature, Calipari was credited in some circles for increased education funding in recent years.[1] One of his closest personal friends was state treasurer Joe Malone.

Nationally, basketball was the most visible extension of the university. Minutemen games were constantly on television. The days of begging for midnight appearances were long gone—UMass had been nationally televised sixteen times in the 1994–95 season, appearing on all three networks, as well as ESPN and ESPN2. College basketball talking heads like Dick Vitale were constantly spreading the gospel that the land grant institution in Emily Dickinson's backyard had become one hot school.

The Minutemen had friends in high places. Governor William Weld sometimes showed up at games. Calipari's secretary, Bonnie Martin, found herself fielding calls from Senator Ted Kennedy and Bill Cosby. National Security Advisor and western Massachusetts resident Tony

Lake always arranged special outings when the Minutemen were in Washington. UPI White House correspondent and UMass graduate Ken Bazinet sometimes filed his on–line UMass basketball newsletter from Air Force One. Above the coach's desk sat a signed photo from President Clinton.

The rise of UMass basketball, though, had not come without costs. Since leaving behind the quirky, packed–with–history–and–atmosphere Curry Hicks Cage in 1993 for the larger, sparkling, more sterile Mullins Center, UMass had instituted a policy of dispersing season tickets according to a "priority points system." A common practice in bigtime collegiate sports, this system is designed to reward prime real estate to people who have demonstrated loyalty to the team. That loyalty was measured at UMass in a lot of ways: by a history of holding season tickets, by having been a student or employee of the university and—significantly—by making contributions to the UMass Athletic Fund. Yes, the school did a better job than many of reserving tickets for students and longtime fans, but without question lots of people who had seen UMass basketball up close for years were now peering at it from behind the well–tailored shoulders of people who couldn't tell Dana Dingle from Kris Kringle.

Up in the rafters, fans noted two numbers retired, both reading "32." One of those belonged to Julius Erving. The other belonged to George (Trigger) Burke. A good scorer during his two seasons in the mid–fifties, Burke was certainly not one of the two greatest players in UMass history. Several others had contributed more on the court than the lawyer from Quincy who often arrived at home games in a limousine. None had contributed close to as much off the court, where Burke's financial contributions flowed well into six figures. He deserved to be honored in a large way for his devotion and generosity. But did he deserve to have his number retired? The same number that was subsequently worn by others, including the great Dr. J? To many observers, this seemed like the consummate sellout. Whenever Jack Leaman looked to the rafters, he felt sick to his stomach.

After the 1994–95 season, WHMP fired western Massachusetts native George Miller, its talented play–by–play man for the past four years. Calipari insisted he had nothing to do with the decision, that it didn't stem from Miller's aggressive questioning about Mike Williams the year before. The station's general manager Rick Heideman explained that he wanted to bring in someone with both broadcasting skill and business acumen to help expand the radio network. The dumping of Miller and hiring of Marc Vandermeer from Michigan showed that money was talking. Such personnel moves, of course, are made all the time in other places. In mellow western Massachusetts, though, Miller's firing seemed startling.

Players, too, had felt the downside of the bigtime. Back in the eighties when the teams stunk, the academic performance and behavior of basketball players were far more questionable than they were now, but few people noticed. Suddenly, the lives and grades of the Minutemen were open books. They were viewed less as college kids and more as public figures, in the same realm as politicians or movie stars. And now that UMass had started to attract players with possible professional futures, shadowy presences began showing up on campus. The "runners" for agents, young people who blended well in a college setting, began to introduce themselves. *Just wanted to meet you, Marcus. Just wanted to meet some of your friends.*

Something had been lost in the UMass basketball program. It wasn't about Jack Leaman and the Curry Hicks Cage anymore. During the 1994–95 season—the one that virtually everyone expected to be *the* year at UMass—a contentiousness and cynicism had started to creep into the mix. For all the success, the innocence seemed to be fading away forever.

•

No one knew what sort of tone to expect when UMass met the press for "Media Day" on October 12, 1995. Media members sat down over lunch on the third floor of the Mullins Center, chatting up the obvious angles for the evening news or tomorrow's papers. Would Marcus Camby be one of the best players in the country? Could the little–known backcourt of Edgar Padilla and Carmelo Travieso get the job done? How would UMass deal with the likelihood of decline?

John Calipari entered the room in a sport jacket, looking tanned and rested. He smiled. "We have a chance of being special again," he began.

Working the room easily, he took questions. Yes, UMass was not as deep as it had been. He was counting on a big year from Camby, but felt strongly that UMass needed to be more than its star. The guard situation was uncertain: "It's a little scary with Edgar at the point. He hits the band. He hits people in the seats. He hits the scorer's table."

Calipari kidded about beginning his eighth year on the job. "You guys thought I'd be here no more than four seasons: winter, spring, summer and fall."2

Without so much as a smirk, he brought up academics: "We had no players in summer school. That's probably not a story, but no one was here all summer. They did very well academically. Nine of the thirteen are on the Athletic Director's Honor Roll. The starting five had a 3.0—probably not a story, but it is a fact."

His goal for the season? "To win a national title."

What about the non–league schedule, which included heavyweights like Kentucky, Louisville, Memphis, Maryland, Georgia Tech, Wake Forest and Syracuse? "We've overscheduled. There's no question. If we finish 7–6 in non–league games, that would be great. When we schedule the way we schedule, I as a coach have to accept the fact that we're going to lose games. We're not winning every game."

His own improvement as a coach? "Every year you get stuff thrown at you. Last year, just think about all the stuff that was thrown at us. The key is: are we staying focused as a staff? Are we keeping the team focused? Are the individual players getting better? The other thing you'd say is, how have they done in school? How have they done in jobs after school? Are they people that we're all proud of? I think we've gotten better with all that stuff."

It was all such a good show—sincere, affecting, winning in a way that John Calipari almost always is. And then, asked about the rewards of his job, he took this media moment to a whole new level:

"I am so excited that the university wants me here. I am so excited to be the coach here. I am the luckiest guy in the world. I'm not going to sit here and lie to you. This is a great country, this America. This is incredible. My dad tries to remind me—'My dad came through Ellis Island, worked in the coal mines of West Virginia, died of black lung at forty–four to give you an opportunity'—and to give my dad an opportunity to do what he's doing. My dad still works for USAir. He will not retire. He's carrying bags down at USAir, and here I am coaching at UMass. Are you kidding me?3

"So believe me when I say, I may not come across this way, but I am so happy and so elated that I have the opportunity to coach here at this school. Why this school? I'll say it again: the mission of the institution. I am not a country club guy. I never have been. I never had a silver spoon in my mouth. My sisters and I were the first college–educated people in our family. My parents were high school educated.

You talk about this campus. How many people on this campus are in the same boat I was? They're not driving around in BMWs like on other campuses. They're not. They're struggling to get through school. They're struggling to get the money to get through school. That's the mission of the institution, and that's why I'm proud to be here.

"Now, we've got an engineering program and a business school, and all the other things that are tops in their field, but we're also giving kids an opportunity to get an education. We're giving socioeconomically disadvantaged—you guys like when I go through this?" He paused to flash a self–satisfied smile before repeating, "socioeconomically disadvantaged students a chance to get an education. And if you want to do something with yourself, you can do that here. That's why I enjoy working here.

"There are some schools that I wouldn't feel comfortable being there. You know with the tweeds and the thing on the. . ." Grimacing masterfully, he slapped his right hand to his left elbow, where a patch might be if he were another kind of guy at another kind of school. Then he smiled, shrugged, looked straight at the reporters and said, "That's just not me."

He was absolutely riveting. John Calipari, still the wunderkind. The year was about to begin. Innocence was back. Now all he had to do was get ready to coach against Kentucky and Rick Pitino.

•

They shared a history. In the summer of 1976 at the Five–Star Camp not far from his home in Moon Township, Pennsylvania, the teen-aged Calipari stood enraptured by the hoop evangelism of Syracuse's young assistant coach. In the spring of 1988, Pitino—then the first–year head coach of the New York Knicks—took time out of his schedule and money out of his pocket to help the moribund basketball program at his alma mater hire the unproven Calipari as its coach. And then there was the night in March of 1992 when UMass, having reached the NCAA tournament for the first time in thirty years, staged a furious rally against Pitino's Kentucky team in the Sweet Sixteen, a rally that fizzled after Calipari was called for his memorable technical by Lenny Wirtz.

But it was more than history that they shared. John Vincent Calipari, thirty–six, and Richard Andrew Pitino, forty–three, had become the prototypes of the modern basketball coach. They were slick and good–looking. They were sultans of spin and sound bites every bit as much as they were Xs and Os experts. They were not father–figure coaches like John Wooden or Dean Smith, but rather the new generation of coaching genius, the gym rat gone GQ. And, of course, they each burned to win a national title.

Calipari's status as a bigtime coach was unquestioned by the 1995–96 season. He had a fat contract with all the accoutrements: the TV show, the radio show, the six–figure sneaker deal. His university package, reworked in the summer of 1995, gave him a ten–year coaching extension and guaranteed him employment at UMass until age sixty–two, yet gave him the option to leave without penalty. Aggressively courted by the NBA, Calipari had chosen to stay with the college game where the coach is the star. He embodied the energy and the passion that made college hoops such a popular product. Among Calipari's endorsements was a Degree Deodorant commercial in which he described coaching as "a war without bullets." Above all, he won. In the last four seasons, UMass had won 111 games, third most of any team in America. Calipari had arrived.

Still, he was no Rick Pitino. In the eyes of most college basketball fans, Calipari was still protégé, still Little Ricky. UMass and Kentucky had met head to head on three occasions. Pitino had won every time.

Kentucky was Kentucky, the Roman Empire of College Basketball, as Pitino liked to call it. The Wildcats were the second winningest team in the sport's history, behind North Carolina. In the forty–five–year history of the AP poll, they had finished in the Top 10 at the end of thirty separate seasons. They had made ten appearances in the Final Four. Five times they had won it all.

To be sure, Kentucky had had its share of dark moments. The Wildcats' 1952–53 team was prohibited from playing interscholastic games by the NCAA after investigations surrounding point shaving[4] revealed that Kentucky had paid its players. More recently, a 13–19 season in 1988–89 was followed by NCAA probation. That's when Rick Pitino rode in on a shining horse, not only restoring the program's honor, but rebuilding Kentucky into a powerhouse. As he had his whole life, Pitino won people over with his charm and competitive drive. In six years he had taken the Wildcats to a Final Four and two Elite Eights. Over the last four seasons his teams had won 114 games, more than any team in the nation.

In the eyes of a growing minority of impassioned Kentucky fans, however, Pitino had not won enough. There was no national champi-

*Rick Pitino (Photo by Jerrey Roberts)*

onship trophy to glisten at the front of a parade in Lexington. Just the year before, in 1995, Kentucky seemed invincible through the first three rounds of the NCAA tournament. Then, like the Minutemen, they lost in the Elite Eight, falling one game shy of the sport's most coveted weekend.

Now, with a new year beginning, the Wildcats were expected to do nothing less than bring home the national title. They would carry the burden of sky–high expectations all season long. After all, the talent level was staggering. There were four players—Tony Delk, Antoine Walker, Ron Mercer and Wayne Turner— who had been McDonald's

All–Americas in high school. A fifth, Roderick Rhodes, had been all but forcibly transferred to California, because Pitino had no room for him on the team. How good was Kentucky? Fresno State coach Jerry Tarkanian, who had been the head coach at UNLV's star–studded national championship team of 1989, said that Kentucky might be the most talented squad in college basketball history. The Boston Celtics had already assigned nine full scouting reports on members of the Wildcats. Even Pitino, spin–master supreme, conceded that this was the most talented group he had ever coached.

But would they be the best team? Throughout the year, the key for the Wildcats would be submerging egos. Rick Pitino, of all people, knew how difficult that could be.

UMass faced a different kind of challenge. It was not clear that the Minutemen had the horses to compete, particularly against the teams on Calipari's maniacal play–anyone–anywhere–anytime schedule.

Yes, the Minutemen had Marcus Camby, the first preseason All–America in school history. Sure, there were steady senior forwards in Donta Bright and Dana Dingle. But realistically this was a team with major questions. Three starters were gone from a year ago, including two–year co–captains Lou Roe and Derek Kellogg. UMass had a most unproven backcourt in Edgar Padilla and Carmelo Travieso, a player who had started only two games in his first two years. There was no depth. In fact, UMass had only ten scholarship players on the roster, a full three below the NCAA limit.[5] What's more, in their last appearance on a basketball court, they had lost an exhibition game to the Converse All–Stars.

After the debacle against Converse on November 17, only eleven days remained before the season opener. John Calipari knew his team needed to improve tactically. The Minutemen were not running an efficient halfcourt offense. They had been confused on defense in the two exhibition games. People really didn't seem to understand their roles. No leadership had emerged.

In Calipari's mind, though, the biggest issue was clear: UMass had to regain its fighting spirit. Loose balls had to become matters of urgency, rebounds passionate quests. The game had to be played, not just as if it were important, but as if it mattered in some fundamental sense. As Calipari often said, UMass had to play as if a loss meant a trip to the electric chair.

To instill this mentality in his players, Calipari felt he had to get them to do things they didn't like to do. In Calipari's eyes, coaching was about overcoming human nature: getting individuals to think about the group first, getting people to do the hard thing instead of the easy thing. The task at hand, he said on his first weekly radio show on November 21, was "breaking through barriers, trying to get them to step out of a comfort level. They play in a comfortable way, and they don't want to break out of that. You've got to be uncomfortable to really get it done."

So Calipari set about making things as uncomfortable as possible. He ran a basketball boot camp, far more about toughness than tactics. "Get ready for football practice," he told the players: hard picks, hard fouls, hard work. Practice had to be harder than any game. The key to winning was making the game tough for the opponent. Nothing easy. As he had done years ago at Moon Area High School, Calipari was riling up his players, bringing out their fierceness.

One afternoon, with streams of sweat pouring down his players' bodies and heavy breathing filling the Mullins Center, Calipari called the team into the center of the floor. In front of everyone he said that he was thinking about starting freshman Charlton Clarke at point guard and putting Edgar Padilla on the bench. Padilla was just not getting the job done, Calipari said. So what if Clarke had missed a bunch of practices with pneumonia and arthoscopic knee surgery? So what if he didn't fully know the plays yet? At least he wasn't playing scared.

After the Converse game, Padilla had talked long and hard with UMass's former point guard Derek Kellogg. The next day they went out to dinner at Bertucci's in Amherst, discussing what it meant to play point guard for Calipari. Padilla had all the physical tools and desire, Kellogg told him, but sometimes he just got too hard on himself. He let mistakes boil too long in his mind. His sensitivity got in his way.

Now Calipari was putting him to the test. Though the words tore into Padilla's heart, he wasn't going to react. He was going to work hard. Stay cool. Show the coach that he could do it.

On the afternoon of Sunday, November 26, the Minutemen tossed their maroon equipment bags into the storage chamber of a King Ward bus behind the Mullins Center and rolled down to Connecticut's Bradley International Airport for the first trip of the season. The first leg of their flight to Detroit took them to Pittsburgh, where Vince Calipari used to fuel planes for Allied Aviation, sometimes bringing his only son with him for a day of adventure. During a brief layover, the players hung out briefly in the concourse, frequenting restaurants with names like "Wok N Roll," and checking out the Upper Deck Authenticated store where an autographed Julius Erving basketball could be had for $199.99.

They then boarded the connecting flight to Detroit, and bused up north to a Marriott not far from the Palace at Auburn Hills. The Kentucky game was scheduled for Tuesday night.

It was pure chance that the Minutemen should open against Kentucky. They were playing in the Great Eight, one of a growing breed of made–for television basketball tournaments. Actually, it was not a tournament in the true sense. Consisting of two nights of doubleheaders, the event was designed to give the teams that made the Elite Eight of the previous year's NCAA tournament one high–profile, measuring–stick game where a loss would be acceptable. Teams were paired by a drawing. UMass just got lucky.

Kentucky had opened its season the week before, ironically enough traveling to western Massachusetts to play fourteenth–ranked Maryland in the Tip–Off Classic at the Springfield Civic Center. At a luncheon just hours before Kentucky's twelve–point victory, Pitino closed his comments by addressing the UMass fans in attendance. "Remember to take it easy on us," he joked. "We're just a bunch of farm kids from Kentucky trying to find our way in the world."

Calipari appreciates the spin game as much as anyone. Deep down, he knew that a victory over Kentucky was not out of the question. The Minutemen had been picked as the preseason Number 7 team by AP. In each of the last two Novembers they had knocked off Number 1, stunning North Carolina in 1993, and Arkansas in 1994. Neither of those victories had been expected.

Still, given Kentucky's overwhelming talent and UMass's wretched preseason performance, another upset seemed highly unlikely.

UMass, after all, was still UMass. No national championships here. No Final Fours. Only one McDonald's All–America—Donta Bright—in Calipari's eight years as coach. The difference between the two schools seemed to be embodied by Kentucky freshman guard Wayne Turner. A Massachusetts product, he attended Beaver Country Day School, and left as the second highest rated high school point guard in the country, behind only Stephon Marbury. Turner was pursued aggressively by the Minutemen, a team that desperately needed guards, especially in-state All-Americas. UMass and UConn were his top choices until one day late in the recruiting season when Rick Pitino showed up smiling at Beaver Country Day. After Turner visited Lexington, the deed was done.

Now, on the morning of November 28, Calipari laughed when asked how many of his players would have been recruited by Pitino. The list, apparently, was not very long.

•

There is a moment before a game begins when a team stands alone. It lasts for several seconds, at most. Starters have been introduced to the public. Coaches await them on the sideline, eager to run through final instructions. Pep bands blast out a tune. Cheerleaders thrust pom-poms to the sky. Fans, abuzz, await the game.

In that moment, at 9:41 on the night of November 28, a funny thing happened to the UMass Minutemen. They coiled into a tight circle and began jumping up and down, leaning into the center, bumping shoulders and chests. From afar, they looked like a bunch of angry hornets on pogo sticks. Tyrone Weeks, the burly junior forward, inadvertently slammed into Carmelo Travieso, opening a cut on the wispy guard's lip. No matter, they continued to bounce and bump, a frenetic team "mosh pit." It was a spontaneous channeling of all the pent-up energy from eleven days of football practice, a focusing of fire as the season began, a gesture at once of unity and aggression.

Funny thing, too, coming from this team. As far as Division I college basketball teams go, the Minutemen were a gentle crew. The starting five included Camby, who had spent a good chunk of the semester tutoring middle-school students; forwards Bright and Dingle, two of the most soft-spoken captains in America; Travieso, who had arrived on campus two years ago with a thick portfolio of drawings and thoughts of being an art major; and Padilla, a player so sensitive he had started crying a year ago after one of John Calipari's tongue-lashings. They were hardly a team with an air of menace. But they were fierce competitors. They did play for Calipari. And the season was about to begin. After Calipari drew the team in and diagrammed some plays on his clipboard, the players put their hands in the center of the circle. Their message was simple: "One-two-three: war!"

Any fan arriving ten minutes into the game would think the scoreboard was broken. It read: UMass 29, Kentucky 10. How on earth?

The Minutemen had found "UMass Basketball." They were rebounding as if the ball were the last scrap of bread on earth. They were defending as if each Kentucky basket were a dentist's drill. They were playing *hard*. The signature play in this stretch came when Tyrone Weeks hurled his 260 pounds over the endline to save a ball, plowing over a pair of terrified UMass cheerleaders. Steph Boudreau and Amy Buswell, both freshmen cheering in their first game, were led off the court with minor injuries: Boudreau had a headache, and Buswell, blood dripping down her chin, had what she later termed "a humongous fat lip—it was so gross."

Emotion, though, is never enough to sustain a team. At a certain point talent takes over. Finally digging in, Kentucky surged back on the strength of its withering press. The Wildcats hounded Padilla and Travieso in the backcourt, forcing several turnovers. They started raining in three–pointers. At halftime the game was dead even, 45–45.

Surely, it seemed, UMass was done. The Minutemen had come out with pedal to the metal, but they had run out of gas. The momentum was all Kentucky's. For UMass, starting a season of so much uncertainty, there would, at least, be something to build on.

Kentucky inbounded to start the second half. The Wildcats were just getting set to attack, to blow past the Minutemen, when Marcus Camby, anticipating a perimeter pass, picked the ball off with a couple of colt–like strides. Flying downcourt with astonishing speed and grace for a six–eleven center, he soared high and slammed the ball down with two hands. It was a play of such beauty and power that it would flash again and again on ESPN all season: the definitive promo for UMass. It was also the ultimate statement play. UMass was not going to go away. "Refuse to Lose" was alive and well.

The Minutemen quickly ran up a ten–point lead. Kentucky surged back. Pitino brought in squadrons of players to try to wear down UMass. Eleven Wildcats played; all scored. By contrast, UMass did not get a single point from a sub all night long. The thin UMass bench had grown even thinner in the first half, when freshman Charlton Clarke, just twelve seconds into his first playing stint, got carried off with what proved to be a broken foot. As a result, Padilla and Travieso, the only scholarship guards available, were forced to go it alone in the backcourt.

Calipari, kinetic as ever on the sideline, exhorted them on, trying to squeeze out every last drop. "GO TO THE BALL!" he thundered on several occasions. His hair, typically the most perfect in the college game, started to frizz. His hard brown eyes locked in on the action. His mouth never seemed to stop. At one point, when he lashed into

Padilla, Calipari looked up to see Camby holding up his right hand. "Will you just chill out?" Camby said. "We're gonna win this game."

They led by just three points with 2:14 to go, but then made all the plays. They grabbed key rebounds. They hit clutch shots. They hit free throws. All five starters scored at critical moments. Somehow, UMass was a team expecting to win.

On the bench in the closing seconds, Rigo Nuñez swirled a towel overhead. Charlton Clarke banged his crutches on the floor and shouted, "Yes, sir!" Calipari took out his starters and hugged Padilla with such emotion that ESPN showed the embrace live, and then moments later, on replay. UMass won, 92–82.

It had been a startling yet definitive UMass victory. All the elements that would come to define this team were in place. There was the balance of fire and composure. There was the ethereal play of Camby, who led everyone on both teams with thirty–two points, nine rebounds and five blocked shots. There was balance, double–figure scoring from all five starters. There was indefatigable guard play from Padilla and Travieso.

UMass had done it again, knocking off Number 1 for a third straight November. Somehow they had beaten Kentucky.

Afterward, Rick Pitino sat in a chair in the Kentucky locker room, showering credit on UMass. He talked about Calipari's building job. He said that Camby might be the best player in the country. Asked about the Wildcats, Pitino took on an edge of defiance. "We are not a great team now," he said. "But we will be in March."

Having finally defeated his coaching Big Brother, Calipari stood on the podium in the postgame press conference. "I was worried about this team playing UMass Basketball," he began, "playing with passion, playing with emotion, diving on the floor, making extra passes, refusing to lose. . . .We had been playing awful, but if you play hard, you have a chance to win."

Later, out in the hallway, he was questioned about Pitino by a reporter from a Lexington TV station. Staring into the camera, Calipari said, "Leave him alone. Let him coach his team. He's the best there is in the business. He will be there in March, and I will be rooting for him—unless, of course we're playing against them."

# 10: "Do You Have the Drive?"

December 6, 1995

Amherst, Massachusetts

The date December 6 had long been circled on the calendar hanging above Marcus Camby's oversized bed on the eleventh floor of the John Quincy Adams dormitory. That night UMass would host Wake Forest, and Camby would tangle with Tim Duncan, widely regarded as the best big man in college basketball. It was a title that Camby himself coveted.

Before you become a big man, you must grow up. For Marcus DeWayne Camby, this had been a gradual process. Unlike a lot of superstars who blossom early, Camby was more goldenrod than dandelion. Physically, intellectually and emotionally, he was a late bloomer.

The Bellevue Square neighborhood of Hartford where Camby spent his first eleven years is not the worst housing development in the country, but for a glimpse of urban desperation in late twentieth–century America it serves just fine. Amid the melange of crack vials, swirls of graffiti and plywood–covered windows, young people try to find their way in the world. Camby's old home, Building 61, is now condemned.

Like plenty of other city kids, Camby started playing basketball by hanging a milk crate from his mother's clothesline. Shooting amid the bleak backdrop of Bellevue, he dreamed the typical hoop dreams: the college scholarship, the NBA, the big bucks. He was a fairly tall and very skinny kid with uncommon coordination, but he was far from a prodigy. There was no reason to believe he'd be good enough, no reason to believe he'd be big enough. Indeed, there was no reason to believe that deep down he even wanted his dreams enough—enough, that is, to really sweat for them. Being a nice guy was never a question; Camby was polite and soft–spoken, exuding a certain sleepy kindness that people liked. He had an especially nice way with younger children. Motivation, though, was another issue.

His mother Janice, raising three children by herself, sought a better life for Marcus and his two younger sisters, Mia and Monica. From early elementary school on, she enrolled them in "Project Concern," a busing program that took the kids to greener, whiter, West Hartford.

Camby had a hard time reconciling the difference between his home life and his school life. West Hartford is one of the most affluent and well regarded school districts in the state. Camby saw schoolmates dropped off in BMWs, kids who took summer vacations in Europe. The lives of people in his neighborhood, a few miles and a solar system away, were so different. It was a tougher world, yet to Camby it was also a safer world. If the bounds were tighter, so were some of the bonds. He felt at home watching UConn basketball games with friends at the modest apartment of "Stevie J" Johnson, a longtime McDonald's worker who served as father figure to many of the boys from Bellevue Square.

Most of the important people in his life were women. Hartford's recreation chief Jackie Bethea taught Marcus how to play basketball at the Kelvin D. Anderson Center and kidded him about the way he "cleaned out" Ponderosa Steak House at an all–you–can–eat meal. His mother scraped together enough money with office temp jobs to move the family to a city–owned townhouse opposite a big graveyard in the north end when Marcus was eleven. She decorated the tiny living room with a ceramic collie, a fish tank, and Marcus's basketball trophies. His grandmother Ruby was always waiting for him when he got home from school. Marcus described her simply as "my best friend."

Though he was raised in the inner city in a house of women, it was in the schools of West Hartford where he was supposed to become a man.

According to Conard High School basketball coach John Benyei, who teaches physical education at the middle school, Camby was anything but a high achiever. None of his teachers came out and said that he was lazy, but the common teaching euphemisms poured out. He "wasn't applying himself." He was a "slow starter." He had "unrealized potential." There was often a gentle quality to him—his smile was filled with shy sweetness—but the effort just wasn't there.

The same was true when it came to basketball. During his first year of high school, the six–one Camby was kept on the freshman team, not because he couldn't help the varsity, but because of lackluster efforts in class and in practice. As a sophomore, he shocked Benyei by not even showing up at tryouts. The team wasn't going to be very good, Camby explained. He'd rather take the afternoon buses back to the city and play with "my boys." As a junior he played just five games—flashing some tantalizing talent—before becoming academically ineligible. Efforts to spark Camby were frustrating. "Kids are ready for lessons at different times in their lives, and Marcus just wasn't ready," Benyei says. "He wasn't a real worker at the time. He was not a kid who loved to practice. Someone said that he needed a good hard kick with a soft shoe, repeatedly, every day. We tried to give him some discipline, but he took exception to it. It was challenging. It was hard. It just wasn't what he wanted to hear. I told him, 'This is not hard. If you want to play in college, you'll learn about hard.'"

Still, Benyei saw Camby's other side. Once when he had players over to his house, he was touched by Camby's genuine warmth toward the coach's young children and little dog. "Strange as it sounds, I really felt that he could make a great teacher," Benyei says. "He had such a nice way."

Forced to repeat his junior year in 1991–92, Camby convinced his mother that he would do better at Hartford Public High School, joining his friends from the neighborhood. He understood that by doing so he would have to sit out a year of basketball because of state rules regarding transfers. The rule was especially important to prevent exploitation with someone like Camby who, seemingly overnight, had shot up to six–eleven.

Unlike a lot of rapid–growth kids, he was in control of his body, coordinated and fluid. He ran with astonishing speed for someone so tall. He handled the ball well. He passed beautifully. His shot–blocking skills were absolutely menacing. Still, he was one of the best kept basketball secrets in the country. After all, he had played only five varsity games in four years of high school. In the high–stakes, scour–every–square–inch world of college recruiting, he was a virtual unknown. He had not, however, escaped the notice of UMass assistant coach Bill Bayno.

Acting on a tip, Bayno drove down to the playgrounds of north Hartford and got a look at the long, lean and lethal game of Marcus Camby. It was a shocking sight. Who was this kid? Though bone–thin and easily winded, he practically oozed with potential. Bayno sped back to Amherst and started gushing to John Calipari. Knowing how rare the true diamond in the rough is, Calipari was skeptical. "Get him in a camp," he told Bayno. "We'll see what he's made of."

In the summer of 1992, Camby attended the ABCD basketball camp held on the campus of the University of California at Irvine. His roommate, Edgar Padilla, didn't get a chance to form much of an impression. "In my room," Padilla recalls, "Marcus was sleeping all the time."

On the court, Camby was wide awake. His game was so multifaceted and potentially explosive that college coaches were startled. John Calipari watched the action, salivating and grimacing at the same time. According to Calipari's friend Steve Rosenberry, a regional scout for the Golden State Warriors and Seattle Supersonics, the UMass coach sweated it out, "hoping the kid would screw up so other coaches wouldn't notice him. He said to me, 'Rose, this kid can do everything,' I said, 'John, he weighs forty pounds.'"

When Camby returned to Hartford, his phone was suddenly snapping with call–waiting clicks. Everyone was interested. Among the most aggressive recruiters were UConn head coach Jim Calhoun and assistant Howie Dickenman. UConn basketball, after all, was the center of the sports universe in Connecticut. Everyone in Camby's neighborhood followed the Huskies. The Hartford Civic Center, where UConn played several home games, was just a few blocks from his townhouse. Most of his friends, teachers and family members expected that he would stay close to home.

He did—in surprising fashion. In October of his senior year, Camby signed his letter of intent to attend UConn's shadow rival, UMass, an hour to the north. Mike Williams, a Hartford playground legend, had given good reports about the Minutemen. Camby felt there would be playing time right away. Most important, UMass had shown interest early. Bayno seemed real to him, comfortable in the inner city, matching the sales job with something that felt like genuine concern. And while Camby knew that Calipari had the reputation of being intensely demanding, he felt ready for hard.

•

To John Calipari, every freshman presents a unique challenge. He comes in with a special set of skills and personality traits that have to be blended into the team concept. Ultimately, though, the challenge is really the same with each player: finding a way to bring out his best. Calipari liked to talk about taking players from their parents as boys and returning them in a few years as men. With Marcus Camby, Calipari knew that he had a long way to go. Camby's baby–faced innocence seemed to border on fragility.

In the fall of 1993, Camby walked around campus in his blue letter jacket from Hartford Public. When the weather turned cold, he added a goofy-looking hat with a pom–pom and ear flaps. In interviews his answers were short and nervous, invariably including the phrase "take it in stride."

During preseason conditioning that fall, Camby hardly distinguished himself. He was the weakest player on the team in the weight room, a point Calipari seldom failed to note. In the afternoon running sessions at the Curry Hicks Cage, Camby would be lagging in the back of the pack, when he'd hear Calipari's thundering voice with just the right amount of taunt: "That's okay, Marcus, if you want to be an ordinary player. But if you want to be special. . . ."

While he was multitalented and eager to learn (Calipari dubbed him "the finest listener I've ever coached"), Camby seemed to avoid the rougher parts of the game. He was easily pushed out of rebounding position. He drifted to the perimeter where there was less banging. His endurance was so suspect that his playing stints sometimes resembled hockey shifts. Camby would raise his fist to ask for a substitute several times each game—a practice Calipari advocated, but only to a point. The coach wanted his players to push through barriers, to work to exhaustion. To be great, he felt, they had to leave the comfort level. One of the coach's pet phrases was "work capacity," a quality he discussed as if it were a muscle that could be developed. Calipari often praised the work capacity of people like Lou Roe and Donta Bright. He never used the term in regard to Camby.

When Camby was a sophomore in 1994–95, a couple of outside events helped spur his development.

In October, he was one of four UMass players cited for being on academic probation in The *Boston Globe* story. He was no dumb jock, never had been. He just hadn't fought hard enough for academic success.

Camby never fully forgave the *Globe*, referring to it a year later as "the paper that hurt my family." He would later admit, though, that the story had some benefits. He sat down with his mother, Janice, and his surrogate mom, Hartford recreation chief Jackie Bethea, for a long heart–to–heart. "It was embarrassing," Camby told *The Hartford Courant* in 1996, "because I know what education means to my mom. I have the head to do the work. And what kind of example was I setting for the kids back home?"

Hooking up with UMass's new academic coordinator Dave Glover, a former Academic All–America basketball player at Baylor who would become a close friend, Camby dug in as never before. He earned a 3.2 GPA in the fall and ultimately shared the team's Skip Connors academic award with his best friend Tyrone Weeks, who had also been embarrassed in the *Globe* story.

The other turning point for Camby came in January when he was told after a game against West Virginia that his grandmother Ruby had died of pneumonia. The team flew west to Saint Louis; Camby stayed home to be with his family. His baby face now covered with a thin line of beard, Camby realized that he needed to be, in his words, "the man of the house."

On the court, UMass was still Lou Roe's team. The senior forward was the team's top scorer, top rebounder and unquestioned leader. Camby, however, was the indispensable element. When he pulled his hamstring at home against St. Joseph's, top–ranked UMass was wrapping up its school record sixteenth straight win. While Camby sat out, the Minutemen lost two of three games, and trailed a fourth at halftime at Rutgers when it was suspended by a student protest.

Back in action, Camby's flashes of brilliance grew more frequent and more sustained. At times he carried the team. His very presence on the court changed the game. His shot blocking allowed teammates to pressure the ball on the perimeter and provided a fearsome psychological weapon underneath, forcing opponents to shoot with awkward angles and unusual arcs that spelled low percentages. Offensively he started showing greater range on his jumper, along with increased aggressiveness in the low post. His numbers—13.9 points, 6.2 rebounds and 3.4 blocks per game—only hinted at his ability to control the action. Increasingly, NBA scouts took notice.

In March of 1995, Camby led UMass through the first three rounds of the NCAA tournament, averaging over eighteen points a game. The Minutemen advanced to the Elite Eight for the first time in school history and stood just one game shy of their season–long goal: the Final Four. That's when they ran into Oklahoma State and Bryant (Big Country) Reeves.

In truth, no UMass frontcourt player had a good day. Roe, playing through a severe hamstring pull, scored just nine points, on three of eleven shooting. Dana Dingle also scored nine, on three of ten. Donta Bright didn't hit a field goal all game and scored just three points. But Camby's struggles were the most painfully visible. He was overwhelmed and worn down almost immediately by the massive Reeves. By game's end, he had hit just two of ten from the field for six points, grabbed only four rebounds and played only twenty–three minutes before fouling out. Reeves, playing the full forty, had twenty–four points and ten rebounds. At the center spot, there had been complete domination.

There was an open–scab rawness to the atmosphere in the small locker room at the Meadowlands. This wasn't just any loss, not even any season–ending loss. It was a loss that felt like failure, a squandered opportunity that might never come again. The Final Four had been so close that UMass players, coaches and fans could taste it. Now the taste was pure acid. Hanging his head, Marcus Camby felt responsible. "I think it hurt me the most," he reflected a few months later. "If I had played just an average game, we probably would have won."

When he returned home, Camby found twenty messages on his answering machine from agents. "It's a funny game they play," Camby reflected four months later.

Was he ready for the NBA? On the one hand, Camby knew there were some lingering questions about his toughness, questions that had only been accentuated by his performance against Oklahoma State. At six–eleven and two hundred fifteen pounds, he seemed frail by pro standards. He had never played a full college season, having missed time with a knee injury as a freshman and the hamstring pull as a sophomore. He had played thirty minutes or more only four times in his two–year college career. The grind of an NBA season—eighty–two games and all that travel—seemed daunting.

Still, turning pro was tempting. After a conversation with NBA scouting director Marty Blake, Camby felt confident he would be picked within the top seven selections in the league's draft. He could become a millionaire overnight, no small thing for a young man who had grown up with so little. He could provide immediate comfort for his mother and younger sisters. Granted, the money would come at some point—Camby, like most players deemed future NBA stars, carried a seven–figure insurance policy against career–ending injury—but by signing now he could realize those boyhood dreams launched while tossing a ball into a milk crate. Why delay? Most of the top college sophomores in the country were opting for the draft: Joe Smith of Maryland, Jerry Stackhouse and Rasheed Wallace of North Carolina, Antonio McDyess of Alabama. It would be easy to follow that path. Besides, UMass was surely headed for a downturn.

In typical low–key fashion, Camby never called a press conference to announce his decision. He merely let the deadline for draft declaration quietly pass. Asked about his rationale after the fact, Camby said simply, "I didn't feel that I was physically or mentally ready to go."

Heading home in late May, Camby carried an autographed photo of Spurs star David Robinson that John Calipari brought back from a visit to San Antonio. The photo, which Camby promptly hung up on his bedroom wall, said, "To Marcus, I've seen you play. You have most of what it takes. Do you have the drive?"

•

Camby often went back to Bellevue Square to talk with Stevie J and some of the neighborhood kids that summer. He even spent a week helping to chaperone a bus trip for children down to Busch Gardens in Virginia. Working at a couple of basketball camps, he often teamed up with his UConn buddy Ray Allen.

Much of his time, though, was spent out of public view. In long hours at the Kelvin D. Anderson Center, Camby prepared for his junior year. Buoyed by an internal drive greater than he had ever felt before, he began to push the envelope. After one particularly spirited workout, Camby and some of his buddies visited a neighborhood tattoo parlor. When Camby emerged, a green and magenta design on his left biceps showed a ball sailing into a hoop. The picture sat atop a two–word message: "Mr. Camby." It was a significant choice of words. When he returned to UMass, he knew, he would be expected to be The Man.

His was a strange campus life. In the fall he was approached by numerous professors who thanked him for coming back to school. Not a day went by without students approaching him for an autograph. Draped over a couple of rows of bleachers at the Curry Hicks Cage before a conditioning workout in October, he said that his goal for the year was simple: "I just want to be a normal guy, a normal college student. I don't want anyone to think I'm any different."

An education major, Camby spent one afternoon each week tutoring middle–school students in South Hadley. It was, he said, his favorite time of the week. The students there did more than worship him. They worked for him. They called him "Mr. Camby."

"I like working with kids more than I like playing basketball," Camby declared during one interview. He said his goal was to become a school principal one day. He liked teaching, but it was the principal who set the tone for the entire school.

In preseason conditioning workouts, Calipari saw Camby setting an impressive tone. He was out there at the front of the pack, leading the way in drills. It was apparent that there was no more need to taunt him about whether or not he wanted to be special. His time had arrived.

Against Kentucky, Camby was breathtaking, leading the way to a startling upset. "That was just a great game by a great player," said Wildcat coach Rick Pitino, shaking his head in the locker room.

Camby went on to win the MVP of the Franklin National Bank Classic in Landover, Maryland. In the opening game against Maryland on December 2, UMass fell behind by sixteen points in the first half, only scored fifty for the game, yet still managed to win, 50–47. After sitting out a good chunk of the first half with three fouls, Camby seemed destined for the bench midway through the second when he landed on a Maryland player's foot and started limping. He held his fist up for a substitute. Assessing the injury from the sideline, Calipari left his star in the game, sending a message. In the end, Camby hit the basket that put UMass ahead, blocked the shot to prevent Maryland from tying things up and grabbed the decisive rebound to seal the win. Asked what the difference was in the game, a weary Maryland coach Gary Williams offered a one–word answer: "Camby." In the championship game the next day, Camby scored thirty points in just twenty–five minutes while UMass rolled over Florida, 80–58. Gator star Dametri Hill confessed afterward, "He's so good I caught myself watching him a little bit."

Three days later, much of the college basketball world was watching. The Wake Forest game was without question the most vigorously covered sporting event ever on the UMass campus. ESPN flashed promos for days. Dick Vitale was set to call his first game from Amherst. Requests came in for 182 media credentials. Reporters from *Sports Illustrated* and *The New York Times* arrived. So did fifteen NBA scouts and general managers.

The excitement had little to do with the matchup of Number 3 UMass and Number 10 Wake Forest, though it did represent the first–ever clash of Top 10 teams in Amherst. The spotlight was shining instead on Tim Duncan and Marcus Camby.

They shared the Number 21, a soft–spoken reserve and a sudden surge to fame. Duncan had been even more obscure in high school. Growing up in St. Croix, hardly a hotbed of hoops, Duncan attracted little college attention despite his muscular six–ten frame and surprisingly sophisticated footwork around the basket. Two of his four college choices were Hartford and Delaware State. In his first two seasons in the ACC, though, he had become the most highly regarded center in college basketball. As a sophomore he had averaged 16.8 points and 12.5 rebounds per game. The consensus among NBA insiders was that if Duncan entered the draft after his sophomore year, he would be selected Number 1. But just nineteen years old, he, like Camby, chose to come back.

Their games were different. Duncan was a classic back–to–the-basket center. Camby, less defined, more versatile, preferred to play out on the wing, to face the basket, to slash. Duncan was the far stronger rebounder. Camby was quicker. Both were supreme shot–blockers.

They downplayed the individual matchup. "The game is five–on–five, not one–on–one" Duncan said.

"I don't want to get in a little personal battle between me and Tim, and get out of the team chemistry," said Camby.

The confrontation, though, was impossible to ignore. Bob Ryan, columnist for *The Boston Globe*, wrote a long story on game day comparing the showdown with some of the top big–man battles in college basketball history, matchups like Lew Alcindor vs. Elvin Hayes in 1968 and Patrick Ewing vs. Ralph Sampson in 1982.

Just before the 9:30 tipoff, UMass players gathered at the foul line, and reached to the center of the circle where Camby held a ball aloft. When they broke, he spiked the ball hard to the ground with two hands. After introductions, the Minutemen did their bump–and–jump routine. Then, for the first time since the infamous Converse game nineteen days earlier, they took the floor at the Mullins Center. The place was buzzing.

Tim Duncan won the opening tap, but little else. Hounded by Camby, he scored just nine points, on four of eighteen shooting, after entering the contest with a gaudy 76.7 percent accuracy. Similarly challenged by Duncan, Camby forced shots early and hit just six of nineteen overall for seventeen points. But the UMass center clearly won the duel. In the end, Duncan seemed worn down. He even allowed Camby a ten–footer without lifting his arms to defend. The game came to an unofficial close with just under a minute to go when Duncan grabbed his own rebound, only to have his putback attempt swatted away by Camby.

Truly, UMass's 60–46 victory was a team effort. Carmelo Travieso played thirty–seven ferocious minutes; Edgar Padilla played forty. Donta Bright slashed through the Wake defense for twenty–two points. Dana Dingle held Wake Forest sharpshooter Ricky Peral scoreless, and made the night's signature play by ripping the ball out of Duncan's hands while lying flat on his back, then flipping a pass to Bright for an easy basket.

"I would say that UMass is headed for a wonderful basketball year," said Wake Forest coach Dave Odom. "They're well–coached. They're well–drilled. They believe in each other. The only thing they've got to watch is peaking too early."

UMass was 4–0, having knocked off three ranked teams. It was a start that no one anticipated. "We're just hustling," Calipari said. "We're playing with emotion. Guys are diving. It's just a habit of how we play. We only know how to play one way. We don't know how to be cool. We only know how to play hard."

As the clock ticked past midnight, a final flurry of questions focused on the upcoming game against Boston College at the brand new FleetCenter. Smiling to a Boston reporter, Marcus Camby said, "I'm from Hartford. I'd rather play UConn."

That would certainly be a date to circle on the calendar.

# 11: "Anything You Do in Life is About Selling"

December 9–22, 1995

Few state universities in America suffer the identity problems at home that UMass has faced almost since its inception. Elsewhere, the State U generally is a showcase, a source of power and pride. Many top students from prominent families go to the State U and extend the fine legacy of the universities of Virginia or Michigan.

In much of the country, the sports teams of the State U are a rallying point for the populace. Visit Indiana or Arkansas or Nebraska, and you'll find support bordering on religious fervor. A big win by Rick Pitino's basketball team swells the pride of people in Kentucky like little else. *Those are our boys. That's what we're about.*

It had never been that way at UMass. Geographically the forty-fourth largest state, Massachusetts was unquestionably at the top when it came to a collection of prestigious and pricey private colleges. Prominent families often sent their sons and daughters to school in–state, but that usually meant Harvard or MIT, Amherst or Smith, Williams or Mount Holyoke, Tufts or Boston College. People at UMass often felt like second–class citizens. State senator Stanley Rosenberg of Amherst once described the university as having a "psychological profile which is something like an inferiority complex."

In significant measure, people at UMass had been made to feel that way. A thinly veiled academic snobbery has long pervaded the state. The university labored under inadequate funding for years; per–pupil spending for higher education in Massachusetts consistently ranked at or near the bottom of the fifty states. "Cow College" and "ZooMass" had been popular terms to describe the school. In the winter of 1995–96, *Globe* columnist Dan Shaughnessy irked the prickly masses with repeated references to "UMass–Hooterville." The power base of the state—the legislature and the major media—sat in Boston, two hours and one enormous psychological chasm from the main

UMass campus in Amherst. In short, the state university had never served as the flagship institution for the state.

As far as athletics were concerned, that role had always been played by Boston College. Bob Cousy and Chuck Daly coached at the campus on Chestnut Hill. The beloved basketball teams with Bob Carrington in the seventies still rate occasional paeans in the Boston press. Boston College meant Doug Flutie and "The Pass" in Miami in 1984—the Hail Mary to Gerard Phelan that made the beer flow in Beantown. BC had the only Division I football program in New England. It had Big East basketball. The stuff that mattered.

Sports at UMass? For years, the teams weren't deemed worthy of much more than cursory coverage in Boston, an occasional passing reference to Julius *Irving*. "[Boston media] thought the state stopped in Worcester," recalled Jack Leaman. "They'd drive to Holy Cross, and that would be the end of it. They thought if they came out any further, they'd fall off the end of the world, like people said about Columbus."

More recently, despite the huge success of the Minutemen, John Calipari's team had never played a game at the old Boston Garden, the marquee arena for sports in the state. Some people felt there was a concerted effort to keep UMass out of the Boston power base. "BC conspiracy theories" were overblown, but it does bear noting that in the summer of 1995 when new WHMP sports director Marc Vandermeer started efforts to expand the Minutemen's radio network, more than one Boston radio station decided not to come on board because of a fear of losing the contract for Boston College football. Without question, UMass's success posed a threat to certain interests.

Ultimately, there was no way to keep UMass out. Calipari's teams were too good, too compelling. There was no better sports story in Massachusetts in the nineties. Boston pro teams had fallen on hard times. The Red Sox never got to the World Series. The Patriots were mired in mediocrity. The Bruins were always watching rivals hoist the Stanley Cup. And the once–proud Celtics, perhaps the most successful franchise in the history of professional sports, had tumbled through one singularly uninspiring season after another.

Calipari charged into the void. His teams were now extremely well covered by the Boston papers (though the grades story in the *Globe* remained a sore spot). His weekly television and radio shows aired in Beantown. In recent years he had started to get top–shelf in–state recruits, one of whom, Monty Mack of South Boston High School, told

Calipari in the fall of 1995 that he had grown up dreaming of playing for UMass: words that would have been comical for any decent player just a few years before. Moreover, Calipari had awakened a feeling of pride in UMass graduates that had long been dormant. It was a feeling familiar to graduates of BC and first–rate state universities across the land. *Those are our boys. This is what we're about.*

On December 9, UMass and Boston College, long–ago rivals who had played only once since 1979, met in the Commonwealth Classic. The first men's college basketball game at the FleetCenter—the new Boston Garden—drew political bigwigs from Governor William Weld on down. Tickets, split equally between the two schools, had long been sold out despite their hefty price tags of $35 and $50, more than twice the top–dollar price for seats at either school's home arena. Even with near–blizzard conditions that made transportation hazardous, the house was packed, 18,974 strong. CBS carried the game on national television.

For a young BC team coming off a 9–19 season, the game represented a chance to play a highly ranked opponent, but, according to coach Jim O'Brien, little else. "In my mind the game has no significance," he said in an interview in late November. "I think it's fitting that Boston College is involved in the first college basketball game in the FleetCenter. But the opposition is of no matter to me."

For UMass, too, the game held little meaning—in one sense. The goal of being the best team in the state, or even New England, had long since become incidental. Those aspirations came from another era. College basketball was no longer a regional game played predominantly by local kids in weathered gyms. For better and for worse, UMass had outgrown the days of Jack Leaman and the Cage. Now the goals were national. Games like UMass vs. BC—"neighborhood games" (to borrow a term from John Chaney)—were of little consequence.

Yet John Calipari knew that to people associated with UMass, few games mattered more. Maybe he was an import from Pennsylvania—maybe he didn't have the same sort of visceral response to in–state rivalries that someone like Leaman (or, for that matter, Massachusetts natives Jim Calhoun and Mike Jarvis) might have—but during his eight years in the state he had absorbed enough of its quirks and had spoken to enough UMass graduates to understand. Out in the Mullins Center hallway after the Wake Forest win on December 6, he told a Boston television reporter with typically penetrating crassness: "Our alumni feel that they've been crapped on for fifty years."

Yes, this game mattered. This was about validation, about belonging, about respect. In a real sense, this game was about the arrival of UMass in the state of Massachusetts. All the gung–ho graduates of UMass wanted for this great coming–out party was the expected: a big win over Boston College.

In the first half, Calipari's match was lit. He quickly picked up a technical foul for arguing a call by referee Tim Higgins. At one timeout, he charged halfway across the court to high–five Dana Dingle after some inspired hustle. At another point, he held his hands over his ears as if to suppress some sort of explosion. By the 3:52 mark of the half, UMass was already down by thirteen points. Sure, Calipari didn't expect to go undefeated. A loss would be just one game in a long season. This loss, though, had implications that cut to the core of a school's reputation.

UMass closed the half with an 8–0 run, then rattled off the first nine points of the second half. Minuteman fans rocked the house.

BC responded. Star junior forward Danya Abrams, a locomotive with Charmin–soft hands, bulled his way inside. Freshman guard Scoonie Penn blazed through the UMass defense. The game seesawed back and forth. The boisterous fans were more energized than any crowd FleetCenter officials would see all year. When the five–ten Penn hit an artistic floater over the long arms of Marcus Camby, the game was tied at fifty–seven with 1:56 left.

UMass worked the ball around the perimeter. The fuel light on, the Minutemen tried to push through fatigue as the Eagles dug in on defense. Camby was bottled up in the post, Donta Bright denied the ball on the baseline. As the shot clock ticked under five, all eyes and hot TV lights bore down on Edgar Padilla, who alone among all players on both teams had not sat for one second of the grueling contest. His face locked in steely focus, Padilla sprang up in the air and backspinned a soft–arching three–pointer into the hoop.

After a BC timeout, the Eagles worked the ball in to the post on the right side, where Abrams backed in on Camby. The UMass center had Abrams by four inches, the BC big man had Camby by forty–five pounds. It was the game's pivotal moment: a matchup of the two best college players in the state. Abrams spun left into the lane and tried to get Camby in the air with an up–fake. The UMass center held his ground. Abrams then leaned in with his left hand, but Camby jumped diagonally and swatted the ball away, knocking it off a BC player out of bounds.

Demonstrating the same composure down the stretch that had closed out wins against Kentucky and Maryland, UMass was flawless at the finish, making all the plays and winning, 65–57.

It had been a staggeringly entertaining afternoon. "This may have been the single best atmosphere for a game that I've been involved with," said BC coach Jim O'Brien, his squad launched on a season that would feature national rankings and an appearance in the NCAA tournament.

Impassioned as ever, Calipari stood before the sea of cameras and microphones. "I heard since the day I got here, 'New Englanders could care less about college basketball,'" he said. "That's all I heard. I told people, 'You're crazy. You've just got to give them something exciting. They love winners.' Now honestly, you've got to do more with less in New England. That's how it is. And you know what? I think our team epitomizes what New England's all about. Work hard. Extra effort. Dive on the floor. Do a little bit more with a little bit less. That's what we try to do."

A team known as the Minutemen had arrived in Boston.

•

The non–league schedule John Calipari had put together for the 1995–96 season was as rigorous as that faced by any team in the country. Twelve of the thirteen teams had known recent national prominence. Eight of them would be ranked in the AP Top 25 during the year. Three were ranked in the Top 10 when they played UMass. "I want to learn about my team," Calipari said. "You don't learn anything by playing Popcorn State."

On the night of December 12, though, the staccato blasts of heating kernels were heard all over the Mullins Center when the University of North Carolina at Wilmington started warming up. The UNCW Seahawks? What were *they* doing here?

Back in 1977–78, half his lifetime ago, John Calipari had galvanized his Moon Area High School teammates to the school's first winning season since 1961. The point guard, the class president, the prom king—"The King of Everything," according to teammate Bill Mazar—Calipari had a knack for getting what he wanted. And while he was too slow and too short (at just under six feet) to attract interest from any prominent basketball programs, his leadership and competitive zeal did not escape notice. Several Division II programs expressed interest. Calipari, though, was determined to play at the highest level. Only two Division I schools dangled scholarships: the University of Vermont and the University of North Carolina at Wilmington. UVM, a former whipping boy of the Yankee Conference, had a pretty good point guard in Dana Carrell. UNCW, finishing up just its second year at Division I, had no returners at the point. Calipari felt that smooth–talking Seahawk coach Mel Gibson gave him some assurances about playing time. The decision wasn't difficult. "Vermont was a better school, no question," Calipari said years later. "I knew that. But it was about playing. I was a gym rat."

"We feel pleased to get John, who will be a big help to our program," Gibson told the *Beaver County Times.* "He is a pure point guard, a tremendous passer and an outstanding ballhandler. He has leadership ability on the floor that is hard to find in a high school player."

In the pivotal year of 1978–79—a year when ESPN and The Big East were launched, a year when Magic Johnson and Larry Bird turned America on to the NCAA tournament—John Calipari got his first taste of Division I college basketball. The taste would prove sour.

He liked Wilmington, a beautiful seacoast city with plenty of Georgian architecture, heaps of southern hospitality and some pretty good basketball. (A local kid named Michael Jordan was just beginning to make a name for himself as a high school player). Calipari was a fireball from the moment he arrived. He quickly ingratiated himself with area children by setting up a youth ballhandling group called the Little Seahawks, a group that survives to this day performing at halftime of UNCW games. Filling out his first sports information questionnaire, he responded to an inquiry about future plans with the fateful words: "Sales, management, coaching possibly." He took courses in business. Mostly he played ball.

"Nobody worked harder," recalls teammate and roommate Dennis Tobin. "He was in the gym seven days a week, in season and out."

Long after the lights went out, Calipari kept Tobin up talking basketball, night after night after night.

Come gametime, though, Calipari was glued to the bench. Unbeknownst to Calipari during the recruiting process, Gibson was also making a pitch for Barry Taylor, a junior college transfer from Florida. Taylor played. Calipari sat. And stewed.

Gibson, now an athletic administrator at UNCW, says that Taylor was the best point guard he ever had in twenty years of coaching at the college level. Calipari? "He was not a high–impact player on a Division I level. He was right on that marginal area there. But his intensity and desire and drive were such that he wasn't content being a backup player on a very good team."

In part, their conflict was no more complicated than a battle over playing time, the annual chopping–down–to–size of high school stars making the adjustment to college ball. This was particularly hard on Calipari, whose combination of charisma and desire had felled every obstacle that had ever come his way.

There was another element to it, however—a painful disillusionment. Calipari felt betrayed by a coach, and coaches to him had always been gods. Increasingly, he felt shut off by Gibson, turned away, as if somehow he didn't matter. According to Tobin, Calipari frequently went in to talk to the coaching staff and returned feeling stung. "It's not that I wasn't up for the challenge," Calipari said later. "But the element of challenge was kind of taken away. It was just, 'You're not going to play.'"

While Calipari now describes Gibson as someone with "a good feel for the game," the old wound comes to the surface when he is asked about what he learned from his former coach: "There are certain times you say, 'I'll never do that as a coach. I'll never be this way.' It's as valuable to learn through those experiences as it is the good experiences. As much as I learned what to do, I learned just as much what won't work, and why it won't work, and how it affects people."

In his sophomore year, the rift with Gibson deepened. Calipari poured his heart out to Tobin, and began having long conversations with his parents Vince and Donna over the telephone. Eleven games into the season he made a decision. The pride of Moon Township, the kid with the "Refuse to Lose" will, was quitting something for the first time in his life. The King of Everything was tumbling off his throne, taking a step down to play Division II ball at Clarion State. He had lost his basketball innocence.

(Granted, Calipari was not the only strong–willed point guard ever to part company with his team in the middle of his sophomore year. Eight years earlier, Rick Pitino had been kicked off the University of Massachusetts squad by Jack Leaman.)

Though stung at UNCW, Calipari lost none of his faith in himself and his future in "sales, management, coaching possibly." He plunged right into life at Clarion State. Coach Joe DeGregorio says that Calipari's blend of tenacity, charm and resourcefulness stood out from the pack.

There was the hard–nosed Calipari, wearing wrestling headgear so that he could play with a fractured cheekbone. There was the gracious Calipari, sending a thank you note to DeGregorio's wife after she hosted a team meal. There was the hustling Calipari, scraping together the money to buy a couple of trailers on campus and renting them out to students: the point guard turned landlord. His major, not surprisingly, was marketing. "I think anything you do in life is about selling," he later said. "Selling yourself to other people—that's what I did."

In summers, he worked the basketball camp circuit, cultivating connections and learning the game. His father Vince tried to persuade him to take a construction job one year, a position that paid far better than camps. "That ain't all, Dad," Vince recalls John saying. "This is what I want to do."

In his senior year, 1981–82, Calipari quarterbacked the Golden Eagles to wins over schools like Mercyhurst, Point Park, Lock Haven, Alliance and Slippery Rock. All the while, he looked ahead to a life of bigtime college basketball. One of his top contacts through the Five–Star Camp was Bob Hill, then an assistant coach at the University of Kansas. When Calipari graduated in four years, he forsook his final year of eligibility[1] and accepted an offer to join the Jayhawks staff at the very bottom of the totem pole as an unpaid graduate assistant.

Kansas was a revelation to him. He was awed by the place's mystique. This *was* college basketball, home of James Naismith, Wilt Chamberlain and national championships. While showering in fabled Allen Fieldhouse after a long day, he caught himself thinking, "Wow, Phog Allen showered here."

Anything but glamorous, his job was full of gopher errands and scut work. He supported himself by working at the cafeteria for varsity athletes. Looking no older than a college freshman, he stood there with a ladle and asked, "Peas or carrots?" At home, he and his roommate debated whether to get furniture or ESPN; they wound up watching college basketball games from the floor. He got his bed by raiding Allen Fieldhouse after the filming of a triage scene for the TV movie on nuclear holocaust called "The Day After." It was classic Calipari, darting in after Armageddon to nab a cot.

He worked for three years at Kansas, one under Ted Owens and two under Larry Brown.[2] Having left the head coaching job of the woeful New Jersey Nets, Brown brought his analytical but intense approach to Lawrence. For twenty–four–year–old John Calipari, Brown was a mentor: "a teacher who challenges guys, a class act." Calipari absorbed as much as he could. According to athletic business office secretary Ellen Higgins, Calipari tried to adopt both Brown's limp and his stylish dressing. The onetime ball boy who sat on the bench at Moon Township in a clip–on tie developed a taste for fine clothing in Lawrence, Kansas.

He and Ellen started to date during this time—going first to a Kansas City Royals game that was rained out. A former high school cheerleader in tiny Osceola, Missouri, she had a no–nonsense toughness about her that Calipari found appealing. She used to type up basketball drill books for him, then sit through the JV games that he coached, surprised at his wild animation on the sidelines. In the summer of 1986 they married.

By that time Calipari had left Kansas for the University of Pittsburgh. While it was tough to leave Brown, the Pittsburgh position was the next step up the ladder: a full–time assistant's job, including recruiting duties, in a league then regarded as the best in the land, The Big East. He was back home again. The ultimate sales job, college basketball recruiting was the most natural thing in the world for Calipari. At home in both tenements and cushy living rooms, the coaching chameleon had charm that was hard to resist. He had the politician's gift of being able to summon a sincere passion for the same words over and over again.

A number of quality players—people like Brian Shorter, Rod Brookin and Sean Miller—came to Pittsburgh thanks in large measure to Calipari's recruiting efforts. His star was rising. In 1988 he made his move, accepting his first head coaching job at the University of Massachusetts.

Now in his eighth season, having lifted the Minutemen to unprecedented heights, he had come full circle: taking the floor against UNCW. Calipari said he scheduled the game because of "my contacts down there"—people he knew from his own ill–fated playing career and fifty–year–old head coach Jerry Wainwright, a former mentor at the Five–Star Camp. For UMass, the game was one of twenty–five during the season that would air on national television. For UNCW it was the first in school history.

After UMass's easy 77–51 victory, Calipari said he only got nostalgic once: "I looked down at the bench and saw guys who were sitting where I was."

Wainwright, thanking Calipari for the favor of national exposure, reflected on the changes that had been wrought in the years since the UMass coach was a Five–Star hotshot. "I remember my first year with him at camp," Wainwright said. "He has the same smile. He has not changed, other than the fact that he has his own drive–up window at one of the banks here."

•

The ten–day break for finals that followed the UNCW game was supposed to be a quiet time, but quiet was never the way for the University of Massachusetts basketball team. On the night of December 13, Calipari got a live call on his radio show asking, "Are you going to choke again in the Big Dance this year?"—the third such call he had received during the year. He strongly suspected people he liked to call "our friends from Connecticut."

The next day, news broke that an attorney representing six players had notified the university that it might be subject to a suit for illegally releasing grades to *The Boston Globe* a year ago.[3]

Then on December 15, *Sports Illustrated* published a mostly flattering profile of Marcus Camby that focused on his showdown with Tim Duncan of Wake Forest. At the end of the story, though, the usually reserved and deferential Camby was quoted as telling friends of his in the parking lot, "Duncan's soft. He's afraid of me." Camby denied making the comments. Still, the whiff of bad public relations was out. On December 18, sitting in his office in the Mullins Center, Calipari dictated to media relations assistant Charlie Bare a letter from Camby to Duncan. Bare was told to fax it back to the basketball office, where Camby could take a look and sign it; then it would be mailed to the Wake Forest student newspaper. During his radio show the next night, Calipari mentioned that Camby had written a letter of apology, and stated, "But that's the kind of kid Marcus is."

After finals the now second–ranked Minutemen bused to New York to prepare for Georgia Tech at the Meadowlands. At a news conference the day before the game, Calipari revealed that junior Tyrone Weeks had recently confided a wild goal at a team meeting: "Let's go undefeated." Upon hearing the words, Calipari said that he laughed out loud.

Returning to the Meadowlands was, for the Minutemen, returning to the scene of the crime. Here, UMass had crashed and burned in the second half against Oklahoma State in March, falling twenty minutes shy of the Final Four in Seattle. More than a journey of redemption, though, the Minutemen hoped that this trip represented foreshadowing—the Meadowlands would also host the 1996 Final Four.

The inaugural Jimmy V Classic was a doubleheader serving as a fundraiser for the V Foundation, a cancer research group founded by the late Jim Valvano. An impassioned coach, Valvano had been a colorful and controversial character. His sprint around the court looking for someone to hug after North Carolina State's stunning win in the 1983 national championship game stands as one of the most enduring images of the sport. Seven years later he resigned amid scandal that landed his school on NCAA probation. Rising again as a naturally gifted broadcaster for ESPN and ABC, Valvano continued to work even as cancer took its toll on him. One of the last games he ever called was a UMass–Florida State contest in December of 1992, after which he and Calipari had dinner. Not long before he died at the age of forty-seven in April, Valvano delivered a wrenchingly powerful address that launched the V Foundation, concluding with the words, "Don't give up. Don't ever give up."

The foundation had struck it big with these games. The opener featured Number 1 Kansas taking on Temple. The nightcap had Number 2 UMass playing Number 21 Georgia Tech.

John Chaney's crew, just 2–4 coming into the game, shocked the undefeated Jayhawks in overtime, 74–66. The door to the top was open, and UMass charged through with stifling defense. Georgia Tech's acclaimed backcourt of Stephon Marbury and Drew Barry was held to combined eight of twenty–nine shooting by Carmelo Travieso and Edgar Padilla. Bottled up by Dana Dingle, Georgia Tech's top scorer Matt Harpring hit just two of eleven. Marcus Camby policed the middle with six blocked shots. Throw in the typical UMass offensive balance—all five starters in double figures—and the result was a more–convincing–than–it–sounds 75–67 victory.

A month before, the Minutemen, still reeling from the exhibition loss to the Converse All–Stars, were getting ready to start the season amid "a crisis within the UMass basketball program." Now they were 7–0 for the first time ever under Calipari, having polished off four nationally ranked teams. Still, the year was young.

"Our goal is to get back here in April," Camby said that night. "If we don't, it's a failure for us."

When the next AP poll came out on Monday, the University of Massachusetts was at the top. It was Christmas morning.

# 12: "A Dream with a Deadline"

December 28–30, 1995

Honolulu, Hawaii

n the late winter of 1994, having lived with Carmelo Travieso for months, freshman Edgar Padilla turned to his roommate and asked when his birthday was.

"May 9th," Travieso said. "Why?"

"No, you're messing around," said Padilla. "That's my birthday. Seriously, when is it?"

"May 9th."

"Yeah, right. Let me see your license."

Travieso reached into his back pocket and flipped open his wallet. Sure enough.

And so the story began to circulate. Padilla and Travieso were all but blood brothers. They had both been born on the same day in Puerto Rico. Maybe even in the same hospital. As the 1995–96 season heated up, and the two junior guards not only started together for the first time but performed superbly in helping the Minutemen gain the nation's Number 1 ranking, their story became a popular one: a "small world" story for the ages.

Problem was, it wasn't true.

Yes, Edgar Padilla was born on May 9, 1975, in Santurce, Puerto Rico. His older sister Millie recalls the day with excitement. "A new baby brother, it was like having a new toy," she says. When proud parents Mariano and Milca led the family out of the hospital a few days later, four–year–old Millie, two–year–old Giddel and baby Edgar were wearing identical red and white outfits. This family would stick together.

May 9 was also a significant day for Carmelo Travieso Sr., and his wife Carmen Peña. It wasn't that their infant son Carmelo was born that day—just that it was then apparent that he would live. Actually born a month before in Rio Piedras, Travieso was a sickly baby. In the atmosphere of crisis and confusion, no paperwork was filed on his birthdate. There were more important things to worry about. A variety of circulatory problems made it look as if the baby would not pull through. Just a few weeks old, he had to endure a blood transfusion. Carmelo Sr. and Carmen said their prayers . . . and they were answered. One month after he came into the world, Carmelo was officially listed as being born. Thereafter, he would celebrate his birthday on May 9th.

Many years later at UMass, Travieso confessed the technicality to Padilla. Both decided not to worry the public with the details. It was too good a story. Besides, they seemed to share everything else.

In both families, the maternal grandmother played a critical role. Pina Bonilla, Edgar's grandmother, was a near–constant presence in the family's house in Toa Alta. The liaison with the hearing world, she helped to arrange doctor's appointments and meetings with school personnel to help the children with spoken language. At night, she intervened when Milca and Mariano couldn't hear their children's cries. She also bought Giddel and Edgar their first basketball.

For Travieso, Victoriana Peña represented the connection with the family's roots in the Dominican Republic. Living in a wooden shack in the southern coast town of Baní, Victoriana served as the family matriarch. In the summer of 1979 she was taking care of her four–year old grandson Carmelo, and his older brother and sister, Raul and Lisa. It was a carefree summer of swimming and games until late one Friday night, August turning to September, when Hurricane David hit.

No stranger to the ravages of storms, the people of Baní thought they were ready for David and took the usual precautions. Carmelo recalls the atmosphere of curious excitement as his relatives cooked food and stored water. A shelter was set up in an elementary school made of brick. The Traviesos brought Victoriana to the shelter well before the storm hit, because her mobility was limited. Then they went back to the shack to wait. For a while all was peaceful. Then the sky began to darken. Winds began to blow. Rain, innocent at first, began to fall. They waited. For a young child, there was something fun about it.

There was nothing gradual about this hurricane, no period of transition. One minute it was a rainstorm, the next a catastrophe. Ferocious winds lashed the village. Raindrops fell like bullets. It quickly became apparent that Victoriana's shack was not sufficient protection, and Carmelo's family, along with dozens of others, ran out onto the road in a desperate race to the school.

"When you're four years old, you don't know what to expect,"

Carmelo said years later. "You're looking for someone to take care of you, but there were a lot of people who were there. We just had to run. I just remember the rain, how hard it was. It was hitting me in the chest, and I was crying. There was a lot of debris flying and light poles falling. You could hear the wind howling."

The road was fast becoming a river. At one point, the surging mass had to leap over a fallen wire crackling in the water. Tree branches slammed down all around them. The wind was strong enough to knock many a child to the ground. Finally, soaked with water and blood, they reached the school, and spilled crying into a packed room of frightened neighbors.

Thousands of Dominicans perished in Hurricane David. Many more were left homeless. The banks of rivers like the Ozama and Yaque overflowed, causing precious plantain crops to rot in the mud. Rice fields were ruined. For weeks after, children lugged pails to cisterns in search of fresh water. Life was reduced to its most raw elements.

Carmelo Travieso Sr. arrived as soon as he could. Navigating his way through the flattened town of Baní, he found his children alive and well, if still a bit scared. His tiny son who shared his name was now twice stamped as a survivor.

•

Later that year, after his parents were divorced, Carmelo moved with his mother and siblings to Jamaica Plain, Massachusetts. Thrust into another world, the family scraped by. His mother cleaned houses to make money. Out of necessity, they lived simply.

A few years later they moved into the top floor of a three-story house in Dorchester on a street alive with diversity. "We had black, white, Cuban, Cape Verdean, Puerto Rican, Dominican, all different stuff," Travieso recalls. "It was good on our street. When you're younger, you don't know any better. The person next to you is the person next to you."

It was here that his passion for basketball started to develop. A neighbor's house had a caged-in backyard, and local boys put together a makeshift basket, using scrap wood for a backboard and a de-spoked bicycle rim for a hoop. They made a foul line and a three-point line by dragging their heels in the dirt. Forced to shoot over the outstretched arms of his brother Raul (almost five years older), Carmelo spent a lot of time behind the three-point arc. "I always liked the long-range shot," he says. "I grew up watching Larry Bird."

Blessed with a springy athleticism, he was good right away. The one–on–one games he played with friends were called "Thirty–two to Zip." In order to beat Travieso, all opponents had to do was score one hoop before he scored thirty–two. While not exactly the recipe for making lots of lifelong pals, the game honed Travieso's competitive spirit.

He was a bright, if unfocused, student at Martin Luther King Junior High in Dorchester. A precocious artist, Travieso had his paintings and drawings hung up all over the school. While the disruptive, sometimes violent environment at school was, in Travieso's words, "pretty wild," he wasn't looking for a way out. That was all he knew. One day, though, he scored forty–two points in a junior high game. Soon after, he had a visitor, Robin Dixon, basketball coach at Thayer Academy in Braintree.

The huge financial aid package offered by Thayer opened up a new world for Travieso. He met kids whose lives were different from those he knew in Dorchester. They dressed differently, talked differently. They had a certain polish. Wide–eyed, Travieso took in the whole scene, feeling a little overwhelmed. "You can do it," Dixon told him over and over. "You can make it here." In time, he thrived. His academic skills sharpened. His artistic talent was nourished by long hours in the studio, dabbling with watercolors, etchings, charcoals.

On the basketball court, he blossomed. His jump shot was picture perfect—the quick elevation, the perfectly tucked elbow, the instant release, snapping his wrist down and sending the ball on a gentle, back–spinning parabola toward the hoop. He was a leaper with great hands and great instincts. So athletic was Travieso that he could stand on one foul line and flip the ball backwards over his shoulder, three–quarters the length of the court toward the other hoop with a frightening accuracy, usually hitting the backboard, sometimes the rim, occasionally sinking the circus shot. At once a serious teenager and a free spirit, Travieso loved to play the game. By his junior year in 1991–92 he was regarded by many coaches as one of the two or three best high school players in Massachusetts. One of the other players mentioned in that vein lived in the western part of the state and intrigued Travieso because of his presumably Hispanic heritage. The kid's name was Padilla.

When they met that summer at the ABCD Camp in Irvine, California, Travieso and Padilla felt an immediate bond. The cultural connections were largely unspoken, but palpable; they seemed to understand each other in a fundamental way. Being able to speak Spanish provided a sense of relief, especially for Padilla, who had moved to the States not quite three years before. They had each endured a certain prejudice against Latino players—*This ain't your game, man; go play baseball.*[1] Mostly they shared a journey. Without any words about transfusions or hurricanes or deaf parents, they realized they had traveled some of the same difficult roads.

While John Calipari was left salivating over the play of Marcus Camby at the ABCD Camp, he also gained interest in the two Spanish–speaking guards. It was always good to get in–state kids, and it was clear they both could play. Recruiting required a little bit of patience. In the Travieso household, Carmelo's older brother Raul translated Calipari's words into Spanish for their mother, Carmen Peña. With the Padillas, Edgar's sister Millie turned the words into sign language. In both cases, Calipari recalls a long pause before parents laughed at his jokes.

In the fall of 1993, Padilla and Travieso arrived at UMass as freshmen, sharing a room in the John Quincy Adams high–rise dormitory. As they grew closer, each recognized a sensitivity in the other that was rarely visible in the macho world of Division I college basketball.

Travieso marvelled at the closeness of the Padilla family. He saw them at every game, and chuckled at Edgar's description of Milca walking around the concourse of the Mullins Center when the score was close, unable to bare the tension. Often he joined an array of Padilla parents and cousins and uncles for a Sunday feast at the Amherst home of Edgar's older sister Millie and her husband Omar. Travieso wanted to communicate with Edgar's parents, and kept his roommate up late a couple of nights to learn some rudiments of sign language. When Edgar's older brother Giddel quit the team and left school in the fall, Travieso sensed the whole family's pain.

Padilla was surprised to find out about Travieso's artistic skill, something he had never before associated with an athlete. Many times he came back to the room and found Travieso calmly sketching or drawing, while the staccato rhythm of rap popped out of the radio. Once, Padilla returned to find a beautifully calligraphed message taped to their door. Entitled, "Our Goal, A Dream with a Deadline," it was Travieso's statement of commitment about the hard work needed to win a national championship. Hell, Travieso even *looked* like an artist, bearing an uncanny resemblance to dancer Gregory Hines.

*Carmelo Travieso (Photo by Kevin Gutting)*

On the court, life was rough. Calipari was hard on Padilla and Travieso right from the start. Playing behind Derek Kellogg and Mike Williams, the two freshmen had opposite problems in the coach's estimation. Padilla was tough, but out of control. Travieso was heady, but way too soft.

Publicly, Calipari extolled Padilla's "fearlessness" as his defining trait. The wiry guard seemed to thrive on challenge. But when Calipari screamed in practice, a part of Padilla froze inside. He wasn't used to yelling. He had a hard time tuning out the tone, and not taking it personally. Sometimes, he would later admit, he feigned misunderstanding, hiding behind his Spanish, even though he understood each knifing word. The criticism stayed with him too much. Often at night he lay awake replaying his mistakes from the day. While he did play every game his freshman year, even starting seven at shooting guard, Padilla expected more of himself. He brooded about his errors far more than he enjoyed his successes.

Travieso was rooted on the bench as the team's fourth guard in a three–guard rotation. Often he didn't get in until garbage time, sometimes not at all. Yes, he had the nice shooting touch, but he just didn't seem ready for the physical nature of the games, particularly on the defensive end. He was used to moving around picks, not fighting through them. His private school game, drifting to the perimeter, shooting jump shots, was ridiculed by Calipari. *I can't fucking play you if you can't be tougher than that!* By year's end, Calipari took Travieso into his office for what the coach later termed "shock treatment"— learn to play hard, physical basketball, or transfer.

"I thought the guy was insane," Travieso would later confess. "The things he said. The way he acted. He told us, 'If I'm not yelling at you, you should worry.' I guess there was no reason for me to worry. He knew what he could get out of us, and he'd say, 'I'm not letting you waste a day.'"

At the time, though, Travieso was stung. He admits that he did give some serious thought to transferring; playing time wasn't looking any better the following year with Kellogg and Williams back as seniors. Also, Calipari was going to be recruiting some other guards. Maybe Travieso would never really play at UMass.

Ultimately he decided to stay, in part because of his friendship with Padilla. If they worked hard, maybe one day they would be the starting backcourt.

Their friendship deepened. While they shared a great deal, they also filled voids in the other. Travieso gained a certain fortitude from Padilla. He admired the way Padilla kept coming back for more, no matter how many slings and arrows he absorbed on the court. Travieso also started returning each summer to Puerto Rico at Padilla's suggestion to play in the Superior League, the island commonwealth's highest level of competition. Games were heated. Town rivalries were explosive. The on–court battles provided a great sharpening stone for college players. Around the edges of games, Travieso also began to reconnect with his father, Carmelo Sr., a man he had seen very little of since the tumultuous hurricane and subsequent divorce years ago.

Padilla's intensity, at once blessing and curse, was lightened considerably by Travieso. While Travieso had a definite seriousness of purpose—a hard worker on the court who was taking upper–level courses in economics—he had an ability to shut things off and have fun. By his sophomore year he had established himself as the team's top prankster. Padilla, reluctantly at first and then with greater and greater zeal, became an accomplice. By midseason, Padilla was up late in a Pittsburgh hotel room, dialing the number of team trainer Ron Laham and putting on his best gangster voice. "Lay–ham," he said, "we're going to get you!" The water fight with Laham that followed culminated in

Travieso and Padilla stranded out in the hallway, locked out of their room and laughing till their bellies ached.

They played more as sophomores, particularly after Mike Williams was kicked off the team in February. Padilla became the starting shooting guard, playing alongside Derek Kellogg. Averaging seven points and three assists a game, he was emerging as an important part of UMass's attack.

His defense much improved, Travieso spent less time as Calipari's whipping boy. When Padilla went down with a sprained arch in UMass's NCAA game against Tulsa, Travieso became the starter in the Minutemen's Elite Eight game against Oklahoma State. That afternoon, while UMass suffered a painful loss, Travieso was the Minutemen's leading scorer and arguably its best player.

After strong summers in Puerto Rico, Padilla and Travieso returned to campus in the fall of 1995 knowing their moment had arrived. Circumstances added both pressure and opportunity. UMass had not had much success recruiting guards the last two years, bringing in only one backcourt player each season while just missing out on several top–notch prospects. Point guard Andre Burks played sparingly in 1994–95 before tearing ligaments in his knee and then running into off–court problems.[2] He wound up transferring after the season to McNeese State, not far from his home in Louisiana. In the fall of 1995, Charlton Clarke, a combo–guard from the Bronx, began his career but got saddled with a maddening array of preseason injuries. Then, in the opening game against Kentucky, he broke his foot after just twelve seconds on the court, sidelining him for half the year and leaving him in subpar condition for the entire season. Thus, UMass was down to just two scholarship guards, Padilla and Travieso.

There was no room for error; any injury or foul trouble would spell crisis. Padilla and Travieso would have to play virtually the whole game, every game. Even if that were possible, the six–two goateed guards each came with major question marks. Padilla had to play point guard, running the offense. He himself entered the season with questions about his ability to fill the role; he felt far more comfortable at shooting guard. In one game the previous year, an important contest late in the season at St. Joseph's, Padilla had pleaded with senior point guard Derek Kellogg not to commit any more fouls because he didn't want to take over that spot. Without question, Padilla's shoddy preseason performance only exacerbated the doubts. For his part, Travieso was unproven. He had started only two games in his first two years. In a hotel room the year before, after a loss to George Washington, Calipari admitted to two reporters his doubts that Travieso would ever be able to deliver in the clutch for UMass.

Now, for better or for worse, Padilla and Travieso were all Calipari had. They had to shoulder the entire load.

Through the first seven games of the season, they were shockingly good. Tireless and tenacious, they worked together with an uncanny rhythm. Defensively, they were a portrait of pesky relentlessness. Offensively, their blend of skills gave UMass a versatile attack from the backcourt, knifing penetration and perimeter shooting. Already they had outplayed two of the most well regarded backcourts in the country, Duane Simpkins and Johnny Rhodes of Maryland, and Stephon Marbury and Drew Barry of Georgia Tech.

While Marcus Camby was the unquestioned star presence, and while Donta Bright and Dana Dingle were the steady and solid senior co–captains, in some ways it was Padilla and Travieso who emerged as the team leaders. Padilla had become the coach–on–the–floor point guard, calling team huddles on the free throw line after fouls were called. Travieso ran the team through stretching exercises before each practice, sometimes zinging in a one–liner or two. Most significantly, when the Minutemen broke from the locker room and ran onto the court in the tense minutes before gametime, it was always the two guards who led the pack.

•

As an indoor game, college basketball can be played almost anywhere. There is no need, technically speaking, for extensive travel. In the modern age, though, travel to glamorous locales has become routine. It's great for exposure. It's great for recruiting.

The year before, UMass had flown the Concorde to Paris to participate in the Buckler Challenge. In 1995–96, Christmas vacation was, to the players, even more inviting—they were headed to Honolulu for the Outrigger Rainbow Classic.

The Minutemen were the last of the eight teams to arrive. Calipari said he wanted all his players to celebrate Christmas with their families. He spent the holiday in Osceola, Missouri, with Ellen, his girls and his in–laws. On December 26, the team convened, somewhat chaotically, in Los Angeles, and flew over the Pacific. Touching down after a long, disorienting day, the Minutemen skipped the leis and macadamia nuts, and went right from the airport to practice.

UMass was slated to play on the last three nights of the four–day tournament, December 28–30. Newspaper previews suggested that three games in three nights against quality competition would expose UMass's limited depth. Padilla and Travieso in particular should show the wear and tear that came from averaging thirty–seven minutes of playing time apiece.

The difference between playing thirty–two and thirty–seven minutes of a forty–minute game might not seem like much. In Division I college basketball, particularly with UMass's emphasis on relentless man–to–man defense, playing close to a full game taxes the reserves of the most finely conditioned athletes. Even in an era of lengthy TV timeouts, a couple of decent breaks on the bench are usually necessary to regain strength. Without these respites, the end of the game becomes a test of will. All of the sport's little decisions—fight through the pick, or drift around it; beat your man to the spot, or play behind him; make the hard cut, or stand on the perimeter—become choices where the path of least resistance gains more and more appeal. Many people start doing the easy thing instead of the right thing, which is almost always the hard thing. Often this is how close games are lost.

UMass opened against North Carolina State, a once–mighty Atlantic Coast Conference team now trying to rebuild after a couple of years of struggle. The Wolfpack entered the game 6–0. Senior center Todd Fuller more than held his own against Marcus Camby, scoring thirty points, yanking down fourteen rebounds and showing—as Bryant Reeves had the year before—that the UMass big man had a hard time with physically bullish post players. The Minutemen rebounded from a second–half deficit to win, 78–67, thanks in no small measure to the guards. Padilla, playing thirty–eight minutes, had nine assists against just one turnover. Travieso, playing the full forty, scored sixteen points.

The next night against a 7–2 University of Southern California team, UMass got a major scare in the opening minutes when Camby fell awkwardly to the floor, grabbing his knee. It turned out he was okay, but the Minutemen had to play the rest of the game without him, a test of the one–man team theory many had espoused in the preseason. Padilla, saddled with foul trouble, was limited to a season–low twenty–eight minutes, but he made the most of them, scoring a game–high nineteen points, with four assists and no turnovers. Travieso had sixteen more points in a thirty–eight–minute stint. UMass coasted to a 78–63 win.

The championship game pitted the Minutemen against Syracuse. The Orangemen, not regarded as one of the top teams in The Big East when the season began, had started the year with eleven straight wins. Ranked Number 13 in the country at the time, they would prove to everyone come March that they were a legitimate national power.

Despite an impressive return by Camby, UMass trailed by a point after a hard–fought first half.

In the second half of their third straight night of basketball, when exhaustion was supposed to be taking its toll, UMass played its most aggressive twenty minutes of the season. The defensive pressure was unceasing. Contesting every pass, the Minutemen sucked the spirit out of Syracuse. In the closing moments, Edgar Padilla and Carmelo Travieso seemed to get their hands on every ball, combining for eight steals. Right down to the end they played with exuberance, doing the hard thing all the time. They each played the full forty minutes in an emphatic 65–47 win. It was the first time in Syracuse coach Jim Boeheim's twenty–year career that the Orangemen had been held under fifty points.

The Minutemen closed out the 1995 portion of the season with a championship and a startling 10-0 record. The early questions about the team had been laid to rest. The depth was sufficient. The leadership was there. The guards were outstanding.

# 13: "Marcus, You Okay?"

January 14, 1996

Busing back to their hotel after the smothering victory over Syracuse, the University of Massachusetts Minutemen were feeling good. They were spending their Christmas vacation in Hawaii. They were undefeated. Number 1 in America. As the bus rolled down Kalakaua Avenue, the four–lane epicenter of Honolulu's sprawl where hotels obscure the white sands of Waikiki, they cranked up the music, poked fun at each other, basked in the warmth of another win. They were college kids having the time of their lives. No one really noticed the little girl toddling out in the street.

From the far right lane, the terrified driver angled the bus to the left to block as many lanes as possible, while the carefree little girl waddled perilously toward the center of the road. Car horns blared as UMass team manager Matt Komer, seated shotgun from the driver in the tour guide's seat, sprang to his feet and frantically pushed on the air–locked door.

A senior from the small town of South Hadley, ten miles from the UMass campus, Komer had become involved with the Minuteman team as a freshman. At first he was low man on the totem pole in the managing hierarchy. When an exhausted player came off the floor and vomited—Dana Dingle was notorious—it was Komer who mopped it up. Before practice, Komer was the guy pouring out the cups of Powerade and putting them on a tray. Wide–eyed and eager, he had earned the nickname "Cheez" because of his perpetual, camera–ready smile. In time he moved up the ranks. The coaching staff recognized his can–do efficiency and put him to work coordinating team travel. He was Cheez at the airport, making sure all those maroon duffel bags found their way to the bus; Cheez in the hotel lobby, getting John Calipari the biggest suite possible; Cheez on the cellular phone, confirming the availability of a gym for practice. When assistant coach

Bruiser Flint arrived at Northampton's Cooley Dickinson Hospital in October with his laboring wife Rene, the first call that he made was to Komer. Neither Bruiser nor Rene had family in the area. Komer stayed with them for hours, right through the golden moment when Jada Flint arrived.

Now another little girl was on his mind. Komer barged through the door, veered left, sprinted in front of the bus and scooped her up just in time. His heart pounding, Komer carried the girl to the sidewalk where a panicked John Calipari said, "We've got to find her mother!"

With Komer right on his heels, Calipari sped into the open–air Royal Hawaiian Shopping Center next to the sidewalk and approached one woman after another, saying, "Ma'am, ma'am, is that your little girl?" Startled, each one looked at the placid toddler in Komer's arms, wearing a dress, tights, a little white shirt. They then shook their heads no. Blazing through the courtyard of the mall, Calipari spotted a distraught young woman and said, "Ma'am, ma'am. . . ." She spoke no English. Racing over to Komer, she held out her arms and swallowed up the little girl. With mother and daughter both crying, Calipari put his arm around Matt Komer's shoulder and said, "You're my hero for the day."

•

The Minutemen spent New Year's Eve in the air, flying into the sun, coming home. On January 4, they faced third–ranked Memphis at the Worcester Centrum. Down 59–58 with 1:15 left, UMass found a way yet again. Donta Bright sped through the defense for a hoop. Edgar Padilla, in his thirty–eighth minute of play after missing two days of practice with a severe stomach virus, hit two clutch free throws, then blocked a three–pointer by Mingo Johnson. UMass won, 64–61.

Their unexpected romp through eleven non–league games complete, the Minutemen set their sights on Atlantic 10 play, which began at home against Dayton on January 6. One of five newcomers to the A–10, Dayton seemed far removed from its basketball glory days of the fifties and sixties when no team in America matched the Flyers' 435 wins. Most recently, they had endured five straight losing years. The 1995–96 season had begun with surprising success: an 8–3 record that already surpassed the win total from a year ago. The key ingredient to Dayton's good start was the tremendously improved play of six-ten senior center Chris Daniels. Polite and popular, Daniels had never before distinguished himself as a college basketball player, averaging 4.4 points per game through three seasons. This year, though, he was averaging 13.5 points and connecting on a sparkling 72.4 percent of his shots. Now he was set to tangle with Marcus Camby.

Daniels was magnificent. He looped little hook shots over Camby, beat him on the baseline, drained a couple of jumpers. Against an imposing defensive force, he scored twenty points, connecting on ten of twelve field goals. "He's a terrific player," Camby said, nodding his head after the game.

Camby wasn't bad himself. Playing with a fluid ease, he scored a career–high thirty–eight, yanked down a game–high eleven rebounds, and blocked four shots. One of his dunks was so emphatic that it bounced off the Mullins Center floor high over the backboard. UMass rolled to a 78–58 win. "He's a hell of a player," said Daniels. "He's all I thought he would be."

They never saw each other again. Four and a half weeks later, after a morning practice, Chris Daniels died of cardiac arrhythmia.

•

It was the snowiest winter on record. Plows were grinding into the night every few days in the East. Hardware stores were doing big business in scrapers and shovels. School kids were cutting a Faustian deal of snow days that would keep them in classrooms until the very end of June.

The biggest blast of snow came on Sunday and Monday, January 7–8. Like everything else, Atlantic 10 basketball was affected. On Sunday, St. Joseph's game at Virginia Tech was postponed because of the thirty–four inches burying Blacksburg. With airports closed on Monday, the Hawks bused back nine and a half hours into Philadelphia—which had received a record 30.7 inches—for Tuesday's game against UMass. Problem was, the Minutemen hadn't been able to make it down from Massachusetts, delaying the game for a day. On Tuesday night, UMass was in transit, arriving at Bradley Airport in Windsor Locks, Connecticut.

Wearing a black leather coat, baggy jeans and a pair of sunglasses perched high atop his head, Marcus Camby ducked under the metal detector. The squealing security checker asked for his autograph. After Camby smiled shyly and scratched out his name on a piece of paper, the woman bragged to a colleague, "This is going to be worth something!"

Walking with his characteristic slow saunter, Camby eased down to USAir Gate A9, only to find out that the flight was delayed. Turning around, he sauntered back to Pizza Hut, returned with two pepperoni Personal Pan Pizzas and plopped down next to Ted Cottrell for a game of Sega.

John Calipari, seeming unusually relaxed, sat by himself for several minutes reading a book called *Managing Values*. Bruiser Flint, kept awake too many nights by two–month–old Jada, slouched down in a chair and closed his eyes. Fellow assistant coach John Robic found a television with UConn and Villanova playing.

Players spread out across the terminal. Dana Dingle, a white headband encircling his forehead, paged through *Vibe Magazine* while swaying slowly to the beat on his Walkman. Donta Bright studied the sports page of *USA Today*. Several players gathered at a magazine rack where an *Inside Sports* cover story on Dennis Rodman commanded more interest than a swimsuit retrospective featuring Kathy Ireland.

Matt Komer collected the gold Frequent Flyer cards from the coaching staff and stood in line to have a USAir employee run them through the computer system.

The team attracted more than passing interest from other travelers. Most hung on the periphery and whispered about Number 1, about Camby, or about Calipari. Some were bolder. The Krasno family from Pottsville, Pennsylvania—Lester and Pam, and their children Faith and Jesse—showed few qualms. After all, they had just finished visiting the UMass campus because nineteen–year–old Faith was transferring from Muhlenberg.

Decked out in a UMass cap and jacket, twelve–year–old Jesse approached Carmelo Travieso and began talking.

"Are you shooting for the pros?"

"Yeah, we all are."

"You start, don't you?"

Travieso nodded.

"Mind if I get a picture with you?"

"Not at all."

Within two seconds, Pam Krasno sprang into action. A heavily made–up woman with piles of black hair and enough bracelets and necklaces to create havoc at the metal detector, Pam started backing up toward a storage closet and clicking photos with one very long red fingernail. Jesse beamed. Travieso grinned. Pam kept clicking away. Asking Camby and Tyrone Weeks to get in the picture, she said, "I'm not embarrassing anyone, am I?"

Finally, a USAir attendant announced boarding for the flight. Jesse asked Travieso if he were flying first class. Travieso said that he wasn't. Jesse immediately told his mother that he wanted to trade tickets with her, that she could sit up front with Dad. His voice pleading, Jesse said, "I want to be in second class with these guys."

•

The next night the Minutemen were gathered in the locker room at St. Joseph's Alumni Memorial Fieldhouse getting prodded by Calipari. *These guys lost back–to–back buzzer games, then they spent ten hours on a bus. They're pissed. They want to take it out on Number 1. You gotta understand that there's a bull's–eye on your backs. You're going to get everyone's best game. Playing Number 1 is a big deal to people. It's their chance for greatness. This building opened in 1949, and they've never hosted a Number 1. They're gonna be crazy out there.*

Just then, media relations director Bill Strickland entered with a somber expression on his face. "I've got some bad news," he said.

UMass swimmer Greg Menton, competing that day at Dartmouth, had collapsed at poolside after the 200–meter freestyle. They had tried to revive him on the deck, and then in the ambulance. He was now at Dartmouth–Hitchcock Medical Center. The situation looked grim.

Truth be told, they didn't know Greg Menton. They didn't know that he held three school records, that he was a top–notch student, or that his fellow swimmers regarded him as a vibrant young man. They did realize, though, that he was a fellow athlete, a fellow UMass athlete. Staring at the floor with an awkward numbness, the Minutemen said a prayer, led by Calipari. Nothing gut–wrenching, maudlin or prolonged: just a few words about there being more important things than sports. *What we do is not life or death, guys. We're lucky to be doing what we're doing. Let's just hope that Greg makes it. . . .*

For whatever reason, the Minutemen lacked their usual fire. Their trademark defensive intensity—their relentless effort to make the game tough on the opponent—was missing for the first time all season. St. Joe's made big shots all night long. Fueled by an overflow crowd smelling a monumental upset, the Hawks played way above the level of a 4–4 team. They responded to every UMass run. If the Minutemen were defined by the motto "Refuse to Lose," the Hawks seemed to draw strength from their mascot, which flaps its wings all game, every game. At least on this night, they too, were relentless.

Neither side led by more than six points throughout the contest.

Finally, with 21.5 seconds left, UMass appeared to lock things up when Donta Bright hit two free throws for a 78–73 lead. All season long the Minutemen had demonstrated great composure down the stretch. Surely, this game was over.

Until UMass somehow committed two fouls on three–point attempts in the final fifteen seconds. First Edgar Padilla fouled Mark Bass, who drained all three shots. Then, after Padilla hit one of two free throws for a 79–76 lead, a wild scramble ensued at the other end, culminating in St. Joe's Terrell Myers heaving up a desperation thirty-footer with 0.9 seconds left. The shot didn't have a chance, but the Hawks did—when an overeager Bright slammed into Myers as he released the ball. With Calipari's jaw dropping on the bench, Myers coolly sank all three free throws to force overtime.

Calipari gathered his team, swallowed his rage and looked ahead. "Play to win," he said. "Don't play not to lose."

For the eighth consecutive overtime game, dating back to the 1990–91 season, the Minutemen found their crunchtime cool. Edgar Padilla put them ahead to stay with a three–pointer midway through the five–minute period, leading to a 94–89 victory. It was the first time in the six games that UMass had played as the top–ranked team during the 1995–96 season when Number 1 seemed to be more of a noose than a badge of honor. Had the pressure started to get to them?

"If you play not to lose, you lose," Calipari explained afterward. "If you play to win, you have a chance to win."

For the first time ever, UMass had started a season 13–0. Later that night, the Minutemen found out that Greg Menton had died.

●

It would be unfair to say that there was any real heaviness in the air when the Minutemen traveled from Philadelphia to Olean, New York, for Sunday's scheduled game against St. Bonaventure. The subdued atmosphere had more to do with the destination, their least favorite stop on the schedule. UMass didn't so much mind the St. Bonaventure fans, even though they were the ones a year ago who had hatched the taunt, "Hooked on Phonics." The Minutemen weren't exactly living in awe of the Bonnies as a basketball power, either. Indeed, UMass had won fourteen straight games over St. Bonaventure, its longest streak against anyone. Sure, St. Bonaventure had had a momentary turnaround a year ago, winning eighteen games and pushing the Minutemen to overtime at the Reilly Center. But these were the Bonnies. Back when the A–10 had been a nine–team league, some coaches used to joke that the "play–in" game between the eighth and ninth seeds to start the A–10 tournament should have been called the SBI: The St. Bonaventure Invitational.

The main reason for UMass's subdued feeling about making the trip was the trip itself. A team that had grown accustomed to glamorous travel—journeys to Hawaii and Paris and Disneyland, staying in Marriotts and Hyatts and Embassy Suites—did not covet the annual winter flight to Buffalo and the two–hour bus ride to Olean for a stay at the Castle Inn. Deep in the New York snowbelt, St. Bonaventure is a Catholic school with a Franciscan Friary right on campus. It's quiet and charming and cold. UMass's strategy was simple: win and get the hell out.

The game was a big deal in Olean. The Reilly Center had a rare sellout of its six thousand seats. Fans arrived early for the two o'clock tipoff. They were there to root for the underdog. They were there to check out the Number 1 team in America and its colorful coach. And, of course, they were there to watch Marcus Camby.

As the season unfolded, Camby was evolving from curiosity to celebrity. The Atlantic 10 had never had a player like him before in its twenty–year history, someone who could so dominate the action on both ends of the court. He had followed his thirty–eight–point performance against Dayton with thirty–four more against St. Joseph's. Hawks coach Phil Martelli couldn't stop gushing: "Camby was marvelous. I really think he's the Player of the Year." That same night Calipari told the press that his advice to Camby was simple these days: "I keep telling him, 'You're the best player in the country—have fun.' There's not many times in your life that you're in something that you're the best. When you're in that position, enjoy it. Have fun with it."

More than an hour before the game, several fans were down at courtside just to gawk as UMass assistant coach John Robic ran the team through stretching exercises. There was Camby on the floor, swinging his long legs over his head, and dozens of people were staring as if they had just seen a flying saucer. Camby was his usual quiet, lethargic self, conserving his energy for gametime. Half an hour before tipoff, he was out with his teammates shooting jump shots as more fans started to descend. The place was beginning to buzz.

Moments later, Camby started walking back toward the locker room, apparently loose and ready. With Donta Bright trailing him by several yards, Camby ducked through the entryway parallel to the midcourt line, turned right down the corridor and out of view from the fans. Then Camby reached up to grab his head and tumbled in a heap on the floor.

"Marcus, you okay?" Bright shouted, racing to catch up to him. "Marcus! You all right, man?"

Bright snapped his fingers in front of Camby's face and called his name repeatedly. Nothing. Reaching down to Camby's chest, Bright felt a heartbeat, then ran into the locker room to tell the coaching staff. Flinging open the door he said, "Come quick, Marcus is down!" The coaches burst out into the hall, where the scene was growing more chaotic. Players had started gathering, trying to get Camby's attention. St. Bonaventure team doctor Ed Griffin had sprinted over to help.

The coaching staff tried to shoo the players back toward the locker room. Several had tears in their eyes. Finally they gathered, panicked expressions all around. Carmelo Travieso brought the squad together in a circle. They held hands and prayed.

Outside in the hallway, as Camby began to show the first signs of woozy recovery, John Calipari nodded Bruiser Flint back toward the players. The game was set to begin in ten minutes. No one out in the stands had the slightest idea what was happening.

Flint headed into the locker room. EMTs strapped Camby to a stretcher. Calipari followed them out into the January afternoon, crawling into the back of the ambulance, which blared its siren and hurtled out into the quiet, snow–bordered roads of Olean.

# 14: "Hey Man, This is Bigger than Us"

Marcus Camby's collapse was an isolated incident, a mere moment in time, ephemeral as anything else. Within and around the UMass basketball program, however, it set up a chamber of echoes.

For Camby's best friend on the team, the collapse was a haunting reminder of loss. Tyrone Weeks, six–seven, two hundred sixty pounds of bear—grizzly on the court, teddy off—grew up in North Philadelphia accustomed to the chorus of the night: "Gunshots, cars, music blasting, loud people." Not included in the cacophony was much comfort or advice from anyone approaching a role model. His father, Tyrone Sr., never married his mother and never lived in the home. "I heard he was in a gang, that he was in jail for a long period of time," Weeks says. "But he's straightened his life out." His mom? Good-hearted and well–intentioned, Delores Weeks was lost too often in a haze of cocaine addiction. There were nights she came home with a frighteningly vacant expression, other nights with scattered animation. Sometimes she didn't come home at all. Her frequent voyages into rehab clinics began with hope, ended with relapse. When Tyrone was thirteen, the situation deteriorated. He and his younger brother Robert moved in with their grandmother.

The only real refuge was Father Dave's House. A priest with a passion for basketball, Dave Hagan has long been a gentle rock for poor kids in North Philly. Father Dave counseled Tyrone never to give up on Delores. She's a good woman, he insisted. She just needs support.

Through Father Dave, Tyrone met Hank Gathers, the hero of the 'hood. Seven years older than Tyrone, the six–seven Gathers seemed ticketed for stardom. An almost volcanic exuberance flowed out of him. His relentless athleticism provided the centerpiece of coach Paul Westhead's frenetic style at Loyola Marymount, a heretofore obscure basketball program that suddenly qualified for three straight NCAA appearances in 1988–90. As a junior in 1988–89, Gathers led the nation in both scoring (32.7) and rebounding (13.7), becoming only the second player in NCAA Division I history to accomplish that feat. Back home in North Philly that summer, he became an almost mythic figure. Kids adored him. One night at Father Dave's House he presented a couple of extra–large Loyola Marymount T–shirts to a wide–eyed Tyrone Weeks.

During a game in December of 1989, Gathers fainted, sending shock waves through North Philly. Diagnosed with arrhythmia, Gathers was put on medication and cleared to return. All seemed well while the season played out. He was dominating again, averaging thirty points and ten rebounds a game. When the calendar turned to March, Gathers began cutting back on the medication, a move he understood to be sanctioned by doctors. On Sunday, March 4, before Loyola's West Coast Conference tournament semifinal game against Portland, Gathers went out running in the parking lot to burn off some nervous energy. In the early moments of the game he played with his usual explosiveness. Six minutes into the contest, Gathers soared high for an alley–oop pass and slammed it home with two hands. The crowd at Loyola's Gersten Pavilion roared its approval as Gathers flashed a big smile to the home bench. Then, in an instant, he was down. The crowd turned stone silent. Gathers struggled to his knees, then slammed back to the floor in violent seizure. His mother, Lucille, and aunt, Carol Livingston, raced for the court, wailing in horror. By the time Gathers reached the hospital he was dead.

The news shook North Philly with the force of an earthquake. Tyrone Weeks, fifteen years old, sat in Father Dave's house for the longest time. How could such a thing happen? No one he had ever met brimmed with greater energy or greater health. No one had seemed more alive. How could it be? Father Dave sat with the neighborhood kids, absorbing the anger and sadness and overwhelming loss, trying to soothe the pain. There was not much he could do.

When Tyrone finally walked back to his grandmother's house, he was struck by the eerie feeling in the streets. "There was," he says, "a big silence in the neighborhood."

●

For Donta Bright, the reverberations of Camby's collapse were just as wrenching. The eldest of three children and the only boy, Donta grew

*Donta Bright  (Photo by Jerrey Roberts)*

up in the projects of East Baltimore. He developed his first–at–practice work ethic from his mother, Patricia. "She never stopped working to try to better me and my two sisters," he says. His love of sports came first from his father Carlton—before Carlton abandoned the family, leaving Donta, like so many city kids (Marcus Camby, Tyrone Weeks, Lou Roe), the man of the house way before his time.

In a neighborhood with what he describes as "a lot of drugs, a lot of killings," basketball was the beacon: the promise of a ticket out. "We had no [basketball] goal in our neighborhood," he says, "so we just made one. We put up a milk crate and any piece of wood that we could nail it to to make a backboard." The basketball team at nearby Dunbar High School was the pride of the community. Consistently rated as one of the top high school teams in America, Dunbar had sent several of its stars off to college on scholarship. Some had gone all the way to the top. NBA players like Tyrone Bogues, Reggie Williams, Reggie Lewis, David Wingate and Sam Cassell held proof of the possible.

College basketball was followed religiously in East Baltimore during the mid–eighties. Not surprisingly, the team of choice was Maryland. Whenever Terrapin games were on television, young, gangly Donta Bright was taking in every nuance. Nothing made him more excited than watching the star forward, a player with the undeniable stamp of greatness. "I loved Len Bias," Bright says.

In June of 1986, thirteen–year–old Bright and his younger cousin Keith Booth reveled when Bias was chosen by the Boston Celtics as the second pick in the NBA draft. This was *their* guy. He would make it big.

Two days later, Bias's friend Brian Tribble frantically called 911 from a Maryland dorm after the star forward went into cardiac arrest brought on by free–basing cocaine. Paramedics could not revive the stricken star. It is a memory that still fills Bright with anguish. "Everybody who loved basketball knew Len Bias," he says. "He was such a great player."

Seven years later, Bright would be slapped again. He had made it big in his own right, starring on a great Dunbar team, getting named to the McDonald's All–America squad, becoming the first member of his family to attend college. Granted, his first year at UMass had been a difficult one. Unable to play or practice with the team because of Proposition 48 restrictions, he spent a lot of time alone. At night, he often walked over to the Curry Hicks Cage with a basketball and his special–issue key. Sometimes it was ten o'clock, sometimes midnight. Soon he would be lost in the sounds of the game: sneakers squeaking, ball drumming on the floor, rim rattling. Next year he would be ready.

One night that summer the news hit him like acid. Reggie Lewis, who had risen from Dunbar dreams to the captaincy of the Boston Celtics, had collapsed and died in a gym at Brandeis University. Another basketball hero was gone.

A year and a half later, Bright was first on the scene in the hallway in Olean, New York, when Marcus Camby went down.

•

For Camby himself, the collapse was at once a source of mystery, a profound nuisance and a message about appreciation. Memories of the incident are dissolved in amnesia. "I just remember getting up and going to the bus," he later said. "After that, I don't know. I just remember seeing myself on TV a lot."

The five days of January 14–18 were long and boring, scary and uncomfortable. First in Olean, and then, after a Medevac flight, at the UMass Medical Center in Worcester, Camby lived in unreal hospital time. Around the edges of hospital food and hospital sleep, he endured a melange of needles and tubes and questions. He felt fine, he insisted. He wanted out.

Sealed off from the public and clusters of media staking out the lobby, Camby spent plenty of time talking to his mother Janice. She told him how scared she had been when the news came across the television, how she had instantly gotten sick to her stomach. People were calling the house all the time.

After a few days, Camby was cleared to visit the pediatric ward, where he became a celebrity patient. He talked basketball, signed full body casts, brought a big smile to the face of lupus patient Harry Tambolleo. The visit, Camby said later, was his only genuinely happy time in the hospital. It provided a blast of perspective, a sense of how quickly everything could be taken away. One minute you're sailing along with seventy-two points in your last two games. The next minute the ambulance siren is blaring.

•

For the doctors thrust into the fray, Marcus Camby's collapse provided a sense of their own limitations.

They knew from the beginning that he was not an ordinary case. The patient was the Number 1 player on the Number 1 team in the country. In Massachusetts in particular, the case was sensitive. Esteemed cardiologist Gilbert Mudge had come under fire for clearing Reggie Lewis to resume workouts after an initial collapse. At UMass, record-breaking swimmer Greg Menton had died just the week before. Public pressure on the physicians was overwhelming. People wanted supreme caution. Above all, they wanted an answer: how could an apparently healthy twenty-one-year-old college basketball player just collapse for ten minutes?

In a sense, people were scared as much for themselves as for Camby. Young athletes, after all, are our society's gods. They seem to have an insurance of a good tomorrow, a stay against the inevitable. With the most finely conditioned of bodies, they have seemingly exerted some sort of control. When they collapse, our collective vulnerability is underscored.

The evaluation went beyond thorough. A host of cardiac tests demonstrated a healthy heart. Brain scans, brain–wave tests and spinal taps revealed no neurological problems. A profusion scan of the lungs ruled out a blood clot. Screening for toxic or narcotic substances produced nothing. There was no sign of tumor, narrowed arteries or aneurysm. It wasn't a seizure.

For all their technological sophistication, medical expertise and thoroughness, the doctors had no explanation for Camby's collapse. Terming the fainting merely "a brief lapse of consciousness," neurology chairman David Drachman told a packed room of reporters at the UMass Medical Center on January 18 that half of all blackouts remain a mystery. "Keep in mind that we're talking about ten minutes out of twenty–one years," Dr. Drachman said. "That is sort of like a needle in a haystack."

Asked if he could guarantee that Camby would be okay when he resumed playing, Drachman said simply, "There are no guarantees."

•

For UMass assistant coach James (Bruiser) Flint, the collapse represented an opportunity. When John Calipari left in the ambulance, missing his first game in his eight years at UMass, Flint was thrust into the head coaching role he had long dreamed about.

No one really called him James. He had earned the lifelong nickname Bruiser as an infant. His grandfather, a man with the appealing name Gentle Lee, tried to assuage parental fears about the sickly baby by saying, "Don't worry: when he grows up, he'll be a bruiser."

Basketball was in his blood at an early age. In high school he was a standout at Episcopal Academy in Philadelphia, where head coach Dan Dougherty had "a way of grabbing you around the neck, but he didn't grab it fully." He starred as a point guard at St. Joseph's, then spent two years as an assistant coach at Coppin State. In 1988, at the strong urging of UMass assistant coach Bill Bayno, he joined the staff of the Minutemen in the second year of the Calipari regime.

Flint had played a supporting role in the dramatic rise of UMass basketball. He was a good recruiter. His rapport with players was excellent. He yearned for a team of his own, particularly after watching Bayno land the head coaching position at UNLV the year before.

The circumstances at St. Bonaventure that day were not exactly what he had in mind. He had to swallow his own fears, acknowledge the shock several players were feeling and somehow refocus the team. Wearing impassive expressions, the Minutemen led from start to finish in a 65–52 win.

At 9:20 that night, Flint and Calipari left the hospital after extensive talks with Camby and the doctors. Out to a late dinner, the coaches finally turned to basketball. "What about the coaching?" Calipari asked. "What did you think?"

"I think I'm ready."

"I think you are, too."

•

For the UMass basketball team, Camby's collapse represented a collective sense of challenge. Off the court, they were dealing with trauma, a terrifying memory that would be imprinted forever. On it, they had to prove that they were more than their superstar.

In charging to the Number 1 ranking, of course, UMass had had to be far more than a one–man show. There had been plenty of contributors. Moreover, the Minutemen clearly had all the intangibles: chemistry, a willingness to submerge individual egos, the courage to deliver when it mattered most. Still, there was no question that they were a team with a star, more so than had been true at UMass since the days of Julius Erving. Now the star was gone.

The Minutemen responded. They played hard, and they played together. Granted, the stretch of games following Camby's collapse did not represent the iron of the schedule, but they were eminently losable. Three of the four games were on the road. There was no Popcorn State to contend with. UMass just kept on winning. Every game out, it seemed that somebody new reached inside and found his very best. In that first St. Bonaventure game, Weeks went wild with fifteen points and twelve rebounds, both figures representing career highs. At home against Rhode Island on January 17, Donta Bright had a career–high thirty–two points in a 77–71 win. On January 20, Carmelo Travieso almost doubled his career high with thirty–three to key a 93–89 victory at Duquesne. During the first 7:31 of the second half, Travieso scored a mind–boggling twenty–three points, hitting all nine shots he attempted: six three–pointers, two two–pointers and a free throw. When Duquesne called timeout, Weeks engulfed Travieso in a huge bear hug, and Bright did a spontaneous jig around them, a moment of joy to celebrate near perfection on the basketball court. At the bench

Travieso was mobbed. "They were touching me," he said later. "They were like, 'Damn, you're still burning.'"

•

For John Calipari, in one sense, Camby's collapse represented no more than a crisis that needed response. While pleading, "Marcus, come on Marcus!" he had no time to calculate. There was only time to react. When he left the game behind and climbed into that ambulance, Calipari wasn't asking for a referendum on his character; he was merely making a snap judgment.

And yet, there was something defining about the incident. In an ultracompetitive business, Calipari had rocketed to the top. While impressed with the ascent, many people felt that it carried a taint. Each of the two big national stories involving Calipari's Minutemen—John Chaney's press conference attack, and the printing of player grades— suggested to some that there were hidden reasons behind UMass's success. They felt Calipari was too belligerent with referees, that he didn't care about academics, that basically he was *too* competitive. His "teaching life skills" seemed like mere spin control to his critics, who thought his true colors were revealed more by his description of his team playing as if a loss meant a trip to the electric chair. This was life or death to him, wasn't it?

Calipari stayed at the hospital all day. He sat in waiting rooms, talked to Camby, made the difficult calls back to Hartford, milked the doctors for every speck of information. The next morning he was back there early. He was on the uncomfortable Medevac plane to Worcester, where he comforted Janice Camby, prodded more doctors, began kidding with his star. Along the way, he wrote an open letter to the people of Olean that appeared in the *Olean Times Herald* on Wednesday, January 17:

"On behalf of the University of Massachusetts, our basketball program and Marcus Camby—thank you. In a time of crisis, good people come together. The good people of Olean came together in a big way to help all of us through a scary situation.

"Let me personally thank Jim and Cindy Baron[1] and all of the officials at St. Bona who visited the hospital numerous times to make sure we were taken care of.

"I've always been fond of your school and your town—now I add your hospital to the list. Thanks to all of you."

Calipari never mentioned the letter to the press.

On Wednesday night, January 17, Calipari returned to the sideline when UMass took on a 9–4 Rhode Island team at the Mullins Center. He knew at the time that Camby was scheduled for release the next day. All his bottled–up energy poured out during the game. Stamping his shoes on the Mullins parquet, leaping into the air in disbelief, dispensing his "aggressive counseling" in large doses, earning a technical foul, he was back to being Coach Cal.

"I love coaching," he said that night. "I love this. This is not work for me. My high school buddies say that I've never worked a day in my life. I laugh and I say, 'You know, you're right: I haven't.'"

Asked to summarize the last few days, Calipari said, "I gave my daughters a big hug and cuddled with them a little bit. It's scary seeing someone you love laying on the floor. You don't know if he's about to pass away on you. . . .This has been an interesting thing for all of us. Spirituality. You end up saying, 'Hey man, this is bigger than us.'"

The team flew out on Friday for games against Duquesne and Pittsburgh, right in the heart of Calipari's roots. Ellen, Erin and Megan Calipari were on the flight: John asked them to come because he wanted them to see his grandmother (Nunny—of the famed pasta sauce), who had been diagnosed with cancer.[2] Marcus Camby was not on the flight. Though released the day before, he was forced to wear a portable brain-wave monitor for two more days. On Saturday, while the Minutemen were beating Duquesne behind Travieso's scoring surge, Camby flew out to Pittsburgh with team academic coordinator Dave Glover, and quietly checked into the team hotel.

On Sunday, Calipari interrupted the family trip to fly to New York. Serving as the studio guest of Pat O'Brien, he was Mr. Smooth at halftime of the CBS national telecast of the UConn–Syracuse game. Playing journalist, he conducted an interview with Camby, who spoke from his hotel room in Pittsburgh.

**Calipari:** "Marcus, how about how our players have responded to you being out and then having you back. How has that been?"

**Camby:** "They've been playing great. I realized that I'd have to get back in time in order to get some more playing time. Thank God they've been playing so well. But it feels great to be out of the hospital and to be here with the team."

**Calipari:** "You went to the mall today. Did you buy anything?"

**Camby:** "Window shopping, you know."

**Calipari:** "You buy me anything?"
**Camby:** "I bought you an Armani suit."

Two nights later, on January 21, Calipari returned to Fitzgerald Field House on the campus of the University of Pittsburgh. As a boy growing up in Moon Township, he used to come here for his first exposure to Division I basketball. Now he was back with the Number 1 team in the nation.

Camby, with a couple of days of light practice under his belt, wanted to play that night. During the day, Calipari had been on the phone with Janice Camby back in Hartford. She said it was fine for her son to play. Calipari had also spoken to Joel Gore, the head cardiologist back at the UMass Medical Center in Worcester; Gore, too, gave his go–ahead.

There were plenty of incentives to play Camby. By now UMass was the only undefeated team left in Division I, an honor that Calipari wanted to maintain. He knew that Pittsburgh was going to be a tough challenge. Their 8–5 record included a one–point loss at the buzzer to mighty Georgetown. At Fitzgerald Field House in particular, the Panthers were tough: 54–10 over the past six years. Calipari had the top player in the country at his disposal.

He didn't use him.

In the early going, UMass fell behind, 15–3. Camby looked up at Calipari. The coach watched the game. When reserve center Inus Norville fouled out with 4:46 left in regulation, Camby turned to the coach and said, "Put me in." Calipari replied, "Yeah, right."

At the buzzer, with the score tied at sixty–six, Pittsburgh guard Andre Alridge's leaning jumper hung on the rim for a tantalizing second, then fell off.

In overtime, with Camby cheering in animated fashion from the bench, UMass won again.

•

On Saturday, January 27, UMass PA announcer Jack O'Neill introduced a starting lineup of guards Edgar Padilla and Carmelo Travieso, forwards Dana Dingle and Donta Bright, and then the center: a six–eleven junior from Hartford, Connecticut, Number 21, "Mar–cussssssss Cam–beeeeeeeeeee."

While Camby started jumping and bumping in UMass's frenetic team mosh pit, Calipari stood on the corner of the bench clapping his hands. The packed Mullins Center crowd stood and yelled. Janice Camby looked up to the rafters. Presumably, a host of relieved agents smiled.

Camby was tentative at first ("It felt like my freshman year all over again—my palms were getting sweaty"), then explosive. He hit six of eight shots from the field, seven of eight from the line, and netted the thousandth point of his career along the way. Defensively he was a menace, tying a UMass single–game record with nine blocks. Just thirteen days after the collapse at St. Bonaventure, he led the Minutemen over the very same Bonnies, 72–47.

"I felt great," a beaming Camby said afterward. "I got the starting nod. The place was going crazy. I had a lot of blocks. I scored my thousandth point. It's been a great day for me."

UMass was 18–0, on top of the world. The crisis was over.

# 15: "That Team is a Team"

February 1–22, 1996

Back in the eighties when UMass basketball was mired in the muck, nobody dared to dream about national exposure. Even getting coverage from the state's largest newspaper—*The Boston Globe*—was unrealistic. Television never flashed its hot lights in Amherst. For two years, there was not even any *local* radio coverage.

As the 1996 calendar turned to February, UMass basketball became the hottest sports story in the country. The extensive coverage in Boston papers, which often double and triple–staffed games, represented only a small part of the equation. Malcolm Moran of *The New York Times* had become a regular at The Mullins Center. Maryann Hudson of the *Los Angeles Times* came east for several days to do a story on Marcus Camby. (Peering up at him before one practice, Hudson said, "Do you hate this attention? You're already kind of a rock–star guy.")

The magazine world descended. Mike Lupica wrote a profile of John Calipari in *Esquire*, quoting one anonymous coaching rival as saying, "There's just something about Calipari; he's like a moth moving toward the light. And he knows how to say all the right things." *Newsweek* staffer Claudia Kalb held her tape recorder up to the treadmilling Calipari in a hotel health club and got a spray of sound bites. *College Sports Magazine* lured the distinguished Curry Kirkpatrick into spending a few days shadowing the UMass coach.

Books? Dick (Hoops) Weiss of the *New York Daily News* became a frequent companion of Calipari's on the road. The author of as–told–to autobiographies of Rick Pitino and Dick Vitale, Weiss had found another lively subject.

Television lights blazed: at practice, on campus, in airports. Before the year was out, UMass would have twenty–five games on national TV. The Minutemen were the darlings of the college basketball world.

In a lot of ways they were an irresistible story. They had the best of both worlds. They were on top, yet they elicited people's sympathies, especially after Camby's collapse. As Ron Chimelis of Springfield's *Union–News* aptly observed, they were simultaneously the favorite and the underdog.

UMass's appeal stemmed in part from its spectacular rise to the top. The team's rags–to–riches theme was mirrored by its star presences. Calipari was the gym rat from Moon whose father still hoisted bags for USAir. Camby was the high school unknown whose boyhood home—Building 61—was now boarded up in Hartford.

Camby's recent fainting saga boosted the team's popularity. America saw a kinder, gentler Calipari, and Camby had become the vulnerable star, the everyman who put a scare into the sporting public. It was impossible not to cheer his comeback. Beyond that, he came across as an utterly appealing hero: polite, soft–spoken, a quintessential team player on the court, a gentleman off of it. Asked during a national teleconference if he considered himself a role model, he replied, "Not really. I'm just twenty–one years old. I think a role model is someone who is older and wiser, and has done a little more with his life."

The team's considerable chemistry—the amorphous sports cliché of the nineties—also increased UMass's appeal. Camby's burgeoning talent notwithstanding, UMass was clearly not a team that overwhelmed opponents with its ability. The Minutemen weren't stockpiled with high school All–Americas or surefire NBA players. They were not a big team, not a strong team, not even a remarkably quick team. They had certain qualities, however, that made them stand out from the pack: a togetherness and a fighting spirit. The balance of the team was exquisite, featuring an inside game, an outside game, a shark–like tenacity on the boards, a voracious appetite for defense and an obvious enjoyment of each other's success.

Calipari's efforts to overcome human nature—to get individuals to subjugate their own egos for the greater good—seemed to be fully realized with this particular blend of personalities. He often said that he had never been around a group like this, a team that wanted success for themselves as much as he wanted it for them. He relished the team's unselfishness, its all–for–one willingness to heed the sign in the locker room: "It's amazing what gets done when nobody cares who gets the credit."

If one player embodied that spirit more than anyone, it was se-

*Dana Dingle (Photo by Kevin Gutting)*

nior Dana Dingle. The son of a Con Edison worker, Dingle grew up in the Bronx—prime recruiting terrain for The Big East. None of the teams in the league were interested, though. After all, Dingle was a six–six kid with no outside shot, average leaping ability and nothing particularly exciting in his game. By the end of his freshman year, though, he was starting. He played the game the way Calipari liked it, with a priority on defense and rebounding. Guarding everyone from shooting guards to centers, he was a position defender, almost never blocking shots or making steals, but constantly making the game hard for his man. Offensively, there was no flash at all. He didn't dunk, didn't shoot the three. All he did was work—hard picks, sharp cuts, non–stop effort on the offensive glass. The little–thing king, Dingle was at once UMass's most unheralded starter and its most durable; he played every game from the beginning of his freshman year on.[1] As a captain he was soft–spoken, setting his example by what he did on the court.

The team's preseason concerns about leadership had vanished entirely, replaced by what Calipari referred to as a "geese mentality": "Marcus leads for a while, and when he feels tired, he peels back and Donta takes over. When he gets tired, Dana takes a turn. Then Edgar and Carmelo...." Everyone benefited from the unselfishness, Calipari argued. Often he made the point by quoting one of his heroes, John F. Kennedy, "As the tide rises, all the boats rise."

If UMass's chemistry was intangible, it was also undeniable. On February 1, after the Minutemen had absolutely dismantled Temple, 59–35, in Philadelphia, Owls coach John Chaney stood before the media with his tie draped scarf–like over his neck, marveling at the Minutemen.

"That is the best team in terms of a team," Chaney said, holding his hand up to his mouth as if savoring the taste. "This is the best team in this country in terms of a team. We've seen a lot of great teams with great athletes, but as far as a team is concerned, that's a team out there. That's what you hope that someday you'll have—a great team, a team of players that look for each other, that feed off of each other. That's a great team. I don't think anybody else in the country [is comparable]. You see the Kentuckys with the great talent, and you see a lot of the others. But that team is a team."

As wins piled on top of wins, the once–unthinkable prospect of an undefeated season began to shimmer in the distance. Sure, Tyrone Weeks had stated that an undefeated mark was his goal as far back as December, but realistically the odds were overwhelmingly against such an achievement.

It had been five years since UNLV had posted Division I's last undefeated regular season, and those 1991 Runnin' Rebels had been beaten by Duke in the NCAA tournament. The last team to go the distance—winning the national title with an undefeated record—had been the Indiana Hoosiers back in 1976. Almost six thousand different Division I teams had opened seasons since then, including some of the greatest college basketball teams ever to take the court, and none had gone through a season without a blemish. Modern college basketball made it extremely difficult. Made–for–television matchups of elite non–conference foes had become pervasive. Many coaches realized that challenging schedules paid dividends: greater exposure, better recruiting, a toughening of the team. No one dived into this fray with greater fervor than Calipari, whose 1995–96 non–league schedule had looked masochistic back in November.

Further diminishing the chances of an undefeated year was the heightened pressure placed on Number 1 teams in the era of Vitale-esque hype. Media distractions were ample. Everyone wanted a piece of the action. The same questions (Do you feel pressure to go undefeated? Would a loss be beneficial? How does it feel to chase history?) were posed day after day after day.

It was easy to be softened by success, to believe the press clippings, to lose the fire that fueled the victories in the first place. Further, road games for top–ranked teams were minefields. For years, Calipari had stretched the truth by talking about UMass being the most important game on every opponent's schedule, but this year it was undeniable. Beating Number 1 represented a chance to be King for a Day, to head the highlights on ESPN's SportsCenter, to earn top billing in *USA Today*. For a lot of schools it was a rare opportunity. Spurred by overflow crowds, teams often reached to their highest level of performance. When UMass visited Xavier, the basketball–crazed city of Cincinnati[2] played host to a Number 1 team for the first time. Before the game, *The Cincinnati Enquirer* quoted guard Lenny Brown as saying, "Ever since high school, you just dream about playing a team like this." Forward T.J. Johnson added, "This is why you play basketball. The Number 1 team coming into your gym? You can't ask for any more than that." In the build–up to UMass's game at Virginia Tech, students pitched more than one hundred tents, and spent five days in line for tickets. Somewhere down the road, it was inevitable that what John Calipari called "the bulls–eye on our backs" was going to get hit. Wasn't it?

In his "From the Editor" column in the March issue of *College Sports Magazine*, Norb Garrett discussed the difficulty in posting a perfect record in the modern era. His piece never even mentioned the Minutemen, no doubt assuming that by the time the issue hit the stands in mid–February, their record would be tarnished. "It'll take a miracle for any team to go undefeated in years to come," Garrett concluded.

For UMass, the wins came in all shapes and sizes. On February 1 in Philadelphia, the Minutemen held Temple to a startling twelve points by halftime in a major blowout. Three days later, facing Xavier in the packed Cincinnati Gardens before a national television audience on ABC, the Minutemen needed a three–pointer by Edgar Padilla in the closing seconds to force overtime, where, as always, they prevailed. Playing lowly Fordham at Madison Square Garden, the Minutemen somehow trailed late in the first half after surrendering a startling 17–0 run, then kicked into gear for an easy win. Back home on February 11, they looked invincible again while burying Temple by twenty–nine. From the Green Room where he had once torn into Calipari, John Chaney again heaped on the praise with his signature style: "You've got five fingers, they've got six holes [that need to be plugged]. You don't stop a team with balance. And [Camby's] smart enough that when you tie his ass up, he kicks it out to someone who's having breakfast, lunch and supper on your ass. And he knocks it down. So you come back to the bench and scratch your head."

Back home against a weak La Salle team on February 15, UMass put together perhaps its worst half of the nineties, committing thirteen largely unforced turnovers and surrendering a bevy of open shots. Down eight points at the break, the Minutemen rallied for an emphatic 70–53 win. Two days later, they crushed Virginia Tech, 74–58, spoiling the tent–city enthusiasm of a 19–2 team then ranked a best–ever Number 10 in the country.

Sometimes the Minutemen looked awesome; sometimes they looked lucky. While their record swelled to a gaudy 25–0, they had been tied or down at halftime in ten games. In five separate games they had trailed by double–digit deficits, once by as many as sixteen points. Three times—all on the road—they were taken to overtime. Always they found a way. The shots they absolutely had to hit, they hit. The shots that opponents absolutely had to miss, they missed. It was easy to feel a sense of destiny.

No, John Calipari kept insisting, there was not any pressure. Being undefeated was not the goal: winning the national title was. If going undefeated was a "byproduct" (as Calipari termed it) of winning the NCAA tournament, so be it. Besides, he insisted, UMass was only focused on the matter at hand. "If you worry about the past, you put pressure on yourself, and it's not fun," he said. "If you worry about the future, what you're going to do a week from now, two weeks, it's not fun, because that's where stress comes in. All you want to worry about is today. That's all. Just be in today. As long as you're in today, you're happy."

Still, it was impossible to disregard the attention that UMass's magical season was generating. On February 15, *USA Today* ran a front-page feature about the Minutemen that was headlined "March Toward Perfection."

Four days later, Malcolm Moran wrote in *The New York Times*, "No matter what happens in March, regardless of whatever future the coach may have at UMass or in the National Basketball Association, Calipari may well look back one day to a snowy winter in Amherst and a single-minded group that became the team of his life."

The next day, February 20, Bob Ryan of *The Boston Globe* opined, "If UMass pulls off this unbeaten season/national championship parlay, it will be the greatest one-season achievement in the history of the sport."

That night, the Minutemen took on a surprising Rhode Island team that sported a 15–8 record after going 7–20 season the year before. Former UMass star Al Skinner had molded a young and fiery group into a winner. This game, he knew, was the Rams' big opportunity to step forward on the national stage.

URI generally plays its home games on the school's Kingston campus in old Keaney Gym, which seats six thousand and seldom fills. The UMass game, which fit the category of special event, had been moved to the Providence Civic Center. All 13,106 seats had been sold out for weeks. The fans saw a tight, riveting drama: basketball game as cause.

How tough were the Rams that night? Three of their *cheerleaders* performed with knee braces. Six–seven freshman forward Antonio Reynolds galvanized the crowd by soaring high to block two of Marcus Camby's shots, and by positively suppressing a third, though he was called for a questionable foul on the play.

Emotions ran hot. Calipari picked up a technical foul. Donta Bright got one for ripping the ball out of Reynolds's hands and flinging the freshman to the floor in the process. The game swung back and forth. The Minutemen were on the ropes as they had been so often, clinging to the narrowest of leads. Camby was playing with four fouls. Up 67–66 as the clock ticked under 1:20, UMass desperately needed a basket. The Rams dug in on defense. The crowd roared.

Bright twisted free and flipped up a shot that caromed high off the rim. All ten players on the court seemed to lean in and up, banging together in a single-minded quest. Camby outreached the pack and tapped the ball just over Reynolds's outstretched hand. It banked off the backboard, hit the front rim and popped up again, unleashing another furious surge. Powerfully positioned in front of the basket, Tyrone Weeks sprang his 260 pounds upward and gently tipped the ball into the hoop. Once again, the Minutemen prevailed.

A disappointed but gracious Al Skinner could only shake his head. "It's rare that you have a team that doesn't have the super talent, for them to play as well together as they do," he said. "John has to be elated about having the opportunity to coach a team like this."

It was late February. UMass was 26–0. There were just three games left in the regular season.

•

On Thursday morning, February 22, Spencer Christian concluded his national weather forecast with the words, "Next, the secret weapon of an unbeatable basketball team—a super coach—when Good Morning America continues."

The camera panned to the UMass Minutemen standing in a group at the foul line, and then focused in on the tall guy in the middle, who said, "Hi, I'm Marcus Camby of the undefeated and Number 1–ranked University of Massachusetts Minutemen." As the camera pulled back, the team shouted in unison, "Good Morning America."

After the commercial break, host Charles Gibson began from the studio: "When a new basketball coach arrived at the University of Massachusetts eight years ago, the team had suffered through ten straight losing seasons. But it's been a Cinderella story ever since that day. Now UMass is rated Number 1 in the country. The Minutemen are undefeated. Their record is 26 and 0 through Tuesday night, although they had a bit of a scare in a nailbiter that ended in a narrow victory over Rhode Island. Just three more wins, and the Minutemen will be the first college basketball team to post an undefeated regular season since 1991. The man who has led this remarkable turnaround is *the* hot coach in college basketball, UMass coach John Calipari. And he's joining us this morning from Amherst, Massachusetts. John, it's been quite a ride this year. . . ."

Calipari was masterful. Dapper in a designer sweater, he smiled at the camera while pushing all the right buttons: Refuse to Lose, teaching life skills, live for today. Asked by Gibson if he believed this kind of turnaround were possible back when he took over the program, Calipari said, "We had to do a lot of dreaming. Charlie, we talked about being unrealistic. Because when you're realistic, too many barriers are put on you. We talk about it with our team all the time and our staff—'Let's be unrealistic. Let's try to get this thing where no one thought it could go.'"

•

Ten minutes up the road from Amherst in South Deerfield, six–year–old Luke Morton sat transfixed in front of a television set watching Calipari work his magic. UMass, after all, was Luke's team. His father, Michael, had gotten a couple of tickets to recent games, and Luke had been electrified by the excitement. He went down to courtside at one point and high–fived the Minuteman mascot. After one of the games he got an autograph and some kind words from his hero, Donta Bright.

Michael Morton left for work that morning with a sense of mission. A mechanic at Bay State Elevator, he had to make a service stop at the Mullins Center. While there, he wanted to see if a friend of his had been successful in getting Luke's basketball signed by the Minutemen. Upon arrival, Morton discovered that his friend hadn't been able to get the ball in the right hands quite yet. So acting on a suggestion, Morton nervously walked up to the basketball office.

Sure, Calipari's secretary Bonnie Martin said, the coach would be happy to say hello, but he was unavailable for another half–hour. That's when the idea flashed in Morton's mind. He flew out of the office, bounded into his truck and sped back to South Deerfield to get Luke.

The eldest of Michael and Barbara Morton's three children, Luke had seemed like a perfectly healthy boy until the previous summer. He was a spirited kid with a passion for computers. After logging off at night, Luke usually had his father read him a story and often fell asleep next to him.

One night in June, Michael was awakened by some piercing cries from Luke. He complained of a terrible headache. After a while the pain vanished, but the following night the headache came back. And then again the next.

At first, doctors diagnosed a sinus infection and prescribed antibiotics. For a few days the medication proved effective. Then with a vengeance the headaches returned. One morning, Luke got up with his hand on his head and started vomiting. Something was terribly wrong.

On July 18, 1995, Barbara Morton took Luke in for a CT Scan. At work that day, Michael knew that no news was good news. For the longest time he heard nothing. Then came the call. Luke had a brain tumor.

"At that point I kind of lost it," Michael said. "That's when the nightmare began."

The months that followed were tinged with the surreal. Hospitalized in Boston, Luke had two brain operations that left a huge scar crisscrossing the back of his skull. Chemotherapy made his hair fall out. Michael and Barbara did everything they could to put on a brave face.

Thank God, they said again and again, for this kid's spirit. When squadrons of doctors kept coming in and leaving Luke their business cards, he wanted to give them something back. So Michael's sister, Lani, had some cards made up: "Lucas Paoa Morton," they said. "PC Wiz." There was a picture of balloons in the upper right hand corner, his address and phone number down below. Every doctor got a card and walked out of the room with a smile.

Winter brought the exhilarating peace of remission. Luke returned home to South Deerfield, gathered some energy and developed an abiding passion for UMass basketball. So when Michael careened into the driveway on that February day and told Luke to get ready to meet John Calipari, the boy's face filled with joy.

Calipari was "absolutely great," according to Michael Morton. He gave Luke a picture of Marcus Camby, invited him back to practice that night, and signed his ball: "To Luke, Refuse to Lose, John Calipari."

Floating home in the truck, father and son discussed the meaning of "Refuse to Lose."

"We talked about it a lot," Michael said. "Killing the bad cells. Luke's got that attitude."

Before practice that night, the rest of the Minutemen signed the ball. Luke got to shoot baskets with Camby. His hero, Donta Bright, came over to him and said, "How you doing, big fella?"

Luke came ready with his business cards, each one addressed to a member of the Minutemen in big, blue, six-year-old scrawl. There was no telling when a player on the Number 1 team in the nation might need a PC Wiz.

For the longest time, Luke couldn't sleep that night, but not because of headaches. "He was just lit," Michael said the following day. "It was a special night for both of us. He'll remember this the rest of his life."

With an unknown prognosis and a smile on his face, Luke finally fell asleep, his arms around a basketball.

# 16: "It's Been a Pleasure, as Always"

February 24, 1995
Amherst, Massachusetts

P ublicly, John Calipari doesn't subscribe to the idea of big games. He will build up the most undermanned opponent as a potential threat. The most imposing of foes—the Kentuckys and North Carolinas—are "only big if we win." But long before the 1995–96 season tipped off—far in advance of the Number 1 ranking, the chase for history, the whole magic carpet ride that the year had become—one game stood out in his mind: February 24, at home, against George Washington University.

If Calipari had become college basketball's Superman, Mike Jarvis carried Kryptonite. If Calipari was Achilles, Jarvis was his heel. There was no coach in America who stuck harder in Calipari's craw. Maybe John Chaney had gone ballistic one afternoon. Maybe Jim Calhoun threw darts from Connecticut. But the shiny pate and hard scowl of the George Washington coach was the most rankling sight of all, for one simple reason: Jarvis had Calipari's number.

In some ways, Jarvis had been part of the equation all along. The unconscious intertwining of his life with the UMass basketball story was filled with an unusual resonance.

Jarvis's accent, sardonic wit and competitive drive were rooted deeply in Massachusetts. He had spent the first forty–five of his fifty years in and around Cambridge. As an African–American youngster, Jarvis appreciated the multicultural sophistication of the town, an enclave of tolerance which stood in sharp contrast to the tense race relations in much of Boston.

In that most academic of communities, Jarvis developed a passion for basketball. He used to watch the great Celtic teams of the late fifties and early sixties practice at the Cambridge YMCA, just a few blocks from his home. In 1956, his older brother Dick took Jarvis to his first Celtics game. Purchasing tickets at the door for $1.50, they watched Bill Russell's professional debut. Many a night, Jarvis would go to bed "counting Russell's rebounds on the old wooden radio." To this day he describes then–Celtic coach Red Auerbach as his idol.

Jarvis was a hard–nosed point guard at what was then called Rindge Tech. In his senior year of 1962, he helped lead his team to the city's "Tech Title." Later that year, he and three teammates accepted an invitation from UMass coach Matt Zunic to try out for a scholarship.

Like Red Auerbach, Zunic graduated from George Washington University, a school Mike Jarvis hadn't even heard of at the time. Zunic played briefly in the NBA before becoming a fiery coach in New England. He led Boston University to unprecedented heights, capped by an NCAA tournament appearance in 1959, when his senior point guard and captain was Jack Leaman. Now, three years later, he had just coached UMass to its first–ever NCAA appearance, with Leaman serving as his first–year assistant. He was looking for players who would continue the success.

Jarvis remembers Zunic as "nice and very hospitable." He and his teammates changed at the Curry Hicks Cage, and then played for three hours with other scholarship hopefuls under Zunic's watchful eye. They ate dinner on campus, stayed overnight and played again the next day.

Mike Jarvis was not offered a scholarship. "And rightfully so," he said thirty–four years later. "I was not at that level. Plus, they weren't offering a lot of scholarships to black kids at a predominantly white university."[1]

Instead, Jarvis went to Chamberlayne Junior College for a year before transferring to Northeastern University in Boston. There, after a mandated year off as a transfer, he became eligible to play varsity as a sophomore in the fall of 1964. When the season began, Jarvis was thrilled to be playing college basketball. That feeling didn't last long, as he found himself languishing on the end of the bench. Jarvis felt that he deserved to play. Coach Dick Dukeshire felt otherwise.

"I don't think there's been a better coach in New England," Jarvis now says. "He had great command of the fundamentals. But at the time, when you're a hotshot, it's tough to sit on the bench. You always blame it on someone else. You blame it on the coach."

Writing the original script for the cocky sophomore point guard battling his coach and parting company in mid–season—played out in different venues in the years ahead by Rick Pitino and John

Calipari—Jarvis dropped out of school. He went to work for his brother's Cambridge eatery, Dick's Fish and Chips. Every day he came in, donned his apron, whipped up a buttery batter and dropped French Fries in hot vats of oil. The job gave him plenty of time to think.

"Reality started setting in," he says. "I wasn't going to be a professional basketball or baseball player, which had always been my dream. It was then that I decided to be a coach."

Jarvis visited Dukeshire that summer and asked for a second chance. He got it. Dutifully taking notes after practice for the next couple of years, Jarvis had found his calling.

Unlike the fast–track path traveled by Calipari, who landed his job at UMass at age twenty–nine, Jarvis toiled for years as an assistant at Northeastern and Harvard, while teaching physical education at his high school alma mater, now known as Cambridge Rindge and Latin School, or CRLS. In 1978–79, while Division I college basketball was seeing the debut of Rick Pitino as a head coach (at Boston University), the debut of John Calipari as a player (at North Carolina–Wilmington) and the swan song of Jack Leaman (at UMass), Jarvis landed his first head coaching job: at CRLS. He did all right for himself, going 27–0. It didn't hurt to have a sophomore center named Patrick Ewing.

After seven years of coaching and seventeen of teaching at CRLS, Jarvis finally got the break he was looking for: a college head–coaching job. Like Pitino, Jarvis got his start at Boston University.

He coached the Terriers in 1985–1990, becoming the school's all–time winningest coach with a 101–51 record. During the first week of the 1988–89 season, Jarvis took his team back to the Curry Hicks Cage, where he had unsuccessfully tried out for a scholarship more than a quarter–century before. This time he found himself encountering a new UMass coach, John Calipari.

"I remember coaching against this young kid," Jarvis recalls. "And I remember he pulled this trick play on us. We were always late coming out of timeouts, and after one he had all of his players lined up on the baseline—our baseline. He had some home cooking with Atlantic 10 refs who were whistling for us to get back on the court before they inbounded the ball. So without thinking where we were going, we sprinted to our baseline, just as one of their players ran in the other direction for a long pass and a layup. I remember looking over at John and laughing, like, 'You got me this time.'"

Even so, Boston University won that night, 70–68. The first coaching loss in Calipari's career was administered by none other than Mike Jarvis.

In 1990, Jarvis moved away from Cambridge for the first time in his life. Accepting the head coaching position at GW, a team that had endured five straight losing years, including an infamous 1–27 in 1988–89 (the "1" against UMass in Calipari's first season), Jarvis told *The Washington Post* that he was reluctant to leave New England. "If I didn't do it now, I'd probably never do it," he said. "If I never did it, I'd wonder forever if I didn't shortchange myself."

Perhaps the turnaround that Jarvis engineered with GW was not yet as substantial as the one Calipari performed at UMass, but it was still impressive. He produced one winning season after another, leading the Colonials to the NCAA tournament for the first time in thirty-two years during the 1992–93 season, and then taking them back again the following year. In 1994–95, his team just missed, but Jarvis scored huge public–relations points with a classy interview on CBS right after the NCAA selections. Betraying no bitterness at all, he came off with an apple–pie smoothness and humility that elicited just a trace of a smirk from Calipari, who watched the show with his team and media members from his living room in Shutesbury.

Theirs had become a rivalry with an edge. Filled with physical play on the court and snippy comments off of it, GW–UMass was one spicy soup. In the decade of the nineties, the Minutemen had become the dominant force in the Atlantic 10 conference and a legitimate national powerhouse. But head–to–head, mano–a–mano, where the true ego of college sports gets played out, Mike Jarvis had more than held his own against John Calipari.

In Jarvis's first year, 1990–91, GW took two of three games from the Minutemen, including a one–point gut–churner in the A–10 Tournament. The following year, UMass's breakthrough NCAA season, the Minutemen posted a 30–5 record, but managed only a split with GW. Then the rivalry really started to heat up. In 1992–93, UMass swept the season series against GW for the only time in the Calipari era. The win in Washington was a 68–65 decision in which Mike Williams hit a three–pointer at the buzzer, then took a victory lap around the Smith Center, taunting the Colonial fans.

Emotions escalated during the 1993–94 season. First, GW visited the Mullins Center on January 22, at a time when the Minutemen were enjoying an all–time best Number 6 ranking in the AP poll. The

Colonials, a modest 8–6 at the time, completely took UMass out of its game and led throughout, by as many as fourteen points. UMass closed to 55–54 on a jumper by Williams with fifty–three seconds left. Then, on a call that would forever rankle Jarvis,[2] UMass got the ball back with twenty–three seconds remaining when Vaughn Jones got whistled for an offensive foul for backing into Williams at center court. The Minutemen won the game, 56–55, on a beautifully executed play that culminated with a Marcus Camby dunk in the last three seconds.

In the Green Room afterward, a composed Jarvis said to reporters, "Tell Calipari he's a lucky son of a bitch." The line was delivered in a lighthearted tone, but the words, not the tone, were what registered with Calipari when the comments were relayed.

Three weeks later, the Green Room hosted a far more charged atmosphere after another late UMass victory, when Temple coach John Chaney erupted at Calipari: "You don't say shit to officials without me being involved in it. You got a game that was given to you by the officials right here with GW on three bad calls, okay?"

Asked for a reaction to Chaney's outburst that week, Mike Jarvis said simply, "He's got a point."[3]

UMass then lost to GW in a highly physical game in late February. Calipari was infuriated when Jarvis called timeout with forty seconds left and a fourteen–point lead, then sent his starters back on the floor.

The rivalry only intensified in 1994–95. The teams met for the first time on February 4 in Washington. The Minutemen were ranked Number 1 and riding a then–school record sixteen–game winning streak, but they were suddenly without Camby, who had pulled his hamstring in the previous contest. Playing before Bill and Chelsea Clinton, UMass fell, 80–78. Calipari walked toward the GW bench to shake hands, only to see Jarvis at center court dancing with glee.[4]

The postgame interview sessions were filled with telling moments. In Calipari's portion, a Washington area television reporter asked, "After the Kansas game (UMass's only previous loss) you gave a lot of credit to Roy Williams for, you said, outcoaching you that day. What about this time around? Did Mike do the same type of thing?"

Calipari smiled and paused, before answering, "He did a good job. Obviously he's got his team playing well." There was no way he was giving Jarvis the edge.

Jarvis was asked about the impact that Camby's absence had on the game. His reply: "I hope that the University of Massachusetts will not use that as an excuse, because that's all it would be. When you're the Number 1 team in the country, as they are, and deservedly so, the reason why is because you have depth and you can overcome an injury....I hope that nobody takes away the credit from the GW Colonials because a player was missing from a basketball game."

Ten days later, they met again in Amherst, with Camby still sidelined. All during the game—the last in the career of Mike Williams as it turned out—Calipari was wound tight. He picked up a technical, barely avoided several others and later admitted that he should have been thrown out.

After the GW victory, Jarvis left the interview room saying, "Thank you very much. It has been a wonderful trip back to the great state of Massachusetts. God bless everybody, and the commonwealth."

The two coaches brought out some of the most vivid qualities in each other. GW's two wins in 1994–95 exposed a comically superstitious side of Calipari. In the game in Washington, the Minutemen unveiled some sleek black uniforms that the players loved. Calipari mothballed them for the season after the loss.[5] After the loss at home ten days later, Calipari ordered the baskets replaced at the Mullins Center. In the past he had often complained about "the tightest rims in America," but he hadn't changed them because UMass was undefeated in the building. New BPI 10,000 backboards had been sitting near the loading dock for weeks. The morning after the GW loss they were installed.

Now in 1996, Calipari wasn't worried about any superstition. He was worried only about Jarvis and the Colonials, who arrived with a 17–5 record.

Calipari often told his players and the media that he didn't want any excuses. "When you have an excuse," he said, "you wind up using it." Now there were none. UMass had a healthy Marcus Camby. The Minutemen were well rested, having not played for four days. They were home at the Mullins Center, where they sported a gaudy 38–1 record.

That "1," of course, had been against GW. The Colonials' mastery over the Minutemen had been shocking. In UMass's last seventy–one games, a stretch covering more than two years and including some of the heavyweights of the college basketball world in both regular season and postseason play, the Minutemen had posted a stunning 64–4 record against everyone except GW. Against the Colonials in the same period they were 0–3. And now, with the precious prospect of an undefeated season dangling before them, they were facing GW for their only scheduled meeting of the year.[6] Was it a big game? Only if UMass won.

•

Players generally appreciated John Calipari's intensely demanding style. Sure, a few had transferred away from UMass,[7] but by and large the young men who came to play for Calipari felt pleased with that decision. They understood that he would push them as they had never been pushed before. They knew that the experience would be difficult. But they came anyway—recognizing that players genuinely improved at UMass. Kids with ordinary talent like Derek Kellogg could become legitimate national performers. In Calipari's tenure at UMass, the Minutemen had consistently played better than their ability. With only one NBA player in his first seven years (Lou Roe, sitting on the end of the bench for the Detroit Pistons), and only Camby looking like a lock from the present squad, Calipari had taken his teams to the top.

Calipari's initial "warrior" Harper Williams had once said, "Hard ain't hard enough for him." Roe, the self–proclaimed "lazy sack of stones" in high school, had become a fierce worker under Calipari. Reserve center Jeff Meyer marvelled after his playing career at UMass that, "If he knows you can do something, he will do whatever it takes. If it means talking about your mother, grandfather, looking you in the eye and calling you the most worthless person in the world, he will get it out of you. He won't settle for less."

The current crew of players felt the same way. Just two weeks before the GW game, Edgar Padilla, a player who had been the recipient of some of Calipari's most ferocious "aggressive counseling," said, "Sometimes you as a player think you can do so much, and that's about it. A lot of times Coach Cal sees you as a player where you never thought you could be. That's why he wants you to work harder than you think you can. It gets to a point where you get used to working at one pace: that's hard all the time."

In a politically correct era when educators and parents often accommodate and adjust and compromise, Calipari didn't. In an era when lots of coaches said you can't yell at players anymore, Calipari did routinely. Sometimes they yelled right back—at UMass it was okay. Calipari liked raw emotion. He coached with it, and he wanted his players to play with it. Paradoxically, Calipari—the most modern of coaches—was also a throwback, a screamer who set the bar high, and made his players rise to it. That's why they came to UMass. That's why they almost always seemed to play harder than other teams. That's why they won.

And yet, there was a flip side to his intensity that the players didn't always appreciate. Sometimes he was wound too tight. He could be too reactive. Just a year before, the players had considered it a huge triumph when they summoned the courage to tell Calipari that they didn't like it when he subbed them so quickly, because it made them tense on the court.

Truly, he had pulled back a fair bit in the 1995–96 season. For one thing, he didn't have a lot of depth. The players *had* to play through mistakes. For another, he had never had a group he liked so much. He trusted this team. There were no chemistry busters in the bunch. Sure, they needed to be pushed—always, there was human nature to overcome—but this group had a genuine appetite for hard work. Calipari had talked a lot in recent weeks about the need for him to retreat. After the Temple game on February 11, he said, "No longer am I challenging them. I'm steering the bus, that's all." The next day, on the Atlantic 10 teleconference, he elaborated, "You're trying to empower your team at some point. The game is now theirs. When they get in the NCAA tournament and huddle, it's got to be sincere. They've got to know each other. I'm not on the court with them."

•

The showdown with GW was set for Saturday at high noon on ESPN. Calipari hated noon games, because UMass had a history of subpar performances at that hour. He particularly despised early games at home. In his mind, it was critical to maintain his team's routine of a pregame shootaround five hours before tipoff. That meant getting up very early, and since the players lived in one of the high–rise dorms where Friday nights were far from quiet, there wasn't going to be a lot of sleep.

Making a snap decision on Friday, Calipari decided to shift the team's pregame breakfast from the school's Campus Center to a room at the Mullins Center. That way the team would be together all morning at the arena: the seven o'clock shootaround, the 8:30 breakfast, the build–up to the game. He had administrative assistant Brian Gorman notify university catering manager Vic Keedy, who scrambled to make the change.

When a couple of players straggled in a few minutes late to the shootaround, Calipari tried to bite his tongue; after all, ESPN commentators Ron Franklin and Clark Kellogg were on hand to glean some pregame material. At the breakfast, though, the tension broiling within the UMass coach found an outlet. "There are raisins in the oatmeal!" he thundered. "I don't like raisins in the oatmeal."

•

Mike Jarvis had taken the unusual step of arriving at UMass on Thursday for a Saturday game. His players, he explained, did not have any classes on Friday. He wanted his team to be rested and ready.

Just before gametime, with the full house at Mullins already churning, Jarvis had his game face on when he looked up and saw Calipari approaching, his hand outstretched. With the clock ticking inexorably down to 00:00, the two immaculately dressed men shook hands and retreated.

While the GW starters were introduced, the UMass students held newspapers in front of their faces in the time-honored "ho–hum" tradition. When the Minutemen were introduced, the place shook with noise. After "Mar–cussss Cam–beee," the UMass team jumped and bumped in trademark fashion, the controlled fury born three months earlier when the uncertain season began against Kentucky. Only Edgar Padilla opted out of the frenzy, hovering on the periphery, keeping his hand on Camby's back, maintaining his focus.

Larry Lembo, one of the most respected officials in the Atlantic 10, tossed the ball into the air. Camby soared to it, beating the seven–one, 296–pound Alexander Koul, and tapping it back to Dana Dingle. With confidence, the Minutemen set up their halfcourt offense. Padilla dribbled with his right hand while holding up his left to call a play, warding off pesky five–three freshman Shawnta Rogers with a well–placed hip. The Minutemen spread the floor. Then Padilla flipped the ball over his shoulder to Camby in the right corner. The UMass center stutter–stepped left and launched a twelve–footer. The ball came right back in his face—flicked away by Koul with an easy nonchalance. Yes, Camby recovered the ball, drove in and scored, but a message had been sent: the Colonials were ready. Two of Camby's first three shots were rejected by Koul, and the fourth was altered embarrassingly into the side of the backboard. Suddenly, it was shades of Big Country all over again. Rather than Bryant Reeves, the crew–cut Cowboy from Oklahoma State, Camby was now taking on the Beach Boy from Belarus, with his floppy black hair and a white headband. The results were the same—the strong wide–body center dominated. Displaying surprising agility, Koul hit seven of ten shots, while hounding Camby into a dreadful afternoon, eight of twenty–one.

Camby had plenty of company. Everyone on the UMass team came out tight and tentative. GW played with a fierceness from the start. By the first TV timeout, 4:10 into the game, the Colonials had a seven–point lead; by the second one, four minutes later, the score was 25–11. Then things got ugly.

In the first play out of the timeout, Carmelo Travieso had the ball on the left wing and brought it down in front of him. Defender Darin Green slapped at the ball. Replays showed clear contact with Travieso's forearm, but nothing egregious. When the ball was tied up, officials whistled a jump ball, giving GW possession. From the bench Calipari erupted, earning a technical foul. Two Vaughn Jones free throws made the score 27–11 with 11:38 left.

Forty seconds later, Padilla fed Donta Bright slashing to the hoop from the right side. Bright gathered the ball in, launched himself toward the hoop, and—for the second time in the game—missed a dunk.

On the other end, Darin Green was dribbling right when a whistle blew. Travieso was called for a reach–in foul.

Calipari couldn't believe it. How could his battle–tested team play with such softness? Never had a game he wanted so much started out so disastrously. How could this be happening? With veins bulging in his neck, Calipari shot forth a stream of vitriol while official Gene Monje got set to hand the ball to Green inbounding on the side opposite the UMass bench. Larry Lembo, standing on the side closer to Calipari, tooted his whistle to halt the game. Regarded as a communicator rather than a reactive ref, Lembo liked to let people know when they were pushing too far. He believed in warnings. Striding over to Calipari, he held up his hands in front of the UMass coach's chest, as if to say, "Chill out." Moments later, Lembo turned his back, retreated a couple of steps and got ready to resume officiating. Calipari offered one more comment, the whistle blew, and just like that, he was gone.

Remarkably, Calipari had never been kicked out of a game before.[8] But now, as the coach buttoned his blazer and headed down the runway, everything had come unglued: the good synergy, the positive physiology, the geese mentality, the life skills. The tide was going out, and all the boats were sinking. The undefeated season was plunging into the sand.

Sitting by himself in the UMass locker room, Calipari watched the

*When John Calipari got kicked out of the game against George Washington,*
*Bruser Flint took control. (Photo by Kevin Gutting)*

rest of the show on television with Bruser Flint once more in command of the team. The Minutemen made some noise late in the second half, whittling a twenty–three–point lead to nine, but ultimately fell, 86–76. GW outplayed UMass in every aspect of the game.

Mike Jarvis was first to the Green Room. He said that he and his players had enormous respect for the Minutemen. "With a real good feeling as a rival you can greet them in a friendly, positive way, knowing that you're going to do battle. I think that's what it's really all about. And then after the game, there are teams that run off the floor that don't show the kind of class that a UMass team does. They left the floor today the same way that they always do. They congratulate the other team just like they've done in the previous twenty–six wins. They've got nothing to be ashamed of. They should still be the Number 1 team in the country."

What was the secret to beating the Minutemen? "You've got to play harder than they do. That's almost impossible, but I think we might have done that today. They've had an unbelievably grueling season. When it's all said and done, as disappointed as they might be, they might look back and actually want to thank us, as crazy as that might sound."

Standing up to leave the podium, Jarvis smiled at the room full of reporters. "Hey listen," he said, "it's been a pleasure, as always, being in the great state of Massachusetts."

By the time UMass got to the Green Room, the atmosphere was subdued. Marcus Camby acknowledged that Koul had the upper hand all afternoon: "I just got outplayed today by a stronger guy. He had his way with me."

Travieso, the game's high scorer with twenty–three points, propped his chin in his hand and said, "Our goal was to get to the Meadowlands and perform there. This was just a game, and we lost. We've got to keep on going."

A slightly chastened Calipari said, "The officials did not play a part in this game. George Washington beat our brains in."

Watching the game on television, Calipari said that he got a "clearer view" of his team. "I think you get a little soft," he said. "I tell them all the time that publicity and notoriety are like poison. As long as you don't swallow it, you're okay. We've swallowed it.

"UMass basketball is playing like if you lose, you're going to the electric chair. Well guess what? It wasn't today. You didn't see the fire. You didn't see the emotion and passion."

Losing could have a positive effect, he acknowledged. "The good news is, there's no pressure. It's 'Play Ball.'"

Deep down, though, this loss stung as badly as any he had ever experienced. He acknowledged to his staff that for all the talk about an undefeated season being a "byproduct" of the team's ultimate goal, it had become a goal in its own right. People would look down at the history books, he said, and see the rare jewel of a spotless season shining next to the University of Massachusetts. To lose out on that hurt. To lose it to GW and Mike Jarvis, at home no less, was positively galling.

It was amazing how this year had turned out. Back in November, ninety–nine days ago, the Minutemen had last experienced a loss, somehow falling to the Converse All–Stars in an exhibition game. That night the prospects for the team looked bleak. Calipari was not kidding when he entered the locker room with the words, "Maybe, if we're lucky, we'll get to the NIT."

Since that night, the Minutemen had made a stunning surge through the world of college basketball. They had won beyond their wildest dreams. Everyone, it seemed, had become enamored of this team. Even Calipari had let go of the reins to watch.

Now though, all talk of empowerment and steering the bus was out the window. In Calipari's eyes, his team had committed the one unpardonable sin—they hadn't played hard enough. He responded as only he could. This time the first words out of his mouth in the locker room were these: "I'm taking this team back!"

# 17: "A Little Bit of a Funk"

February 28, 1996

Amherst, Massachusetts

U Mass had lasted at Number 1 for nine weeks, the longest stint since Duke's national championship squad in 1992. Before the new poll came out on February 26, it appeared likely that the reign was over and the Minutemen would fall to Number 2 behind Kentucky.

The Wildcats had pulverized all comers since the loss to UMass in November. They were 24–1, winners of twenty–three straight. Their average margin of victory in the streak was a staggering 25.1 points. Only twice had opponents come within ten. Rick Pitino's Wildcats looked every bit the team they were supposed to be all along: the over-whelming favorite to win the national title.

Still, Pitino lobbied aggressively for UMass to retain the Number 1 ranking. Speaking on ESPN Radio, Pitino said, "I wouldn't vote us Number 1, and I really mean it. I'm being very sincere when I say that, because they have only one loss. We have one loss. And they beat us. Why should they lose it?"

Two of the AP voters agreed with Pitino's logic and picked UMass at the top.

The other sixty–four voted for Kentucky.

•

After the loss to George Washington, Marcus Camby stated matter-of-factly, "I just feel sorry for St. Joe's."

Following a team meeting on Sunday and a couple of intensive practices on Monday and Tuesday, UMass was primed for action. St. Joseph's coach Phil Martelli recognized that he was jumping into peril. "UMass coming off a loss," he said in Monday's A–10 teleconference. "That should be fun."

As the last home game of the year, the St. Joe's contest was desig-nated "Senior Night." Continuing a Calipari tradition, the UMass coach put all of the seniors in the starting lineup. Two of them, Donta Bright and Dana Dingle, were starters anyway. The other three, Ted Cottrell, Giddel Padilla and Rigo Nuñez, had never started a game in their careers. Bit players in the big drama, they had scored a combined total of thirty–one points all season, a number exceeded by single–game totals achieved already by Bright, Marcus Camby and Carmelo Travieso. Of course, there was no significant risk in starting players who usually sit far down on the bench; they would only stay on the floor for a few minutes, and UMass would surely pummel the Hawks anyway.

Cottrell had managed to move quietly through the program, no small feat at UMass. At twenty–four years old (having taken a post-graduate year of prep school and then having red–shirted his first year of college), he was the team's senior statesman. A lean six–nine, he wore glasses and spoke very softly, lending him an almost scholarly air. Off the court, he had some rather pleasant quirks. He was the unofficial team barber. He enjoyed aerobics and mountain biking, and when the team traveled to Hawaii, he was the only brave soul to head out on a surfboard. On the road he played hours of electronic Sega games. On the court he had never panned out, one of few Calipari players not to blossom over the years. As a senior, he was actually getting less "garbage time" than he got as a freshman. His teammates liked to poke gentle fun at Cottrell, calling him "Pooky" because of his resemblance to a movie character, but they all liked his gentle spirit. It was hard not to.

Rigoberto Nuñez was an immensely popular player with his teammates and UMass fans. He was radiant Rigo, the emperor of enthusiasm. Off the court, he was the team's most uproarious comic, a quick–witted, offbeat and enormously uninhibited presence. During a team visit to Pittsburgh's Children's Hospital in 1995, Nuñez and his teammates were riding a large elevator down to the lobby. Two elderly women were also on board, one of whom whispered to the other through the elevator quiet, "These must be basketball players." Right on cue came Nuñez' deadpan response: "Nope, field hockey."

He was the school's Number 1 fan, a towel–swirling maniac on the bench at basketball games and an outrageous supporter of other teams on campus. At everything from swim meets to, yes, field hockey games, Nuñez maintained a non–stop banter with his impossibly loud voice, cadenced with a Dominican accent. Watching the baseball team

*The incomparable Rigo Nuñez (Photo by Kevin Gutting)*

play Harvard one spring, Nuñez banged a stone against metal bleachers and got fans to sing Queen's anthem, "We Will Rock You." He offered his opinion of the Ivy Leaguers: "They've been pampered for too
long. Whip 'em now!" When the Harvard hurler faked a pickoff throw,
Nuñez bellowed, "Tricks are for kids. We're men! Minutemen!" When
another Crimson pitcher had trouble throwing strikes, Nuñez roared,
"He's getting wild! Soon he'll be hanging with Clint Eastwood in the
West." On it went without interruption for nine innings.

He was serious about basketball. A gangly six–seven with long arms
and springs in his feet, Nuñez had very little in the way of an offensive
game. Through his first three seasons as a walk–on, he had been used
by Calipari partly for defensive help, and mostly as an emotional sparkplug. He often galvanized the team and the crowd with his spirited
play. For his senior year he was given a scholarship—in part because
the team had a recruiting shortfall—but ironically enough, he, like
Cottrell, was getting less playing time than he did in previous years.
On a team whose chemistry was so good, where the intensity almost
always seemed to be there, the need for an energizing force had been
reduced.

For Giddel Padilla, starting on Senior Night was a proud moment.
As he was escorted onto the floor by his parents Mariano and Milca,

Giddel knew that he was nearing the end of an intriguing basketball odyssey.

Back in Puerto Rico, Giddel had been the first Padilla to play ball. He was the first star, the first to bring acclaim to the determined family with the two deaf parents. Even as he taught the game to his younger brother Edgar, Giddel was hatching dreams—he would play in college, then in the NBA.

Real life had not kept pace with the dreams. After moving to Massachusetts and starring at Springfield's Central High School, Giddel began a zig–zagging journey of disappointment: chasing a star at UNLV for a few months, sitting on the end of the UMass bench as a walk–on for the second half of the 1992–93 season, quitting the team the following fall when Edgar arrived as a scholarship player. Lacking a real outside game, Giddel had not been able to make the tough transition from six–three forward in high school to six–three shooting guard in college. Though he was a scrappy defender, his offensive game was still best around the basket—a tough place to play at his height. Further, he had alienated people with his brashness. While he felt that John Calipari had misled him about opportunities for playing time, he knew that Calipari didn't trust him, either. And watching his younger brother become a standout was a mixed blessing.

In the summer of 1995, Giddel rediscovered his love for the game when his tip–in basket for Bayamón won the Puerto Rican Superior League championship before fifteen thousand fans. Suddenly, he realized that he wanted to play for UMass during his senior season—even though he knew it meant a year spent buried on the bench. So he asked Edgar to make the awkward trip to Calipari's office to plead his case.

The season had played out mostly as Giddel had expected. Despite working hard in practice, he had played only twenty–four minutes all season, exclusively inconsequential time at the end of long–decided games. Though he felt sure he could help the team, he never complained. After all, a year ago he had been playing intramurals. Sometimes on the road, he would step into a fancy Hyatt or Marriott and joke with first–year assistant coach Ed Schilling (who had been coaching at the high school level the year before), "Is this paradise, or what?"

True, there were times Giddel's feistiness had flashed to the surface, bringing him to the front porch of Calipari's doghouse. In one particularly physical practice, he got into a scrap with Marcus Camby. Infuriated, Calipari called the whole team off the floor, muttering, "He doesn't know how expendable he is."

Deep down, though, Calipari knew that Giddel had been a hidden part of the team's success. The emergence of Carmelo Travieso as a star–quality player had been facilitated in no small part by daily practice duels with Giddel. No one on the team could push Travieso as hard. The day before the Xavier game in Cincinnati, Giddel stole the ball from Travieso on three straight scrimmage possessions and went in for dunks. In the overtime game the next day, Giddel, as usual, sat for the entire contest.

On February 14, Edgar Padilla gave his brother a Valentine's card, telling him he was glad to be on the team with him. Now, during introductions two weeks later, Edgar came out to hug Giddel, whose arms were slung around the shoulders of their parents. Mariano, wearing a gray suit and glasses, and Milca, standing tall in a blue skirt and blazer, were out on the court with their sons, while daughter Millie cried happily in the stands.

For the first time in so long, this was Giddel's moment. On his twenty–third birthday, he was getting the starting nod. He had no illusions; he would play for a couple of minutes, then join Cottrell, Nuñez and freshman walk–ons Andy Maclay and Ross Burns for a long night of sitting. The starting crew played for the first two minutes and thirty–nine seconds, holding serve against the Hawks at 2–2. Then Calipari went to the bench for his usual lineup. Edgar and Giddel Padilla, passing in the night, exchanged a high five.

•

On the night when the Minutemen were determined to put the awful performance against GW behind them, they played even worse. The guard play, brilliant for most of the year, was positively dreadful. Carmelo Travieso and Edgar Padilla each shot one of eight from the field. From the foul line they combined for an embarrassing two of nine. Padilla, leading the league in both assists and steals and sporting a stunning assist/turnover ratio of 2.72/1, dished out two assists on this night, while committing five turnovers. It was Converse All–Stars time once again. From the bench, Giddel Padilla watched somberly, chin in hand.

As unthinkable as it seemed, UMass was trailing, 58–55, with 34.4 seconds left. The Minutemen had blown one precious opportunity after another, missing five of eight free throws in the last 1:06. Now the game seemed lost. John Calipari looked on in a mixture of fury and disbelief. The capacity crowd sat stunned as St. Joe's got set to inbound the ball.

Calipari had just inserted Rigo Nuñez back in the game, hoping that his long arms and frenetic style could wreak a little havoc. In the pack of eight players struggling for position before the ball was inbounded, Nuñez vigorously moved his arms around St. Joe's guard Terrell Myers. There was plenty of jostling and bumping. Then Nuñez went down to the floor, thoughtfully rubbing his head as the whistle blew. There were several seconds of confusion while the three referees conferred. Was it a foul on Nuñez, sending Myers to the line, or the other way around? Calipari and St. Joe's coach Phil Martelli glared at the refs. Ultimately, official Thom Corbin came striding over to the scorer's table with an explanation that absolutely shocked Martelli: not only was the foul on Myers, it was a flagrant foul— meaning that Nuñez would shoot free throws, and then UMass would get possession.

Had Calipari's squeaky wheel just received the ultimate shot of grease?

For a while it looked as if the controversial call wouldn't matter. Nuñez missed the first free throw and hit the second, closing the gap to 58–56. Then UMass, which had been missing all manner of shots, continued the trend. With eight seconds left, Padilla's tying bid rimmed out. So did Donta Bright's tip. The ball was batted around and flew toward the foul line. Bright grabbed it with his back to the basket, turned around, and let fly.

This time the ball sailed right into the hoop.

Overtime was another epic struggle. After an ugly turnover, Padilla was briefly benched in favor of freshman Charlton Clarke. UMass twice fell behind, twice came back. Up 67–66 with 16.6 seconds left, the Minutemen had a couple of chances to extend the lead. Padilla missed two free throws, then got another chance after a big offensive rebound by Camby. This time he hit one of two for a 68–66 lead. The Minutemen had to hold their collective breath as Terrell Myers, the player called for the controversial flagrant foul, launched a three–pointer at the buzzer. It was dead on line, but smacked hard off the back rim. UMass had survived.

An incensed Martelli raced onto the court after Corbin, but the official was whisked away by UMass security. Afterward in the Green Room, Martelli looked composed. He said that his team was not jobbed by the officials, blaming UMass's staggering thirty–two offensive rebounds instead. Asked specifically about the call, he said, "[Nuñez] may have to go to L.A. for the Academy Awards."

In a stunned St. Joe's locker room, Myers's voice shook as he said that he was sure Nuñez had taken a dive. "Basically he was holding me," Myers said. "I pushed his arm. He fell like he was trying to get an Oscar, and the ref fell for it. It's the worst call I've ever seen in college basketball."

"He definitely pushed me," Nuñez said. "They're saying I took a dive, I should be in Hollywood. I wish I was that lucky."

When John Calipari took the podium, he opened up with a tacit admission of the monumental gift: "It's unfortunate how we got back in it there, but I've been on the other end, like Saturday [against GW]."

Yes, they had won the game. They had shown some fight. But there was no question that vulnerability had crept its way into a special season. The magic was slipping away. They were no longer playing to win, they were playing not to lose—"playing scared" by Calipari's own admission. They had lost their crunchtime cool. They seemed out of sync, out of sorts.

Usually Mr. Control, Calipari seemed mystified. "As a teacher, it's not what you know—it's what they learn," he said. "And as a coach, it's not what you know—it's what you're getting across. The last two weeks I've done a poor job. I'm looking at a team that doesn't even look like anything I've ever seen."

He had felt confident that when he grabbed the wheel of the bus once again his team would respond. Whenever he had faced a crisis, he relied on his will. Most of the time it was enough. Standing before the media that night, he remained convinced that the secret to regaining the team's high–level performance was no more complicated than cracking the whip a little harder.

"Hopefully, I can get this thing righted and get these guys playing the way they can play," he said.

Did he have doubts now about his theory of empowering the players?

"I don't have doubts, but what I told them was this: 'Think about where you were three years ago, and where you are now. Are you a better person?' They all nodded their heads. I said, 'Are you a better student?' They all nodded their heads. 'Are you a better basketball player?' They all nodded their heads. Then I said, 'You've got to believe what I'm telling you. I've been honest with you since you've been here. You have to believe what I'm saying and what we have to do. Let me lead you through this again.'

"They'll do whatever I ask them to do: that's the great thing. We're just..."

The longest pause Calipari had ever made in the middle of a sentence followed. His eyes softened as he rapped a twirled–up stat sheet from one hand to the other. Anguished seconds passed as the most verbally facile coach in the business remained quiet—"...in a little bit of a funk right now."

It was time to turn the calendar to March.

# 18: "Winning and Losing are Both Imposters"

March 8–10, 1996

Any team coached by John Calipari will be well–schooled in public relations. In the high–profile world of college basketball, where reporters and fans invest great weight in the words of not always sophisticated young men—some of them still teenagers—it is important to recognize that words have consequences. Sometimes blandness and evasion are important. Sometimes it helps to follow the advice of former Minuteman star Jim McCoy, who once talked about "blowing some media smoke." Candor can be dangerous. Play with emotion and passion; just don't talk with it.

So as UMass prepared to face George Washington University in the semifinals of the Atlantic 10 tournament in Philadelphia on March 8, there was no talk about "payback" or "statement games." There was nothing to prove. The game was no big deal.

In a sense it was true. At 29–1, UMass did not need the win. The second–ranked Minutemen had almost certainly locked up one of the NCAA tournament's four Number 1 seeds. Ultimately, people weren't going to remember the A–10 tournament. These were community games. So you're the biggest bully on the block—so what?

But any team coached by John Calipari will also be fiercely competitive. Even with national goals, it *is* important to be the biggest bully on the block. This was not just another game. There *was* something to prove. When the Minutemen entered the NCAA tournament, they wanted to feel that they had the edge on the other sixty–three teams in the field. There was a certain psychological necessity about beating GW and burying the whole Mike Jarvis jinx. While Calipari certainly couldn't guarantee a win, two things were certain. This time GW would not play harder than the Minutemen. And without question, there would be no raisins in the oatmeal.

•

In the week before the GW game, UMass had righted its ship. After the shaky performance against St. Joe's, the Minutemen traveled to Louisville to close out the regular season with a non–conference matchup against one of college basketball's most famous teams, one that had won two national titles in the eighties. This was going to be a tough game to win, and not just because the Minutemen were slumping. Freedom Hall, host to six Final Fours and several in–state crusades against Kentucky, was packed with a record crowd of 20,076 fans. They were there to bid the senior class farewell, to wish Hall of Fame coach Denny Crum a happy fifty–ninth birthday, to help give him his twentieth twenty–win season. Earlier in the week, star center Samaki Walker had returned from a ten–game absence during an NCAA investigation regarding the possibly illegal gift of an automobile to his father. Walker had responded with twenty–four points and twelve rebounds against nationally ranked Marquette. At 19–9, ranked Number 21 in the nation, Louisville wanted nothing more than to leapfrog into the postseason with an impressive win over UMass.

The opening tip sailed behind Marcus Camby's head to Louisville's Tick Rogers. All five UMass players retreated on defense—in the wrong direction. Rogers turned upcourt toward the retreating players, thought for a second, then spun around and went in for an unmolested dunk. A UMass team that once seemed so full of focus suddenly didn't know which way it was going. It sure didn't look as if the Minutemen were ready to play.

They were. Camby hit all manner of tough shots. He spiked Walker's first attempt straight down to the floor. He dominated. Edgar Padilla shook off his recent slump to lead the offense with heady aggression. The Minutemen were not perfect, but they found their former ferocity. They rebounded like crazy. They applied their withering man–to–man pressure. And they closed out the regular season just as it had begun, with a tough win over a storied team from Kentucky, 62–59.

After a couple of days back home, the Minutemen traveled to the Atlantic 10 tournament. For the first time, the entire affair was to be played at one site, the Philadelphia Civic Center. No more stacked decks with the championship game played at the home site of the highest remaining seed. On Wednesday, March 6, while the league's lower–seeded teams played preliminary–round games, UMass's four Latino players—the Padilla brothers, Carmelo Travieso and Rigo Nuñez—were honored by a group of more than one hundred Latino organizations in Philadelphia with an assembly at the Roberto Clemente Middle School. "The purpose of this salute," said Angel Medina, coordinator of the event, "is to thank them for making us proud." The next day, UMass breezed past St. Bonaventure in the quarterfinals, 69–56, with Travieso's twenty–one points leading the way. That night George Washington polished off St. Joe's behind an overpowering performance by Alexander Koul (twenty–nine points, eleven of fourteen shooting, nine rebounds). The showdown was set for Friday night.

The pregame cauldron bubbled. Two late eighteenth–century mascots—George Washington with a powdered wig and a Minuteman with a three–cornered hat—sparred absurdly at center court. Opposing starters were introduced by position, meeting stiffly at center court while bands blasted and cheerleaders thrusted pom–poms in the air. GW retreated into a coiled circle, reaching up to the center, while UMass bounced frenetically. Mike Jarvis stared onto the court, vigorously nodding his head. John Calipari, arms folded, waited for his team.

Two minutes into the game, with Camby shooting free throws, GW cheerleaders standing behind the basket unfurled a large banner to remind the UMass center of his struggles with Koul two weeks earlier. It read: "'He had his way with me,' M. Camby."

The banner proved to be more than just good college fun; it forecast Camby's evening. In the midst of a stupendous season that saw him outplay some of the top centers in the land—Tim Duncan of Wake Forest, Lorenzen Wright of Memphis, Samaki Walker of Louisville—Camby was dogged again by the big guy from Belarus. Koul hit eight of thirteen shots, scored a game–high twenty points, pulled down a game–high eleven rebounds. Just as important, he hounded Camby into a stat–busting (six of twenty–three) night. For significant stretches of both halves, Camby was benched in place of unheralded sophomore Inus Norville.

UMass, though, had transcended its star. The one–man team myth had been debunked months before. With Camby struggling in the first half, the rest of the Minutemen just dug in on defense. Dana Dingle stymied top scorer Kwame Evans, who featured a tattoo on his biceps saying, "NBA, My life." Carmelo Travieso thwarted diminutive but explosive point guard Shawnta Rogers, who had controlled the floor game at UMass. Offensively, Edgar Padilla threaded the Colonials for five assists by intermission. Norville gave the Minutemen a lift with his most inspired play of the season. UMass dominated the hustle plays, those grinding, jostling moments when the ball is up for grabs. By half-time, UMass had hauled in a startling eighteen offensive rebounds and built a 37–27 lead.

GW surged back in the second half. When Rogers hit a pair of free throws with 8:22 left, the Colonials took a 54–53 lead. At one point an exasperated Calipari screamed, "Somebody get a rebound!" He and Jarvis both exhorted their players on for the final push.

With Calipari's proverbial electric chair humming, the Minutemen sprang to life. They put together one key play after another: Bright slashing in for a hoop on a great feed from Camby, Padilla pocketing a steal and a layup, Dingle lunging to strip the ball from Koul's hands. A bottled–up GW team was held without a field goal for more than seven minutes. Jarvis pleaded with officials on several occasions, insisting that they had missed several walks by the Minutemen.

As the clock ticked under a minute with UMass comfortably in front, first–year assistant coach Ed Schilling sat next to Calipari, tapping his mentor's knee in quiet celebration. Months earlier, Schilling had sat in Calipari's living room in the wee hours, trying to suppress his yawns while breaking down the Converse All–Star tape and wondering just what he had gotten himself into. Now it seemed like a pretty good situation.

The 74–65 win had been a full–throttle UMass effort, every ounce expended. The GW rap had finally been laid to rest. Now anything seemed possible. At least, that's what Calipari told his team in the locker room.

By the time he reached the postgame press conference, however, Calipari had his media face on. "That was a good win for our program," he began. "All I said was 'Let's play hard. . . .' We rebounded the crap out of the ball."

Was it special to finally beat GW, Coach?

Calipari would allow only this much: "This was a game to break a barrier. We've been breaking barriers all year. The barrier was, they're the only guys that beat us. They're the only guys that give us trouble. Let's break that barrier going into the tournament knowing there's no team in the country we can't play against."

Mike Jarvis was less guarded. Asked by Atlantic 10 communications director Ray Cella for an opening statement, Jarvis said, "The only statement I guess I want to make is, first of all, I guess the percentages favored UMass—they had to win one game sometime against us. It's too bad it had to happen here. Obviously they're 30–1, and they're a great basketball team, and will use this game to get even better. If the good Lord will have it, maybe we'll see 'em again for the [last game of the] best–of–three–game series. But we've got nothing to be ashamed of. We played a hell of a basketball game, and scared their butts off, as we always do."

Asked for the key to UMass's breakthrough play at the finish, Jarvis responded, "Well, it helps when you don't get key fouls called. They also had a couple of travels mixed into that. Every time a travel was missed, a three–point play followed. I think that had as much to do with the outcome as anything, if you want me to be honest."

•

There was one more game to play before the NCAA tournament began. The following night the Minutemen faced Temple for the A–10 title.

John Chaney had done a masterful job with a thin, depleted team, playing most of the season with just one scholarship guard. After inconsistent play through the first few months of the year, the Owls had strung together seven straight victories. With a 19–11 record and early–season wins over teams then ranked Number 1 (Kansas) and Number 2 (Villanova), they were assured a seventh straight trip to the NCAA tournament.

Still, the Owls had been absolutely hammered in both games against UMass. The once hotly contested rivalry had dissolved in the face of 59–35 and 84–55 thrashings. For the last three years in a row, Temple had made it to the league championship game only to lose to the Minutemen.

"I was hoping we'd lose," cracked Chaney after Temple's impressive victory over Rhode Island in the semifinals. "I'm sick and tired of getting my butt kicked by UMass."

But five minutes into the second half, Temple's Lynard Stewart took the ball away from Tyrone Weeks, then buried a three–pointer at the other end. Somehow the Owls were leading, 44–38. A disgusted John Calipari called a twenty–second timeout. Were the Minutemen overconfident? Sapped from the emotion of the previous night? Worn down at the end of a grueling season in the spotlight? In the huddle, Weeks and Calipari got into a screaming match. Things were looking ugly.

Out of the timeout, the Minutemen came out smoking: a Donta Bright three–pointer, a Marcus Camby block on one end and jam on the other, a three–pointer from Carmelo Travieso, another from Edgar Padilla. Just like that, in barely over two minutes, UMass had put together an 11–0 blitz that culminated with John Chaney calling timeout, putting his hands over his head and looking to the heavens.

After the 75–61 win was in the books, the Minuteman mascot stood before Calipari doing salaams, while the UMass coach pumped his fist toward the team's fans. The players, usually contained in the aftermath of victory, let loose with some wild dance steps, hugging and hollering. When the tournament's Most Outstanding Player award was presented to Travieso (seven three–pointers against the Owls), the Minutemen were particularly boisterous—none more so than Camby. An impassive John Chaney stood watching the whole show, his arms folded. His team sat glumly on the bench.

Moments later, Chaney launched into another valedictory about the Minutemen. "I don't remember players who always had an answer," he said in his trademark throaty way, continents of sweat darkening his mostly unbuttoned shirt. "If you look at those guys, they look like no–man people. They look like the no–man gang, until you get out there and play against them, and you find that they are truly blue–chip players in their heart and in their skill."

Chaney's decision to once again watch UMass during the awards ceremony, rather than retreat to the locker room, was never in doubt. "I made them sit there and look at the ones who benefit from hard work," he said. "Because I want them to know the next time they go out, that if they ran a race and they wanted to win that race, they might have to run a little faster and work a little harder. That's why I make them sit through that. Most teams walk off. I will never let my kids do that. You learn from losing—it's the best teaching time of all when youngsters lose, not just to teach humility, but to teach them how to deserve being a winner. Rudyard Kipling once said, 'Winning and losing are both imposters.'"

Chaney, looking tired at age sixty–four, saw all the tape recorders and cameras, and smiled. "You have to stay up late at night to figure out what that means."

"Have you?" somebody asked.

Instantly, combativeness hardened Chaney's features. The man who had won more than three hundred games at Temple, more than five hundred in his career, a coach who had once led his team to a Number 1 ranking and twice taken the Owls one step away from the

Final Four, wheeled toward the reporter and said, "I know, because I've won before." Then his voice softened again as he continued, "As we face the tournament, I'll try to prepare them so that they know we have to run a little faster. Winning is not always found in that score. It's found in your deeds. And once you can teach that to the kids, they play much better each time they go out, believe me."

When John Calipari stepped to the podium, he stood at a crossroads. Behind him was an improbable 31–1 season, already the most wins in school history. His team had just won five straight league titles in both the regular season and the postseason tournament, a feat matched only once in the annals of college basketball (by North Carolina State in the long–defunct Southern Conference in 1947–1951). It had been a remarkable ride.

Ahead of him, though, lay the team's only real goal. Sixty–four teams would begin play in the NCAA tournament the next week. One of them would win six more games and end the year as the national champion. UMass burned to be that team.

"It's going to be a sad day for me when this season ends, whenever it is," Calipari said. "I hope it's after six games. It may be after one or two games, three games, who knows? I have absolutely enjoyed being around these guys, because I think you can see they enjoy each other. You can see they respect each other. You can see they look out for each other. It's a unique group. It is a very unique group. It's been a pleasure coaching them, and it's going to be a sad, sad day for me when this season ends."

The wins had been sparked by different people in different ways. On this night against Temple, Calipari and several players credited the impassioned words of Tyrone Weeks during that timeout, after his turnover had led to a six–point lead for the Owls. Back in early December, the spirited Weeks had dared everyone to dream big by saying the team's goal should be to go undefeated—words that even Calipari initially dismissed as unrealistic. What had he said this time to fire up the team? No one was willing to say.

Several days later, standing before his locker, a sheepish Weeks spilled the goods. In the face of Calipari's stinging criticism, he had delivered these emphatic words: "Fuck you!"

•

On March 10, the day after the Temple game, Calipari hosted his traditional "Selection Sunday" party. Players in sweats and jeans, the coaching staff and their families, and members of the media descended on Calipari's house in the heavily wooded town of Shutesbury, population 1,654. Outside, amid mounds of snow and tall evergreen trees, several TV trucks had parked with their dishes pointed skyward. Inside, Calipari sat on the hearth, sipping a Diet Coke and looking relaxed in a black no–collar shirt with a Nike swoosh. Six–year–old Megan sat propped on her dad's knee. Players lounged around the living room and watched basketball on the coach's big–screen television. They looked confident.

Any sense of invincibility, though, had to be squashed by the events playing out on that television. Two games commanded the team's primary interest. In one, the Chicago Bulls, en route to the winningest season in NBA history, were absolutely throttled by the New York Knicks, 104–72. The other game showed the championship of the Southeastern Conference tournament where an unheralded team from Mississippi State was blasting its way to an 84–73 victory over top–ranked Kentucky. It was clear that in the one–and–done cruelty of the NCAA tournament, absolutely anything could happen. "There's no pressure," insisted Donta Bright. "Absolutely no pressure."

The next day the final AP poll came out. Of the 305 teams competing in Division I, the squad voted Number 1 at the end of the 1995–96 season was none other than the University of Massachusetts Minutemen. That was nice, of course, but the Minutemen well knew that unlike college football, which had always awarded its national championship through a vote, basketball titles were won in only one fashion: on the court in the NCAA tournament.

# 19: "You Must be so Proud"

March 10–22, 1996

The NCAA tournament provides American sports fans with a fix when they need it most. The Super Bowl is a distant memory. Real baseball games haven't been played since the fall. The languid regular seasons of the NBA and the NHL are yawning along, still several weeks away from any games that matter. In March, with the long winter's grip still holding tight in much of the country, college basketball brings heat right into the living room, seemingly twenty–four hours a day.

CBS, paying its $1.75 billion to the NCAA over eight years, provides blanket coverage: sentimental profiles, hype–filled previews, cut–ins to upsets in the making. In factory cafeterias, bankers' back chambers and teachers' conference rooms across the land, office pools are collected with dollar bills paper–clipped to anguished choices.[1] Debates spill past the lunch hour. Can anybody beat Kentucky? Does Princeton have any chance in hell against UCLA? Is this UMass team for real?

Many forces conspire to make the NCAA tournament such a great product. It is filled with underdogs and vivid personalities. The packaging is slick, complete with memorable alliterations: March Madness, the Sweet Sixteen, the Final Four. The one–and–done nature of the tournament provides both its cruelty, because the best team doesn't always win, and its beauty, because the urgency creates a sense that these games are vitally important. For most of the athletes, the tournament represents the largest stage they will ever know, their "one shining moment" as CBS terms it.[2] Mostly though, the play's the thing. The championships of other sports are often over–hyped duds that don't get inside the soul, but in college hoops never a year passes without genuine joy and heartbreak.

Ultimately, it doesn't really matter which teams successfully navigate The Road to the Final Four. At the time, though, it sure seems to matter. In the small speck of the world that is college basketball, the Final Four represents Valhalla.

The University of Massachusetts, for all it had accomplished, had never been there.

Making his fifth straight NCAA appearance, John Calipari was still struggling to find the right approach. Back in 1992, the psychology of the tournament didn't really matter; UMass was thrilled to be there. Winning two games and getting to the Sweet 16 iced an already delicious cake. Not even the loss to Kentucky and the infamous technical foul call by Lenny Wirtz could sour the experience.

By 1994, though, the novelty had worn off. The stakes had gotten higher. With UMass cracking the Top 10 and beating Number 1 North Carolina during the regular season, Calipari thought his team had a genuine chance for greatness. To really be considered one of the big boys in college hoops, he knew it was necessary to make some noise in March. "We're going to be judged on what we do in this tournament," he said. "We know it. We accept it." After the second–round sayonara against Maryland, Calipari stood out in the hallway of the Kansas Coliseum looking stunned.

In 1995, he tried to back off, suspecting that his players might perform better. "There's no pressure to win," he said. "No one has told us we have to win. It's not like we have to win or we're done. What this is about is, let's just do our best, let's prepare, and let's see what happens. We call it letting it fly. Just let it fly." It crashed to earth, however, in the second half against Oklahoma State, twenty minutes away from the Final Four.

There is no right way to approach this most inscrutable of sporting events. It begs for contradictions, and that's just what Calipari and the Minutemen provided. "Live for today," he'd say in one breath, "Don't be afraid to dream" in the next. It was all about empowerment, giving the team over to the players—and all about imposing his will and taking the team back. The players couldn't help but be pleased with what they had accomplished. And yet, Marcus Camby's words from December's victory over Georgia Tech at the Meadowlands rang truer than ever: "Our goal is to get back here in April. If we don't, it's a failure for us."

Surveying the tournament brackets at his Selection Sunday party, Calipari decided to keep his theme simple for the players. "Two great weekends, and we get to the Meadowlands," he said. "That's all it is, guys. Two great weekends."

•

UMass's Number 1 ranking and 31–1 record earned the Minutemen some advantages. For the first time in school history they received a Number 1 seed. They were able to stay close to home for the first two games of the East Regional in Providence, Rhode Island. In addition, they got a first–round matchup with the team considered to be the weakest in the entire NCAA field, Central Florida.

The Central Florida Golden Knights had endured a dismal 8–18 regular season. In the Trans America Athletic Conference tournament, however, they got hot at the right time, winning all three games and earning the league's automatic bid to the NCAAs. Thus, they became one of the obscure darlings of March, ready for the chance of a lifetime, however unlikely. Since the tournament had expanded to sixty–four teams in 1985, no Number 16 seed had ever knocked off a Number 1.

"It's nice being the underdog because no one has any expectations of you," said Central Florida senior forward Howard Porter. "Except losing."

"This would be like the biggest upset in NCAA history," acknowledged Marcus Camby.

The irony of Porter meeting Camby on the court could not be appreciated by anyone at the time, but it would prove to be a poignant coincidence.

Porter's father, also named Howard Porter, had played in the NCAA tournament twenty–five years before with Villanova. In fact, the elder Porter had earned the Most Outstanding Player award of the Final Four after the Wildcats lost to UCLA in the national championship game. He never saw the trophy, however. Porter had signed with an agent during the year, accepting what he called "fringe money." Secretly, he had signed with the Pittsburgh Condors of the American Basketball Association. Such under–the–table arrangements were common in those days of talent wars between the ABA and the NBA, according to a lengthy profile of the elder Porter that Leigh Montville wrote in the March 25, 1996 edition of *Sports Illustrated.* "A Wild West atmosphere pervaded," Montville said. "Do anything. Don't get caught. Porter signed and got caught. Other people assuredly took the money too, but they never suffered the public humiliation that Porter did. Howard Porter. . .did something wrong."

Porter's Most Outstanding Player award, and Villanova's tournament victories were deemed "vacated."

On this Thursday afternoon at the Providence Civic Center, however, there seemed to be no real resonance with the UMass experience. The elder Porter watched his son's team play well against the Minutemen for a half, trailing by just four points. Marcus Camby had a rough afternoon, once having his groin stepped on after falling to the floor, and another time having his forehead sliced open by some overaggressive defense. Blood criss–crossing his face, Camby walked back to the bench and needed four stitches.

In the second half, UMass took over. During the first 1:58 after intermission, Edgar Padilla contributed five steals, a spree of larceny that sparked a 92–70 victory. The tournament's one "gimme" was out of the way.

•

For the second consecutive year, UMass drew Stanford in the second round. In 1995, the Minutemen delivered a great effort, opening up a twenty–point halftime lead and rolling to a 75–53 win. Afterward, Stanford's burly forward Darren Allaway described the experience of playing against UMass as "disheartening."

Allaway felt that this year could be different. An obvious underdog with a Number 9 seed and a 20–8 record, Stanford had proved its mettle by sweeping the season series with Arizona and splitting with UCLA. "We've played Top 10 opponents before, and we've been in the Top 25 all year," said Allaway. "So we belong. There's no question about that in my mind. It won't be a ridiculous upset if we win."

John Calipari knew that Allaway was right. In the press conference the day before the game, he seemed subdued. "It's not how you play," Calipari said, refuting the advice of Little League coaches everywhere. "It's whether you win."

UMass played very well. All of the statistical signs of a superb effort were there. The Minutemen had five people in double figures. They shot fifty–four percent from the field, outrebounded the opponent, and had twenty–three assists against thirteen turnovers. Moreover, their star player was brilliant; Camby scored twenty points on nine–of–fifteen shooting, grabbed eight rebounds, and added seven blocks.

Still, it was a battle to the buzzer. Stanford point guard Brevin Knight turned in the best individual showing by a UMass opponent all season. A fiery and flamboyant performer, Knight came onto the court for warmups spiking a ball hard off the floor, an attitude of confidence he carried all the way through the game. Just five–ten, he fearlessly made a number of acrobatic drives into the teeth of the UMass defense. Sometimes he twisted past Camby for a basket, or set one up with an artful pass to a cutting teammate at the last possible second. Other times, Camby sent his shots flying.

After one second–half drive was emphatically redirected out of bounds, Camby glared at Knight and said, "I'm gonna be here all day. Take it to the perimeter."

Knight glared right back and said, "I'm gonna keep coming."

UMass seemed to be in control with a 66–53 lead and seven minutes left. Then Knight went to work. In the next six minutes he scored seven points and assisted on five baskets, including a gorgeous draw–and–dish to Dion Cross for a three–pointer with fifty–four seconds left. Suddenly, UMass's lead was trimmed to the narrowest of margins at 75–74.

Everything was on the line. A loss here would leave a bitter taste after this sweetest of seasons. "Nice team during the year," basketball insiders would say. "Can't get it done when it matters most."

Trusting his team to perform, John Calipari did not call a timeout. He shouted the same piece of advice he had been yelling all year in what seemed like a thousand close games: "Play to win!"

The old adage about teams taking on the personality of their coaches certainly held some truth at UMass. The Minutemen played with passion in large measure because Calipari coached that way. But there was another piece of their coach's make–up that the Minutemen had absorbed, a cool under pressure. For all his seemingly out–of–control emotion, Calipari almost always summoned composure in moments of crisis. He never lashed out at Lenny Wirtz or John Chaney when others certainly would have; he got in the ambulance when Camby fell. On the court, UMass had demonstrated tremendous poise at the finish—four straight overtime wins this year (eleven in a row overall), numerous clutch performances, almost never a choke job.

Edgar Padilla called out the play "Kansas," designed to get Camby the ball in the low post. Stanford did a great job of bottling Camby, though, and Padilla looked for the second option. Donta Bright cut hard behind a jarring pick from Dana Dingle, flashing to the free–throw line and taking the pass chest–high. Bright went right up, backspinning a jump shot over the extended hand of Peter Sauer, who was late fighting his way off Dingle's pick. The shot dropped right in for a 77–74 lead with thirty–two seconds left.

On the other end, Knight got the ball to Sauer for an open three–point bid, but his shot was off the mark. Camby soared high for the rebound, got fouled, and shrugged off any pressure or fatigue by hitting both ends of the one–and–one. UMass won, 79–74.

"They're a great team," said a somber Knight, who had scored twenty–seven points and distributed nine assists. "They're a great finishing team."

With plenty of sighs of relief, the Minutemen were moving on to the Sweet Sixteen to take on Arkansas.

First, though, Calipari had to take care of some business. On Sunday, he attended UMass President William Bulger's annual St. Patrick's Day breakfast in South Boston. The colorful Bulger, who had just taken the UMass job after seventeen years at the helm of the state senate, roasted Calipari. He also had a surprise for the UMass coach, handing him the phone.

"You must be so proud, not only of your record, but of the way you've done it," said the huge fan of the Arkansas Razorbacks. "The teamwork this year to me has been astonishing. It's really been amazing the way they all do what they do. It's a great tribute to you and to your coaching staff."

The fan then pleaded with Calipari for leniency when UMass took on Arkansas on Thursday. "Only two of our starters have started to shave," he said. "You've got to take it easy on us." Actually, he continued, a UMass victory might not be so bad because western Massachusetts resident Anthony Lake, the national security advisor, was so attached to the Minutemen. "If UMass ever loses a game, he goes into mourning. It endangers the national security. I mean, I'm almost going to pull for UMass on Thursday just to keep something bad from happening in the world."

The gym rat who still spoke to reporters with terms like "jagoffs" and "testicles the size of a hippopotamus" was now yucking it up with the President of the United States. The Man from Moon and the Man from Hope.

One great weekend was over.

•

On Wednesday, March 20, snow fell in Atlanta, big swirling flakes that chilled the soft petals of flowering magnolias. It was the first day of spring in the Deep South, and things were just a bit out of kilter. The snow, as it turned out, presaged a couple of other unexpected falls, those of Carmelo Travieso and Marcus Camby.

Gearing up for Arkansas, the Minutemen knew that they were taking on the most surprising team in the Sweet Sixteen. On paper, the Razorbacks were the least imposing squad left chasing a national title. They had barely made it into the tournament at all with an 18–12 record. Coming off back–to–back appearances in the national championship game (winning in 1994, losing in 1995), the Razorbacks had entered the year without a single returning starter. In February, they seemed to lose any hope of postseason success when leading scorer Jesse Pate and leading rebounder Sunday Adebayo were declared ineligible because of a conflict surrounding their transcripts. Starting four freshmen, Arkansas entered the tournament as a Number 12 seed, and was expected to exit quickly.

That hadn't happened. In Providence they had stunned Number 5 seed Penn State and Number 4 Marquette with the chaotic end–to–end pressure that coach Nolan Richardson termed "Forty Minutes of Hell."

"It's just harassing," Richardson explained after the victory over Marquette. "If you were to be harassed for forty minutes, there's going to be some wear and tear. We all bend to pressure, all of us. There's not a single person alive who won't bend to pressure."

The Minutemen had to respect Arkansas. The Razorbacks, after all, had proved themselves a great tournament team in the nineties. Surely, that's what the UMass players were getting ready to say when they prepared to meet the press on that snowy Wednesday afternoon. Fate and Carmelo Travieso, though, had other ideas.

The makeshift interview room at the Georgia Dome was a "turf–storage facility" that housed huge coils of green artificial turf. In the back of the room, the interview platform was erected some five feet above the ground. A table sat atop the platform with chairs for designated players from each team. Behind the chairs, just on the far side of the platform, hung a blue banner plastered with NCAA logos. There was no railing between the end of the platform and the banner.

UMass players came on for their meet–the–press session at 2:30. First Marcus Camby ascended the platform, followed by Travieso. The UMass guard, instructed by the press conference moderator to sit on the other side of Camby, started to walk behind him. His left foot went over the back edge of the platform, and he reached for the blue banner, assuming there must be a wall behind it. There was nothing, and Travieso plummeted awkwardly to the floor. He landed with his back slamming into a metal–support rail.

While initially frightening, this quickly became a Laurel and Hardy moment, filled with a pull–the–trap–door–and–laugh–like–hell quality. Here was perhaps the most athletically gifted player on the Number 1 team in the country falling off a stage. A ubiquitious TV camera caught the entire thing, and ESPN played it over and over, as if Travieso were Neil Armstrong taking the first steps on the moon. When he emerged from the UMass locker room with a slight limp and an embarrassed smile, Travieso was ambushed by some thirty reporters from around the country. When he came out to join his teammates at practice, he received a razzing cheer. Meanwhile team trainer Ron Laham filled in reporters. Travieso had "a contusion to his lower back in his gluteal muscles." Translation: a pain in UMass.

The next night when the Minutemen tipped off against Arkansas at 10:45—pushed back by the combined greed of the NCAA and CBS, coupled with a lengthy foul–fest in Georgetown's win over Texas Tech—UMass fans were relieved to see Travieso on the court. To their astonishment, though, there was no Marcus Camby.

How could this be? UMass was playing one–and–done, everything–on–the–line basketball in the NCAA tournament, and John Calipari was benching the player who had just been named the top vote–getter for the AP All–America team?

After the game, reporters and fans would find out what happened—sort of. Calipari explained that he had instructed all his players to get out of the hotel during the day. He didn't want them groggy come gametime. Camby, though, had been late coming back from the mall, "caught in traffic" according to Calipari's description. He had been late for the team bus to the shootaround. While emphasizing that his star player had been a model citizen all year, Calipari felt he needed to take a stand. "As a coach, I've got to be consistent," he said. "I've got to let the players know that I'm not changing because of the importance of a game. When you're teaching life skills, you've got to be consistent. You've got to be that way with your best player and your worst player."

As it turned out, he was not alone at the mall. Some of his close friends from Hartford were with him, buying clothing at trendy shops like the Ralph Lauren Polo Store. According to Camby's account in June's *Hartford Courant* story that broke the news of his involvement with agents, his friends were flown to Atlanta and given a shopping spree by Hartford lawyer Wesley Spears, who was trying to become Camby's agent.[3]

At the time, though, no one was looking for warning signs about Camby's poor judgment or the avarice of agents. It was all about basketball and UMass's magical season. Camby was benched for exactly a minute and thirteen seconds, during which UMass built up a 7–0 lead. Moments later, it was 13–0. Maybe Nolan Richardson's claim that "we all bend to pressure" had some merit, but this game was never close. UMass led by sixteen at the half, pushed the lead to twenty-eight after intermission and coasted to a 79–63 victory.

In the wee hours of Friday morning, the Minutemen were now just one game away from the Final Four. All they needed to do was beat Georgetown.

# 20: "IT FELT SO GOOD"

March 23, 1996

Atlanta, Georgia

"Jack Leaman, will Jack Leaman please report to center court?" Sitting high in the Philadelphia Spectrum stands back in 1976, the UMass coach turned to some colleagues and asked them if they heard his name. Moments later, the PA system blared out the same message. Leaman ambled down, wondering what could possibly be wrong. Down on the floor he was met by a grinning Michigan coach Johnny Orr, whose team was getting set to play Rutgers in the national semifinals. "Just thought you'd want to see what the bench looks like for the Final Four," Orr said. "You're never going to get there at UMass."

More than anyone else, Jack Leaman was identified with the University of Massachusetts basketball program. He had watched it from up close, through good times and hard times, for thirty–five years. He had made it his life.

Back in 1961 he arrived as an assistant to his hero, Matt Zunic. He later served as an assistant to Orr, a man who would become a lifelong friend. When Orr left in 1966, disgruntled with the UMass administration's unwillingness to build the new basketball arena it had promised, Leaman became head coach. For thirteen seasons he filled that post with astonishing commitment, winning as no one had ever done before at UMass. Those wild, heady days in the early seventies with Julius Erving and Rick Pitino were unforgettable. By the late seventies, though, it all came crashing down for Leaman, suddenly, jarringly. "Coaching," he would later reflect, "made me a bad person."

He had several opportunities to leave, but he never left. Just couldn't do it. Gritting his teeth at first, he coached the Stockbridge School of Agriculture, did radio broadcasts of high school games, and realized that he still loved basketball. On UMass game nights, he stepped across the dirt floor at the Curry Hicks Cage and climbed up into the bleachers,

*Jack Leaman still coaches golf at the Stockbridge School of Agriculture.*
*(Photo by Gordon Daniels)*

where he usually sat alone and watched. Through middle age, he followed the awful UMass teams of the eighties, often feeling more pain about their embarrassing performances than they did.

When summoned, Leaman offered advice to the parade of unsuccessful coaches who followed him: Ray Wilson, Tom McLaughlin, Ron Gerlufsen. In 1988, John Calipari arrived, seeming brash and confident, yet he often sought out the wisdom of the former coach. On Leaman's suggestion, Calipari shifted one of his first recruits, Anton Brown, from shooting guard to point guard. A few years later, Leaman convinced Calipari that unspectacular Derek Kellogg was just what he needed at the point; flashy athleticism was not what counted.

Leaman watched UMass's rise under Calipari with fascination. On the one hand, Leaman felt the world changing—Calipari's stylish–

salesman approach was so unlike his own. Yet when it came to basketball, it was like looking in the mirror. Calipari was almost old–fashioned as a coach, emphasizing defense, the critical role of the point guard and above everything, team play. Leaman marvelled at Calipari's ability to get his players to accept their roles. He remembered all too well the battles he had fought with Pitino on that very subject a generation ago. Calipari's motivational ability also impressed Leaman. Once on a local sports talk show, Leaman referred to Calipari as coaching "like an old–time evangelist, riling up the masses."

In 1995–96, at sixty–three years old, Leaman was in his second year as the color analyst on WHMP's radio broadcasts. The job was hard for him in some ways. He hated the travel. For long, dull hours he'd sit in hotel lobbies. On the air, his habitual hacking cough sometimes forced him to lean away from the microphone for several seconds at a time. There were aspects of bigtime basketball that made him uncomfortable. It bothered him that players missed so many classes because of the schedule, no matter what academic–support systems were in place, no matter how high the graduation rate might be. He questioned some of the changes that money had wrought. Once, surveying the crowd at the Mullins Center, he observed, "It's gone from being a students' game to being a sponsors' game."

Still, there was much to love, and Jack Leaman couldn't help himself. His thick Boston accent and high–pitched voice took on a sing-song quality as he heaped praise on the team's hustle and defense. "Dingle did as Dingle does!" he liked to exclaim after the UMass co–captain battled hard on the boards.

In all his years in the game, he had never seen a team quite like this UMass squad. For a basketball purist like Leaman, they were a dream come true. He didn't want to wake up quite yet, because he knew just how much one more win would mean to his beloved University of Massachusetts.

•

For John Calipari, the prospect of coaching against John Thompson was "the ultimate challenge." Sounding downright reverential, Calipari said, "He's a Hall of Famer, there's no question. You're talking about a coach who always gets his players to play hard. They respond to him like nothing I've ever seen."

Any talk about the greatest building jobs in college basketball history has to include Thompson's career at Georgetown. In 1972,

Thompson inherited a team that had gone 3–23 the year before. His first season, the Hoyas improved to 12–14. They haven't had a losing year since.

By 1996, Thompson's teams had won more than five hundred games. They had gone to nineteen NCAA tournaments. In one four-year stretch during college basketball's explosion in the eighties, Georgetown made it to the national championship game three times: winning once, and losing the other two by a combined total of three points.

Beyond the success, Georgetown had built a mystique. The Hoyas were a team that inspired fear. Their game was clean, but highly aggressive. Intimidating shot blockers from Patrick Ewing to Dikembe Mutombo to Alonzo Mourning set the tone. Their pressure defense was swarming and panic–inducing. On the sidelines, the six–ten Thompson stood taller than any coach in the land, the trademark towel draped over his right shoulder, the glare melting rocks.

In 1995–96, the Hoyas emerged as a team with frightening capabilities. When they hosted a third–ranked UConn team that was riding a twenty–three–game winning streak in mid–February, the Hoyas took the game over with ferocious pressure, building a 30–12 lead en route to an easy 77–65 win. Looking in the eyes of the Huskies, *Hartford Courant* columnist Jeff Jacobs wrote that he "saw terror."

The Hoyas were led by sophomore point guard Allen Iverson, the most explosive player in the college game. Regarded by some scouts as the quickest basketball player at any level, Iverson averaged twenty–five points a contest, twice scoring forty. There was no doubt that the prospect of getting to the Final Four by beating the Minutemen had Iverson's competitive juices flowing. "I wanted to play UMass so bad when they were Number 1 and nobody could beat them," he said the day before the game. "I just wanted the opportunity to play them."

True, Iverson and the Hoyas could be erratic. Composure was a question mark, underscored when they blew an eleven–point lead in the final two minutes of The Big East tournament championship game against UConn. Still, they entered the NCAA tournament as the most feared Number 2 seed in the field, ranked fourth in the country with a 26–7 record. They were widely picked to win the East Region by experts from Dick Vitale on down.

Did that fact bother Calipari? After all, UMass was the Number 1 seed, the top–ranked team in the land.

"Part of it is we're still UMass," Calipari said the day before the game. "You're talking about two programs that are high profile. One program has won national titles and been to Final Fours, and one program has not. You're talking about one program that's coached by a Hall of Famer, and one program that's coached by a young guy that's trying to learn the game."

"All that talk and stuff don't matter now," said Thompson. "Ratings and rankings and all that crap. You've got to play—it's just that simple."

The two teams had never played before, though they did share some minor history. During Jack Leaman's first year as an assistant coach, the glory season of 1961–62 when Matt Zunic led an overachieving team all the way to the NCAA tournament, UMass played a Providence squad whose center was the imposing John Thompson. Asked thirty-five years later what he recalled about the contest, Thompson said, "I don't ever remember playing the University of Massachusetts."

For the record, Thompson's Providence team won by thirty-four points.

•

What a year it had been! Just four months before, after the exhibition loss to Converse, Calipari sounded defiant at the Mullins Center, when he stated, "We will win. . . .I'll settle for nothing less than that." Sure, he thought they would "win," but in what sense? Fifteen games? Eighteen? An NCAA berth? Not even Calipari could have imagined twenty-six straight victories, a 34–1 record, a Number 1 ranking.

The wild ride of success had been juxtaposed to several close brushes with tragedy. Marcus Camby's terrifying collapse came just days after UMass swimmer Greg Menton died. Weeks later, Dayton center Chris Daniels—who played the game of his life against Camby in January—collapsed and died. The Minutemen remembered the little girl that Matt Komer saved in Hawaii, and Luke Morton, the six-year-old "PC Wiz" with the brain tumor. Just two days before the Georgetown game, Calipari had Carmelo Travieso read an article to the team about the death of Harry Tambolleo, the lupus patient whose life Camby had brightened when they were both hospitalized in Worcester.

They had known glory and fragility, and they seemed to wear them both. Just twenty-four hours away from a chance at the Final Four, the Minutemen left practice and lengthy interview sessions at the Georgia Dome, and headed over to the Shepherd Spinal Clinic to visit Travis Roy.

Most of the players knew Roy's story. He had been the quintessential All-American boy, a mixture of effervescence and innocence, a kid with a big smile, huge dreams and an old-fashioned work ethic. Growing up in Yarmouth, Maine, he had been skating before he was two, playing hockey by three. He yearned to play Division I college hockey, and then to launch a pro career. Arriving as a scholarship player at defending national champion Boston University in the fall of 1995, he seemed to be on course. On October 20, BU opened at home against North Dakota, unfurling its national championship banner. The Terriers scored 1:45 into the game, and then coach Jack Parker put Roy in for his first collegiate hockey shift. Just eleven seconds in, he tried to check a North Dakota opponent, but only brushed against him. Off balance, Roy careened into the boards headfirst. Moments later, he was sprawled on the ice, eyes wide open, unable to move. When his father, Lee, scrambled down to the ice, Travis told him that he was scared, that he had no feeling in his arms or legs. "But Dad," Travis said, "I made it."

Roy had shattered a vertebra in his neck. In an instant, his life had changed from being a college athlete to being a quadriplegic. An enormous outpouring of support flowed to Travis and the Roy family in the months that followed. Everyone from Al Gore to Wayne Gretzky visited. Mail poured in from little kids and old ladies. Piles of money were raised. While the prospects for significant recovery were bleak, there had been some progress. By March, he had used a mouth brush to paint a picture of the American flag.

When John Calipari heard that Roy was getting treatment in Atlanta, he decided to take his team.

The Minutemen did not know what to expect. Tyrone Weeks, the strongest player on the team, later said that he was scared when he arrived. Some players even expressed guilt. Here they were, getting worked up about playing a game.

What they found was an absolutely beaming Travis Roy. "I thought he might have been jealous," said Carmelo Travieso. "He wasn't. He was happy for us. He was so happy just to be alive."

•

Fans back home in Massachusetts churned with anticipation. They heard CBS analyst Quinn Buckner open the broadcast by saying he was "dying for this game." More than thirty thousand fans poured into the Georgia Dome, including filmmaker Spike Lee, who sat behind the Georgetown bench wearing a replica Allen Iverson jersey.

The Hoyas arrived on the court first with determined, impassive expressions. UMass followed, running in behind the Minuteman mascot. As always, the guards led the pack. Padilla blazed in to start the layup line, then missed his shot. Travieso followed and also missed. The butterflies were raging.

By tipoff, though, order had been restored. The Minutemen played a hard first half, battling on the boards, fighting through the Hoyas' pressure defense. By the 5:37 mark, UMass was up by a startling fourteen points. Then Georgetown surged back. Iverson, who had been well contained by Travieso, erupted for eleven points in under three minutes. The Minutemen guards faltered against the press. At halftime, UMass led by just 38–34.

The Minutemen were faced with almost the exact same situation as a year ago. In 1995, they led Oklahoma State by five points with just twenty minutes of good basketball left to get to the Final Four. No one needed a reminder about how *that* drama turned out.

Georgetown emerged first from its locker room and started striding through the narrow hallway that led back onto the court. From behind, a running band of young men in sweatsuits that said "Refuse to Lose" came surging by.

The second half was a dream. Camby took control, hitting the first three shots, and sending a hook shot by Georgetown's Othella Harrington right back in his face. Bright darted and blasted his way to the hoop. Dingle kept balls alive on the offensive glass. Weeks guzzled rebounds. Padilla pushed the offense, and pocketed one steal after another. Travieso poured in three–pointers, and, with some great help from his teammates, absolutely stymied Iverson, whose second–half line included one of ten field goals, no assists, four turnovers.

The lead mushroomed to ten points, then fifteen, then twenty. All facets of what Calipari liked to call "UMass Basketball" were on riotous display. The Minutemen created easy baskets for each other. They played stifling team defense. They spent every ounce.

From the bench, Calipari almost couldn't believe his eyes: "I looked out there, and I said, 'That's us. That's how we should be playing. That's the blueprint.'"

On the bench, there was pure delirium. Rigo Nuñez, swirling a towel with glee, turned his thoughts back home: "What is everybody in Amherst, and back in Massachusetts doing? I was just thinking, 'All our fans, they must be going crazy.'"

Charlton Clarke, whose freshman year had been all but negated by the broken bone in his foot he suffered in the opener, was lost in the moment: "When the clock was winding down, I didn't want it to end because it felt so good."

On the end of the bench, Marcus Camby shared a big laugh with team manager Matt Komer.

In the final minute, UMass scored the last two baskets of the game. First, freshman walk–on Ross Burns passed up a shot to feed Giddel Padilla for a hoop. Then freshman walk–on Andy Maclay, who had played just fifteen minutes all year, scoring a whopping two points, had the ball ahead of all five Georgetown players. There was no time for Maclay to think about just what this would mean to him in the years to come, to say that he scored a basket in the game that took UMass to the Final Four. Noticing Burns streaking ahead of him, Maclay gave up the ball. Burns hit the layup for the final points in an 86–62 rout. It was the UMass way.

They let loose. Parading around in gray Final Four caps, they beamed into the CBS cameras, holding four fingers aloft. They did a rare postgame version of their team mosh pit. Donta Bright took the shirt off his back and offered it to Spike Lee, while the usually soft–spoken Dana Dingle said, "Hey Spike, what's happenin' Spike!" Quinn Buckner of CBS pointed out to Edgar Padilla that Kentucky had won its game, setting up a rematch of the season opener in the national semifinals. "Yeah, we beat them once," said the generally modest Padilla. "We'll beat them again."

What Bob Ryan of *The Boston Globe* termed "the greatest day in the history of UMass athletics" spilled over to the postgame press conference in the turf–storage facility, the site of Travieso's comical fall a few days back. "I'm just so pleased for these guys here," said Calipari, pointing to his players. "They worked so hard. They've been challenged so much by our staff, occasionally aggressively by me. They've responded, and this is their reward. And it's not over yet."

Asked about the personal significance of reaching the Final Four, Calipari said, "I've said before I won't judge myself the way you guys do—winning national championships or getting to Final Fours—it'll never happen. I enjoy what I do. I enjoy my team. I'm teaching life skills, and keeping winning and losing in perspective. I think these guys know I'm that way. It's not life or death for me. I enjoy it. I don't know if it has any significance. It may to you. It doesn't to me."

The questions kept coming. Calipari had the room rapt. Finally, someone asked him if he ever truly believed he could take this program—the University of Massachusetts—to the Final Four.

"I don't know, but I dreamed it," he said. "When I'd be jogging, when I had free time, I dreamed about being in the situation we're in. Dreaming about playing North Carolina and Duke in the championship game. I played the game all out in my mind. I'd smile when I'd wake up, and say, 'Oh geez, we're getting ready for Lowell.'

"One of the things I tell these guys all the time is, 'You got to be able to dream. You got to be able to have a visual picture. And don't be afraid to be special. Don't be afraid to be special!' These guys, with the way they are off the court, being nice and making people feel good, that's all part of it. I think they responded to what we're trying to teach, and what we're trying to get across to them."

He left the room to a loud ovation. Out in the hallway, a good friend was waiting.

John Calipari and Jack Leaman embraced each other with the biggest bear hug imaginable.

# 21: "He Taught Me How to be a Man"

March 25—April 1
East Rutherford, N.J.

The dilemma of Christine Todd Whitman was splashed across the front page of *The New York Times* one Sunday in March. As Governor of New Jersey, Whitman controlled fifty tickets to the Final Four. Unfortunately for her, everyone seemed to want one. Among those trying to wheedle their way into the event courtesy of the governor were Senator Bob Dole and House Speaker Newt Gingrich.

The tickets carried a face value of $70—$140 for both the national semifinals on Saturday night and the championship game on Monday night. Scalpers commanded at least $8,000 for courtside seats, and $2,500 for the worst seats in the house.

For the first time in forty–six years, the Final Four had come to the New York metropolitan area. Back in 1950, City College of New York won the title at the old Madison Square Garden, only to be rocked with the revelations that players had been involved in point shaving. The scandal badly tarnished the sport's image in New York. People were aghast that money had polluted the college game. But now, after almost a half–century of exile, the sport's premier event was back.

This time it would be held at the Meadowlands Sports Complex in a facility that was known as the Brendan Byrne Arena when UMass played there in December. Now it was called the Continental Airlines Arena after the company purchased the naming rights for a cool $29 million.[1]

CBS Sports geared up for the big weekend. The network expected fifty–two million viewers, which meant fat advertising dollars to help turn the $1.7 billion TV contract into hefty profits.

The men's college basketball championship, a nice little amateur sporting event, was set to begin.

•

All week, John Calipari was singing, "I want to wake up in a city that never sleeps." Sinatra he wasn't.

"In church we talk about 'a joyful noise unto the Lord,'" said assistant coach Ed Schilling. "He was joyful. And it was a noise."

A moth to a flame, Calipari couldn't get to New York soon enough. The other three teams arrived on Thursday. UMass, with the shortest distance of all to travel, checked in on Tuesday night. Calipari explained that his team wanted to cheer on St. Joseph's in the NIT semifinals at Madison Square Garden. Traveling in a brand new bus with "GO UMASS" and "REFUSE TO LOSE" painted on the outside, the Minutemen arrived in time for the second half of the Hawks' hard–fought win over Alabama.

For most of the week the Minutemen were holed up at their hotel in Teaneck, New Jersey. They practiced at Fairleigh Dickinson University, met for their required team meals and massive interview sessions, killed some time by going to a shopping mall in Secaucus and by watching the film *Girl 6*. The coaching staff broke down tapes and put together the plan. On Thursday night, the coaches of all four teams met for a Final Four tribute at Radio City Music Hall. Performers included Aretha Franklin and UMass graduate Natalie Cole. The UMass staff also made an appearance at the New York Hilton, where the National Association of Basketball Coaches was headquartered. The Final Four is the Capistrano for college coaches, and Calipari flocked back as a celebrity. The NABC had just selected him its National Coach of the Year, and he basked in the festival of back–slapping and chop–busting. A few blocks south at Times Square, beneath a sign that said "Happy New Year 1996! The Best is Yet to Come," a "Jumbotron" flashed continual college basketball games and highlights all week. Reporters and TV cameras followed Calipari everywhere. One day the *New York Post* printed a back–page rumor that proved unfounded about Calipari's interest in a vacant Big East coaching job. The headline, next to a large picture of Calipari, read simply, "St. John." He was soaking it up.

Back in western Massachusetts, it was a week of giddy anticipation. Talk of The Game seemed to find its way into every conversation. At the University Store, merchandise manager Mary Ellen Martin saw UMass souvenirs flying off the shelves and exclaimed to a reporter, "It's like Christmas." Homemade signs of support were erected in front of hundreds of homes, including the bucket of Kentucky Fried Chicken nailed to a piece of plywood in Shutesbury by seven–year–old Hannah Perlmutter, who painted on the message, "UMass is the winner, Kentucky is fried for dinner." Adopting a similar theme at a "UMass Day" at the Leeds Elementary School, third–grader Jessamyn Rising penned the following poem, which later appeared on the front page of the *Daily Hampshire Gazette*:

*UMass are the Winit-men*
*Kentucky is fried chicken*
*Kentucky are the scaredy-cats*
*UMass will surely lick 'em*

•

Ah yes, Kentucky.

Sure, the national semifinals were about more than UMass and Kentucky. This was the Final *Four*, after all. Fans of Syracuse and Mississippi State were also filled with anticipation, following their teams to the sport's greatest extravaganza. The Orangemen, fourth-seeded in the West Regional, and the Tigers, fifth-seeded in the Southeast, had been significant surprises, leaving a trail of broken hearts from higher-seeded teams in their wake. Anyone familiar with NCAA history knew that sometimes the little engine roared its way all the way to the title. Surely, North Carolina State hadn't been the best team in America in 1983. Several teams were better than Villanova in 1985. Still, the clash between Syracuse and Mississippi State was the decided undercard, almost an afterthought. In the eyes of most fans and writers and basketball insiders, the national title would be decided in primetime on Saturday night when UMass and Kentucky tipped it off.

The spin-fest began right away. Upon hearing that Rick Pitino had declared UMass's lack of depth to be an advantage (because of greater chemistry), and had stated his intention not to double-team Marcus Camby, John Calipari laughed. "This is Opposites Week for Rick Pitino," Calipari said. "Whatever he tells you, it's the opposite."

What about for Calipari?

"Probably the same," the coach admitted.

To be sure, there was a sentimental side to their showdown. Pitino couldn't help feeling pride in UMass's accomplishments. This was his alma mater, a university that had permanently grabbed a place in his heart on that long-ago night at Madison Square Garden when he watched the Julius Erving-led Redmen almost topple mighty Marquette in the NIT. Pitino had seen the basketball program wither, then grow beyond his wildest imagination. "We didn't have enough money for a budget: camp, stationery, secretary, nothing," he said in a coaching teleconference on Wednesday, March 27. "[Calipari] had an arena built when the state was broke. He helped build this program in a very difficult fashion. If you said to me he can get them in the Top 20, I would say that's almost an impossible task. So to say I'm a happy alumnus today would be putting it mildly."

When Calipari looked at Pitino, it was hard not to feel a sense of gratitude. His Five–Star Camp mentor had helped open the door at UMass. Without him, the whole magical ride might never have taken place. "I'm the head coach at the University of Massachusetts because he was on the committee, and he thought I would be good for the job," Calipari said in the same Wednesday teleconference. "He made calls to make sure it would get done. That will always be with me and my family. My wife knows it. My children know it. We're in a position right now as a family because of what Rick Pitino has done for me."

But the nice–nice only went so far. If Calipari and Pitino looked alike and dressed alike and shared both an Italian–American ancestry and a gift for coaching gab like few others, they also shared something far more fundamental. Both had a positively infernal drive to win, a drive that pulled at them almost all the time, bringing out their best, bringing out their worst.

It was almost time to compete.

•

The headline of Mike Lupica's column on the back page of Saturday's *Daily News* said, "Rick's Gotta Have It." On the back of the *New York Post*, the kicker for Mark Cannizzaro's column was even more blunt: "Pitino is Failure if 'Cats Lose."

The pressure on the Kentucky coach stemmed from three different sources. One was the widespread belief that the Wildcats had greater talent than any team in the game. Bob Ryan of *The Boston Globe* pointed out that eight Wildcats had been ranked as top–fifty players in the country when they were in high school. UMass had one such player, Donta Bright. Granted, players develop at different rates—high school unknown Marcus Camby had rocketed to the top of the college game—but the overall talent disparity was undeniable.

In the four games in the NCAA tournament thus far, Kentucky had obliterated the opposition by an average of more than twenty–eight points. "Pitino has the best group of players, a whole bench full of kids who were drop–dead high school stars," Lupica wrote. "He knows it. Everybody knows it. Time to cut the nets down."

Also pressuring Pitino were the enormous expectations on the part of Kentucky fans. For decades, the Wildcats have had the most loyal and the most demanding fan base in the country. Nothing fills the state with more pride than the achievements of the Kentucky team. The Wildcats had been to ten Final Fours and they had won five national titles. But as just about anyone in the Bluegrass State could tell you, they hadn't brought home the goods since 1978. Even with the most victories in the nation in the nineties, Pitino had not delivered what fans wanted most. In the Roman Empire of College Basketball, there was a restlessness in the air. "The people love basketball so much," Pitino said the day before the UMass game, "that they're starving for another championship."

Most of the pressure on Rick Pitino, though, came from Rick Pitino himself. He knew that in an undeniable if horribly unfair sense, his status as an elite coach was on the line, more so than at any point in his career. Sure, he had experienced dramatic, almost stunning, success at every step. He was beloved at Boston University, the pride of Providence, the wunderkind of the New York Knicks. At Kentucky he had rescued a team on NCAA probation, restoring not only a sense of excitement, but a sense of honor. Everywhere he turned, he brought a winning combination of style and success. He was mentioned in the pantheon of the great college coaches of the day: Dean Smith, Bobby Knight, Mike Krzyzewski. And yet, they all had something that he didn't have—a championship.

Pitino knew that some people referred to him as the coach with two autobiographies and no championships. He knew the joke about his team's visit to Italy the previous summer, a visit in which he and his wife Joanne met Pope John Paul. *"May I kiss your ring?" Pitino asks. "Sure," says the pontiff. "May I kiss yours? Oh, I forgot: you don't have a ring."*

Pitino could laugh, but only to a point. The jokes stung for a reason: it was less about the titles themselves than about what they represented. They stung because he was Rick Pitino, the man his college roommate describes as "pathologically addicted to competition." They stung because of the *Sports Illustrated* story just a month before, where a frazzled-looking Pitino graced the cover next to the words "A Man Possessed."

A championship meant simply that for one moment in time, you were the best. It was a moment Pitino had yearned for all his life.

Sure, judging coaches or teams solely by a standard of winning championships is cruel and unfair. Titles are fickle things. The best teams don't always win. Luck plays a maddeningly significant role. Greatness is measured more fairly over time. Yet most of the truly great coaches had managed to win, at least once, when it mattered most. Though he was only forty–three, Pitino had been coaching since the late seventies. As Lupica pointed out in his "Rick's Gotta Have It" column, "He has been the wonder boy of his profession for a good long time."

The holy grail was just two games away.

Closing the press conference the day before taking on UMass, Pitino got philosophical. "You don't know if it's ever going to happen, a championship," he said slowly. "It may happen, it may not. So you have to enjoy what you have when you have it."

With huge rings under his raccoon eyes, though, Pitino did not look as if he were enjoying anything.

•

Publicly, Pitino chafed at the description of UMass as the underdog. The Minutemen, not Kentucky, were ranked Number 1 in the country. UMass, not Kentucky, had Marcus Camby, who had made a sweep of all of the important National Player of the Year awards. When the teams met head to head, Pitino pointed out, it was UMass who had come out a winner. So how was it that Kentucky was favored to win by a comfortable eight and a half points?

Deep down, though, Pitino knew he had the better team. All things being equal, Kentucky *should* win. If the two teams were to play a long series, the Wildcats *would* win. But on one night, playing UMass was the scariest prospect imaginable—for two reasons.

One was that the Minutemen had unparalleled teamwork. Pitino had learned the Jack Leaman Lesson long ago, and when he looked at UMass, he feared the power of their unity.

"This is a truly great team," he said. "No matter what coach—you go back to Vince Lombardi and take some of the best coaches in the game—if you ask them to give you a definition of 'team,' as far as understanding roles, as far as defense, as far as togetherness, as far as all the attributes you would say a great team would have, you can kind of use Massachusetts as an example of that word."

There was one other factor that helped carve the hollows under Pitino's eyes. Years before, he had been instrumental in helping an unknown coach take over the reins at his alma mater. To Pitino's deep joy and absolute horror, he realized that he had created a monster. If anyone could match Pitino's work ethic and passion, if anyone could instill his team with as fierce a fighting spirit as Pitino could, John Calipari was the man.

And yet, wasn't this Opposites Week?

Sure, UMass had great chemistry, but hadn't Pitino molded all of the egos of his standout players into a thoroughly unselfish basketball unit? Didn't he have superstars coming off the bench without complaining? Hadn't he instilled a sense of sacrifice for the greater good?

"What Rick's been able to do, to get the collection of talent to play together, you don't understand how hard that is," Calipari said. "As a basketball fan, it's great to see, because that's what this is all about. You talk about teaching life skills. . . ."

And this notion of UMass being the underdog with no real pressure? Hadn't the Minutemen said all along that winning the national championship was their only real goal? Wasn't it the Minutemen, not the Wildcats, who had refused to cut down the nets after winning their regional final and getting to the Final Four? "They can have them," Carmelo Travieso explained after UMass beat Georgetown. "We want the ones at the Meadowlands."

Beating Kentucky was only a byproduct of UMass's season–long quest. To a man, they had their eyes on those New Jersey nets.

•

Saturday, March 30, dawned clear and cool, a welcome hint of spring in the air, the most bitter of winters finally relinquishing its grip. The New York skyline sparkled. The final weekend of the college basketball season had arrived.

As fans filed in to the Continental Airlines Arena, they saw the railing beneath the upper deck covered with an enormous circular banner. On it, the names of the sixty–four teams in the NCAA tournament were prominently displayed. Drexel and Valparaiso, Colgate and Wisconsin–Green Bay, Princeton and Connecticut were all featured on the fabric in bold colors of blue or red. All had had special seasons, memories that would not easily fade.

In the center of the arena, on either side, four schools had their names featured in gold. It was time to play ball.

UMass, like the other three teams still playing, had 2,500 tickets to the Final Four.[2] Using a lottery system, the school sold 816 of them to students, some of whom resold the tickets for more money than they had ever known. Another 731 went to season–ticket holders who were high on the totem pole of "priority points," thanks in significant measure to contributions they had made to the athletic department. The remaining seats were filled by an intriguing array of people who helped define the tapestry of UMass basketball.

The UMass section was sprinkled with members of the athletic department, people ranging from academic coordinator Dave Glover to basketball secretary Bonnie Martin to assistant women's softball coach Mona Stevens. University president William Bulger was on hand, as well as former president Michael Hooker, who had left UMass for North Carolina less than a year before. UMass's two players with the retired Number 32 hanging from the rafters—Julius Erving and George (Trigger) Burke—came to root for the Minutemen. Politicians were out in force, from Amherst state senator Stanley Rosenberg (who once referred to the university's "psychological profile [as] something like an inferiority complex"), to United States Senator Ted Kennedy, to national security advisor Anthony Lake.

Interspersed among the crowd were fans with strong personal connections to John Calipari, who had ninety–two tickets to distribute. Several went to friends. Two of his former teammates from Moon Area High School showed up: Bill Mazar, who had described Calipari as "The King of Everything," and Mike Bartels, who remembers getting suckered into rebounding shots in the Moon gym because Calipari was "always scamming and scheming on something." Calipari also invited high school coach Bill Sacco, who described his former point guard as "the gym rat of all gym rats," and Dennis Tobin, his roommate at the University of North Carolina at Wilmington. Former Clarion State coach Joe DeGregorio, who never forgot the thank–you note his former point guard sent to his wife, came to root for the Minutemen. There was also longtime family friend Mike Toney, an alleged scalper who had run into trouble with the Nevada Gaming Control Board; Ed Jenka, the national promotions director for Nike; and Mike Francesa, co–host of the popular New York sports radio talk show, "Mike and the Mad Dog." Craig Fenech, agent to both Calipari and Francesa, also boarded the gravy train.

Calipari flew several family members in to New Jersey, including his parents Vince and Donna. He also invited a host of former UMass players, a group that included everyone from Derek Kellogg—who had missed making the Final Four by one half of a game a year ago—to Ben Grodski, who had described some of the coach's techniques as "dehumanizing."

Guests of players also filled the stands. There was Janice Camby, who had stopped watching games on television after seeing her son prone on the floor at St. Bonaventure. Janice's living room had started to overflow with trophies, crowding up against the fish tank, the ceramic collie and the prom photos of Marcus and longtime girlfriend Ceylon Cicero (who was also in attendance).

For the family of Tyrone Weeks, the Final Four was a hard–won reunion. Tyrone's mother Delores came from Philadelphia, where she worked at a rehab clinic. It was the same clinic where, a few years back, she had finally broken free from the desperate battle with cocaine addiction that long ago forced her two sons out of the house. Tyrone ultimately left North Philadelphia for the more suburban condominium of a summer–league coach with the unusual name Tennis Young—at first, it was hard to sleep because of the peculiar sounds of birds chirping in the morning. Young, the surrogate father, came to the Continental Arena with Tyrone's brother, Robert Weeks. Robert was still struggling to let go of the anger he felt toward his mother. He had asked Tyrone over and over again how he could forget about the past. "It's not that I forget it," Tyrone said. "I just don't worry about it. If you worry about the past, it will drag you down. I try to worry about the future. Just let the past be the past."

Dana Dingle's father Willie had swelled with pride all week when his colleagues at Con Edison talked about the game. *Yep, my boy's in the Final Four.*

Patricia Bright was up from Baltimore. She had seen her only son walk a tightrope of trouble, saddened by the abandonment from a father he hadn't seen in years. Now she could hardly contain her pride.

Carmen Peña, mother of Carmelo Travieso, came down from Boston with her other son, Raul. The terror of Hurricane David was now but a distant memory, as were the days when, freshly arrived from Puerto Rico, she cleaned houses to help the family scrape by.

With two brothers on the team, the Padilla family was well represented: plenty of cousins and uncles. Just three rows behind the UMass bench sat Edgar and Giddel's sister, Millie, with her husband, Omar. Right next to them were father Mariano Padilla, wearing a backwards hat with Edgar's picture sticking high above his forehead, and mother Milca, wound tight even before the game began.

•

There was nothing fancy about the Minutemen's strategy. They would play their customary aggressive man–to–man defense, with Camby as the last line, ready to swat or alter any shot that came his way. They would try to maintain a halfcourt game, preventing Kentucky from turning the contest into a track meet where the Wildcats could exploit their superior depth. At the same time, Calipari wanted his players to attack the Kentucky pressure. Rebounds and loose balls had to be pursued relentlessly. Deep down, the Minutemen felt that mentally they were a little tougher than their opponents. If the game got close, they would really see what Kentucky was made of. The Wildcats hadn't had to deliver at crunchtime all season; the Minutemen had been doing it all year.

Kentucky had made one major change since playing UMass back in November. At the beginning of the season, Pitino moved top scorer Tony Delk to point guard, reasoning that his athleticism would galvanize the team. Besides, Pitino said in the Kentucky media guide, point guard was where Delk would have to play in the NBA. When the Wildcats opened their year in Springfield with a victory over Maryland, Pitino was questioned about the strategy by none other than his old UMass coach Jack Leaman, who suggested that the far less spectacular, less offensive–minded Anthony Epps might be the better choice. A few days later, after Kentucky fell to UMass, Pitino agreed. Ever since, Epps had been the point guard, and Delk had played shooting guard. As Pitino watched film over and over into the wee hours during the past week, he concluded that posting up Delk might pay dividends against UMass. Sure, it was unconventional to bring a six–foot, three–point shooter into the lane, but Delk was so strong physically that he might be able to overpower Carmelo Travieso. Pitino thought if he moved big men Walter McCarty and Mark Pope away from the basket (where each had to be respected, even to three–point range), the Minutemen would have to move Camby out of the lane. Pitino also resolved to wear down UMass as much as he could; he would run one fresh–legged defender after another at Padilla, and see just how much iron this ironman had. Defensively, he knew he couldn't let Camby dominate the way he had in November; the double–teams had to be lightning quick.

•

Syracuse defeated Mississippi State in the opener, 77–69. While the Orangemen blew kisses to their section of the crowd and coach Jim Boeheim stood on the court getting interviewed by CBS's Jim Nantz and Billy Packer, Edgar Padilla emerged from the locker–room tunnel.

He looked ready for a prize fight, his right wrist bound in tape wrapped around his thumb, the index and middle fingers of his left hand taped hard together. He lifted up the CBS television wire in front of him, ducked underneath, and led the Minutemen on to the court.

As the clock ticked down, the tension thickened. Hands were clapping, feet were stomping, pep bands were rocking, cheerleaders were hurtling into the air. The players fired up streams of jump shots, discarded warmup tops, got the sweat flowing. The two coaches came out looking resplendent. They shook hands, shared a couple of words. As John Calipari watched his team bounce in the now familiar mosh-pit routine—born against Kentucky back in November—his arms were folded, his stare fixed. Rick Pitino watched his blue–clad Wildcats pull together on the foul line. At courtside, above the WHMP banner, Jack Leaman took in the scene. "This," he said moments before tipoff, "is absolutely incredible."

•

UMass had to weather a couple of crises in the first half. Travieso picked up two fouls before the first television timeout, and wound up sitting out seven minutes. Dingle caught an elbow in the lip, and had to go back to the locker room for three stitches; he missed eight minutes.

While the Minutemen were able to set a halfcourt tempo, they had trouble containing Delk, who scored twelve points. Kentucky proved every bit as tough as UMass on the boards. It was hard to find an edge.

Still, UMass held on. Padilla lacerated the Kentucky pressure, handing out seven assists in the first half alone. Camby had trouble shooting over the double–teams, but played strong on the defensive end, blocking five shots. Bright hit a number of tough hoops. The bench provided some key moments.

Kentucky scored the last two baskets of the half, opening up a 36–28 lead, its largest of the game.

For the ninth time this year, the Minutemen trailed at halftime. They had come back to win every game except one. But they never had to come back against a team like Kentucky.

The beginning of the second half is always a critical time. It is a moment for setting a tone (as Camby had done in the season–opener with his memorable steal and dunk against the Wildcats), and in many cases, for establishing momentum that carries through to the finish.

For the Minutemen, the start could not have been much worse. First, Derek Anderson hit a layup to extend the lead to ten. Then, in a span of just thirteen seconds, Travieso picked up both his third and fourth fouls. All season long, he had been a defender without peer, shutting down guards from Allen Iverson to Stephon Marbury, but he seldom had to defend physical guards who got the ball in the paint. On this night, he seemed overmatched by Delk. With 18:25 left in the half, Travieso found himself on the bench. Just seconds later, the scoreboard read: 43–28. The Minutemen were trailing the most explosive team in college basketball by fifteen points. Pitino was on his feet, riling on his team, smelling blood.

Freshman Charlton Clarke, guarding Delk, found himself thrust into the biggest game of his life. His exuberance gave UMass a little lift, as he set up a basket by Bright, then scored one of his own with a strong drive into the middle. But his candle burned quickly. Never in the shape he wanted to be in after breaking his foot in the season opener, he quickly spent all of his adrenaline and found himself gasping for air. Before he had even played two minutes, Clarke was holding his fist high for a substitute, and Calipari was scrambling on the bench.

The coach knew that it was really too much to ask an unproven freshman to contribute for any extended period of time, but he didn't know what else to do. Travieso quickly hopped out of his seat, assuming Calipari would put him back in the game, four fouls and all. What options did he have? This was a desperate situation. He had to risk it all.

Calipari reached out to Travieso, then took a long look at his bench. Funny, this situation had never come up before. Padilla and Travieso had been so good, so steady. They had played hard all year without ever fouling out, hardly facing any foul trouble at all. The lack of depth at guard—the problem every expert seized upon in preseason—never materialized as a problem, until now. What options *did* he have? He could go to Rigo Nuñez, all gangly eagerness, but Nuñez was not really strong enough to guard Delk, and he wouldn't be able to provide any offense. And then, with his hand on Travieso's uniform, Calipari saw Giddel Padilla staring up at him, his eyes burning with a simple message: *Put me in.*

It would be the ultimate wild card, a maverick move unlike any he had ever made as a coach. Giddel had played only thirty–four minutes all year, none when the game was in doubt. To put him in now, in the Final Four, when UMass desperately needed a spark, seemed positively ludicrous.

Yet hadn't he been a warrior in practice all year, pushing his brother, challenging Travieso, helping to make them as good as they were? Hadn't he known pressure before, hitting the championship–winning shot in Bayamón the previous summer? And even when he was a pain in the ass, almost getting into that scrap with Camby in practice, hadn't it been because Giddel was such a tough competitor? He was, after all, a Padilla, and that meant one thing—the kid was fearless.

Uncertain for a split second, Calipari turned to Bruiser Flint to get the opinion of his right–hand man. Flint nodded his head. In an instant, Calipari sent Travieso back to the bench and turned to the elder Padilla. "This is your opportunity, Giddel," Calipari said. "We need you."

While he reported to the scorer's table, action played out on the court. Clarke missed a jumper, but Camby soared high to slam in the rebound. Then, on the other end, there was a scramble for the ball, and Camby flung his long body to the court to cause a tie–up that gave UMass possession. On the whistle, the officials signaled a television timeout with 15:38 left and Kentucky leading, 47–36. Calipari didn't wait for his team. He charged onto the floor, crossing midcourt, going right in front of the Kentucky bench, where he slapped the back sides of all five of his players. It was time to ignite them with every ounce of his will.

•

When play resumed, the UMass backcourt consisted of Number 11, with "Padilla" printed on the back of his jersey, and Number 10 with the name "G. Padilla." UMass fans could not believe their eyes. What in the hell was Calipari doing?

Dana Dingle scored right away to cut the gap to nine. On Kentucky's possession, Giddel Padilla left his man when the pass went into the post to Mark Pope and slapped at the ball. The whistle blew, and Calipari almost lost control. *What the fuck is he doing?*

The call, though, went against Pope for pushing off, and UMass got the ball back.

Edgar Padilla set the offense, standing behind the top of the key. He zipped a pass over to his brother on the left wing. Giddel instantly made a move toward the hoop, spinning aggressively past Jeff Sheppard and soaring in toward the basket. Pope leaped high to try to block the shot, but just before releasing, Giddel dumped the ball back to Camby for a gorgeous basket and a foul. The UMass crowd was beside itself with joy. When Camby hit the free throw, it was a six–point game.

Those watching on television saw the camera pan to Mariano

*Giddel Padilla (Photo courtesy of UMass Media Relations)*

Padilla—on his feet, clapping his hands, still wearing the backwards baseball cap and the big picture of Edgar over his forehead. There was no sign of his wife, though. Where was she?

The tension had long ago proven too much for Milca. She had left for the concourse, walking in circles, unable to watch. But this moment—this most glorious of moments—had to be seen, or so thought her daughter, Millie. When Millie saw Giddel report to the scorer's table, she pressed her hand up against her father's and screamed out, "Oh my God!" As the action played out, tears streaming down her face, Millie bolted up the steps in a desperate search for her mother. She went racing around the arena, wanting to scream out, "Mom!" and knowing that Milca—wherever she was—would not have been able to hear a word.

•

The second half played out with escalating intensity as the two best teams in college basketball pushed each other to the extreme. Every possession became a matter of fundamental importance. Every rebound was a crusade. Bodies were flying. Calipari and Pitino hollered and pleaded, gesturing wildly, seeking any sliver of an edge. In the stands, fans from Massachusetts and Kentucky screamed at the referees, absolutely convinced that they had been robbed, that there was no justice at all. When a ball would hang on the rim for a split second, urgent pleas of "Get in there!" and "Get the hell out!" rang through the arena.

Kentucky weathered UMass's surge, and built the lead back to double digits. Calipari, who had taken Giddel Padilla out when it was still a six–point game, returned him to the court briefly, then went for broke with Travieso. On successive possessions, Edgar Padilla found Travieso with beautiful passes for long, arching three–point baskets. Camby began breaking free for one tough basket after another, splitting double and triple teams, putting all of his game on glittering display. With 4:56 left, Dingle missed a hard drive to the hoop, but Bright soared high and tipped home the rebound. UMass had pulled within three points at 63–60. A haunted–looking Rick Pitino called timeout.

UMass's defining "Refuse to Lose" spirit had come to the fore. Kentucky, for the first time all year, had to deliver.

Derek Anderson of Kentucky missed the front end of a one–and–one free–throw opportunity. Edgar Padilla lost the ball for UMass, then stole it back from Anthony Epps. Steaming downcourt, he saw Travieso on the left wing and zipped a pass to him. Travieso didn't hesitate, letting fly without really getting his feet set. The tying bid was an airball.

Kentucky then ran off eight of the next nine points, extending its lead to 71–61 with 2:35 left, when UMass called a timeout. It appeared that the Minutemen's last gallant surge had been blunted.

Millie was back in her seat by now, unable to locate her mother, and brooding about the apparent loss. Moments earlier, though, she had seen Giddel pop off the bench yet again, this time to replace Donta Bright, who had fouled out after a noble game: fifteen points, nine rebounds and the kind of fight that seemed to define his team at its best. Calipari had elected to replace him with Giddel, employing a three–guard offense for one of the only times all year, playing out another hunch. It was time for the season's last gasp.

On the next possession, Camby made a beautiful move through a Kentucky double–team, banking in a shot to cut the gap to eight. The ensuing inbounds pass went to Jeff Sheppard on the left side of the floor between the UMass foul line and midcourt. As soon as Sheppard turned, Edgar Padilla swiped at the ball, knocking it over to Travieso, who flipped it back to his teammate on the left wing. Before Kentucky could adjust, Edgar fired a forty–foot diagonal pass, threaded through four Wildcat players. Giddel gathered it in, soared high and dropped the ball in for two. Just like that, it was 71–65 with 2:05 left, and UMass was charging to the bench for a timeout.

Assistant coach Ed Schilling felt a hard lump in his throat. During the year, he had grown closer to Giddel than to any of the other players or coaches. Their special code flashed back in his head: *Is this paradise, or what?* He could not believe what he was seeing. Looking Giddel in the eye as the team broke back onto the floor, he said simply, "Go get 'em."

With 1:49 left, Giddel almost swiped the ball away from Sheppard, knocking it out of bounds. On the ensuing inbounds play, Edgar stole the pass and flew back upcourt. He hit Camby with a pass. The UMass center was fouled on his drive, and dropped in both free throws to make it 71–67.

On the sidelines, Calipari and Pitino squatted just thirty feet apart, both far out of the coach's box.

Again, the UMass defense forced a turnover as Dingle and Edgar Padilla hounded Derek Anderson into a mistake. Camby leaned in for a turnaround over Pope, but the ball caromed off the front rim. Giddel Padilla, all six–three, soared high for the rebound and put the ball back up—only to have it rejected by Antoine Walker.

Anderson hit two free throws, then Edgar Padilla launched a three–pointer that sailed through the hoop just before the public–address man announced, "One minute, one minute remaining." UMass was down, 73–70, scratching and fighting, yearning, absolutely refusing to lose.

The Kentucky Wildcats, though, were far more than an aggregate of great talent. As befits a true champion, they played to win; they did not play not to lose. Immediately, they attacked the basket, and Mark Pope got fouled. He hit both free throws with fifty–two seconds left to extend the lead to 75–70.

Edgar Padilla again blazed upcourt, again let fly for three. This one

*Charlton Clarke, Tyrone Weeks and Donta Bright watch the bitter end.*
*(Photo by Jerrey Roberts)*

rattled in and out, and Kentucky point guard Anthony Epps hauled it in, and sent it sailing the other way, where Antoine Walker's dunk basically ended UMass's season.

With nineteen seconds left, Edgar Padilla fouled out for the first time since the Converse All–Star game. Since that night, he had grown immeasurably. He had emerged as one of the best point guards in the country. On this night, against the most relentless pressure any college team could muster, he had delivered twelve assists and committed only four turnovers. He had played every second of the contest, fighting through exhaustion, pushing out of the comfort level, never stopping. Now it was over. Holding his hands over his head, he walked to the bench and hugged John Calipari.

Moments later, the final points of the game—and UMass's season—were scored by his brother Giddel. The Minutemen had come up short, 81–74.

•

In the aftermath of good college basketball games, rival players often congratulate each other, slapping high–fives, saying some kind words. On this night, players on the two teams hugged. So did the rival coaches.

Several minutes later, Marcus Camby came back to the court with a towel over his head, and took a slow, meandering walk. In the biggest game of his life, he had lived up to every bit of his billing: twenty–five points, eight rebounds, six blocks. He had been the best player on the floor. It wasn't enough.

Outside the locker room, Dana Dingle and Donta Bright sat together, their college careers over. Approached by a reporter and asked to reflect on what his UMass basketball experience had meant, Bright almost burst into tears. "Coach Calipari has meant so much to me," he said. "He pushed me when I thought I couldn't go any more. I came in here as a little kid. I'm leaving as a man. He taught me life skills: never take things for granted, always respect people. It's been great. It's something that will stay with me for the rest of my life."

Wearing black parkas, Carmelo Travieso and Edgar Padilla walked out toward the team bus, taking one last glance at the Final Four. "We'll be back," Travieso said.

"It's been an honor for me to be a part of this team," said Padilla. Asked what it was like for him to play with his brother that night, Padilla choked up. "He's the guy who worked the hardest in practice," he said. "I felt very, very good to see all his hard work pay off."

Giddel, his college career having essentially started and ended on the same night, sat for a long time in the locker room, still wearing his uniform and a white hat that proclaimed, "Meadowlands, Road to the Final Four." No, he said, he wasn't nervous. He had always been ready for his opportunity, preparing as if he were going to play forty minutes. That's why he often had trouble eating or sleeping after a game— too much unspent fuel. Sure, he said, it wasn't easy accepting his role at first, but he had grown to understand. No, he had not had a chance to hook up with his family yet, but they were all going to meet at the hotel. He had plans to tell Edgar that he was proud of him: "Keep doing what you're doing. You're going to have a chance to play at the next level. I really believe that."

He was not sure what his own plans were. In the spring, he would graduate, and then he hoped to play professional ball somewhere. "I believe in my talent," he said.

In some ways the most memorable part of the night for Giddel had nothing to do with his playing. What had really shocked him came afterward, while the team was alone in the locker room, when he saw John Calipari break down and cry.

"He's a great kid—a great guy," Giddel said. "And I'll always have happy memories about him."

The formal postgame interviews took place on a platform down the hall from the locker room. Coaches and players were ushered into a private passage behind a blue curtain, and led up the back of the platform to meet the press. Calipari came out with his hair oddly mussed, the top button of his shirt undone, his eyes red–rimmed.

"We gave ourselves a chance to win against a great basketball club," he said. "We refused to lose. We never stopped playing. We played right down to the end. And I'm proud of them. I told the team after this game in the locker room that I learned more about myself as a coach and a person this year than I have in all my other years of coaching. I thanked them, because you're talking about unbelievable human beings that I coached this year."

What exactly had he learned?

"Well, I honestly learned that it isn't life or death, winning basketball games. And I learned that when you're coaching, you understand that when you have good people, it's very fun to coach. When you have guys that you're struggling with, it's not very fun to coach. And the record of your team doesn't matter as much as that."

When Calipari finished, he headed out behind the blue curtain. There he spent a private minute with the winning coach.

While Rick Pitino made his opening comments—saying with his first words that he was so proud of Massachusetts, his alma mater—Calipari walked back into the hall. He spoke to reporters for a few moments, then turned to walk away.

Jack Leaman was waiting. The two men walked to the bus together, holding hands.

•

Two nights later, Kentucky defeated Syracuse for the national championship. The UMass coaches and players were long gone by that point. Most would say later that they had not even watched the title game. It was too painful.

The only member of the UMass entourage to stick around was Jack Leaman. But once he had congratulated his former point guard, Leaman headed home. He wasn't even around when Pitino came out from behind the blue curtain to answer questions, including one from Craig Handel of Springfield's *Union–News*: "Coach, one of the people most happy for you tonight was Jack Leaman, your former college coach. And I was just wondering what you most learned from him."

Pitino looked out at the room full of reporters and said, "What he did for me was he taught me how to be a man. And that's the most important thing to me. He made it very tough—back then discipline was extremely stringent. Without Jack Leaman, I don't think I would have ever grown up. He taught me the fundamentals, taught me about defensive discipline, but he taught me how to be a man and care about the team before anything else."

# AFTERWORD: "I AM READY TO PURSUE MY LIFELONG DREAM"

Summer, 1996

n the fall semester of the 1891–92 school year, when the game of basketball was invented in western Massachusetts, the region's first famous "Cal" arrived on the scene. A reserved youngster from Plymouth, Vermont, Calvin Coolidge enrolled in classes at Amherst College. Later, in nearby Northampton, Coolidge met his wife, served on the city council, and became the mayor. Years afterward, once his political career was over, he returned to live out his life in the area.

As President of the United States from 1923–29, Coolidge became famous for his terse sayings. Nicknamed "Silent Cal," he is best remembered for one statement: "The business of America is business."

Western Massachusetts's second famous Cal—seldom accused of silence—stood before a lectern at the Mullins Center on April 29, 1996. It was John Calipari's task that day merely to introduce Marcus Camby. This was Camby's moment, the day he would announce his decision about whether to enter the NBA draft or remain at UMass for his senior season of 1996–97. Glistening on a table next to the lectern were Camby's National Player of the Year awards.

The room was filled not just with reporters, but with some of the most important people in Camby's life. His mother Janice was on hand, looking just a little bit nervous. So was "Stevie J" Johnson, a bedrock of the community back in Bellevue Square. Camby's teammates, in slightly disheveled streetclothes, sat in a row behind the lectern.

After Calipari's brief introduction, the man of the hour walked to the microphone wearing blue jeans, a denim shirt and a pendant sparkling with the numeral "21." (No one made any mention of the pendant that day; weeks later journalists suddenly became appraisers.)

"Today," Camby began, seeming relaxed and at peace with himself, "I decided that I'm going to transfer to UConn."

Once the laughter subsided, Camby got on with the business. "This

*Marcus Camby thanks his teammates after announcing his decision to enter the NBA draft. (Photo by Jerrey Roberts)*

decision has been very hard," he said, "but I feel that I am ready to pursue my lifelong dream, to play in the NBA. . . . This last season was incredible. But it was not about winning games and advancing to the Final Four that made it special. It was the fun that we had together. I will never leave UMass in my heart. I will never leave this team. They will always be with me, and I will be with them."

Camby kissed his mother, gave a big hug to academic coordinator Dave Glover and another one to Calipari, then shook hands with each of his teammates. Afterward, he stepped back to the lectern to field some questions, the last of which dealt with the kind of legacy he'd like to leave.

His diffident, little boy's smile curled over his features as he replied, "Probably as a nice person, a guy who helps out kids, that type of image. I don't want to be remembered as a basketball player. On the court, I'd like to be remembered as a player who has a lot of class, plays by the book, plays the game hard, helps his team try to win."

Calipari almost gushed with pride when he stepped back to the microphone. He described Camby's announcement as "just a fabulous day for our program," even though the prospects for the 1996–97 season had just taken a serious nosedive. The reason he was happy transcended wins and losses, Calipari insisted: "I want to be defined not as a coach who wins basketball games, but as one who develops people."

Asked whether he might consider joining Camby in the NBA, Calipari smiled. "I'm going to be here," he said. Yes, he needed a break right now. He was going to go down to Florida with his wife and daughters for two weeks of "rollerblading, biking, running and swimming," but he'd be back. "My intention is to be here for a long time."

•

Within a few weeks, Calipari's agent, Craig Fenech, was involved in serious discussions with the Philadelphia 76ers about their coaching vacancy. Meanwhile, the New Jersey Nets were scrambling to find a new head coach for their beleaguered franchise.

The first choice of the Nets was Rick Pitino. The club's owners felt they had a good chance at luring the Kentucky coach. After all, he had just won a national championship—what else was left to accomplish? Pitino had always displayed an appetite for adventure and challenge; the seven years he had been at Kentucky represented his longest stint at any job. Besides, Pitino was good friends with principal owner Joe Taub. In coaching the Nets, Pitino would be returning to his roots in the New York area. And money was almost no object. When Pitino met with the team's management at the Cincinnati Airport on Friday, May 24, he received an offer of almost $30 million over six years to be coach, general manager and part owner of the team. Such a contract was far in excess of what any other NBA coach was making, and it would dwarf his package at Kentucky—one thought to be the most lucrative in the college game. It would be a hard offer to turn down.

Pitino said that he wanted to think about it. He and his wife Joanne were headed for a golfing trip in Ireland on Sunday, May 26, with a bunch of Kentucky basketball boosters. He would let them know his decision when he returned in a week.

It didn't take that long. Three days into his trip, Pitino said he got some advice from his wife: he should listen to his heart. "I realize now," he said in a prepared statement, "that my heart is with the players of Kentucky."

Miffed, Nets president Michael Rowe set his sights on another candidate.

Two days later, on Friday, May 31, Rowe drove up to New England to have a preliminary meeting with Calipari. By the end of the weekend, negotiations were underway.[1]

On Monday, June 3, talks hit what Calipari later described as "a pause" when he was notified about some startling news: *The Hartford Courant* would be running a story in which Camby admitted taking gifts and money from agents. Before proceeding with any further contract details, Calipari said he wanted to assure himself that both Camby and UMass were not in any jeopardy. After talking with Camby, the coach said he felt better. *Yes, Marcus showed some poor judgment, but it was mostly those scumbag agents, trying to make money off his talent. And UMass should not be penalized. We monitor the agents on campus, make them register. Nobody knew about this situation. How could we? Marcus lived in the dorms. He didn't drive a car. His mom still lived in the projects. Yeah, he wore that necklace, but lots of kids on this campus wear gaudy jewelry, and most of it's fake.*

The *Courant* story ran on Tuesday, June 4, spread out over most of the front page and two full inside pages. In it, Camby was described as making a tear–filled confession that was tape–recorded in his hotel room in Rosemont, Illinois, site of an NBA predraft camp where he was being tested and measured. Slumped against the bathroom sink, wearing only a pair of maroon and black UMass basketball shorts, Camby admitted to *Courant* reporter Desmond Conner that he had accepted money and jewelry from two agents—Wesley Spears and John Lounsbury—who hoped to represent him in his professional career. Some of those gifts were given to friends of Camby's from Hartford. Others, he admitted, he had accepted prior to the end of his college career, a violation of NCAA rules.

Camby claimed that he had never agreed to sign with anyone before inking his pact with Washington–based ProServ on May 20. He insinuated that Spears was trying to blackmail him. "He was like screaming mad," Camby said. "'If you don't do this, I'm going to the press.'" The *Courant* did not indicate where it had received the evidence about Camby's dealings. Spears refused to comment in the story.

While Camby flew from Chicago to Hartford, Calipari took the opposite trip, heading out to Chicago on Tuesday afternoon. His plan, he said, was to watch Donta Bright participate in the scrimmages at the NBA predraft camp.[2]

Calipari also attended to some other business. He spoke with Larry Brown, head coach of the Indiana Pacers, and Bob Hill, head coach of the San Antonio Spurs—two former mentors at the University of Kansas. Calipari, who had started out supporting himself by spooning peas and carrots to college athletes, now had another professional opportunity to consider.

On Wednesday, June 5, details were being hammered out between Nets president Michael Rowe and Calipari's agent Craig Fenech. The coach sat in a hotel room with Bob Ryan of *The Boston Globe* that afternoon and indicated he expected to be back at UMass. "Someone could come along with the right offer," Calipari said. "Someone could come along who is willing to make the complete investment in building a championship team I think would be necessary to get the job done. If something like that came up, I'd be honest—I'll listen. It may happen. It may happen next week. But I don't expect it."

Calipari watched Bright play in the predraft camp and went to the Bulls game against the Seattle Supersonics in the NBA Finals. For the first time in his life, Calipari watched Michael Jordan perform live.

Late that night, Mike Francesa of radio station WFAN in New York broke the story that the deal was done.

Still, there was no confirmation from either Calipari, Fenech or Michael Rowe. Was it really true?

On Thursday morning there were conflicting reports coming over the wire. *The Record* of Hackensack, New Jersey, reported that Rowe had said on Wednesday evening that Calipari had not even been considered for the job. Rowe stated that he had interviewed two candidates in Chicago, but hadn't even met with Calipari, adding, "I would take a lie detector test, and I'm sure he would, too."[3]

Later on Thursday morning, though, confirmation came from Fenech that the deal was done. "Everybody wants to test themselves at the highest level," Fenech said.

UMass had long ago planned some other business for that Thursday morning. Under ordinary circumstances the press conference to announce the resumption of the basketball series with UConn would have been enormous news. After all, this was a burning rivalry that hadn't been played in six years, not since each school had grown from regional program to national power. The antipathy between the two coaches and the two sets of fans was not even thinly veiled; it was naked. But a four-year agreement had been hammered out—there was too much to be gained. So at eleven o'clock, as scheduled, the press conference went off in Springfield at the Basketball Hall of Fame, the site more than eight years before of John Calipari's introductory press conference, where he had promised to "create a love affair" at UMass. On one side of the lectern sat UConn athletic director Lew Perkins and his hugely successful basketball coach, Jim Calhoun. On the other side sat UMass athletic director Bob Marcum next to an empty orange chair.

Dave Gavitt, former Providence coach and founder of The Big East Conference, had brokered the peace between the two schools. He stood before the microphone and told assembled journalists, "This is a great day for New England college basketball."

The next day there was another press conference, this one back at the Continental Airlines Arena at the Meadowlands, home of the New Jersey Nets. Long ago, when they were playing on Long Island in the American Basketball Association, the Nets had been a power, thanks mostly to former UMass star Julius Erving. Since joining the NBA in 1976, though, the Nets had been one of the league's true laughing-stocks. In twenty years, they had posted only six winning seasons. Only once had they made it out of the first round of the playoffs, never getting even remotely close to a championship. In each of the last two years they had posted identical records of 30–52.

Michael Rowe introduced the new coach. He began by saying that he hadn't studied his quotes recently, but that he was proud to have hired a coach who didn't need to take a golfing trip before deciding whether the job was right for him.

Calipari, his glittering 193–71 record at UMass behind him, looked resplendent, if a bit nervous. He began by saying that this was a job he really wanted. Then he thanked Pitino for not taking the position. (Having facilitated a job for Calipari once again, Pitino didn't need to make a financial contribution toward the package this time. After all, as new head coach, executive vice president and director of basketball operations, Calipari signed a contract for $15 million over five years, making him the second–highest–paid coach in the NBA behind Pat Riley of the Miami Heat.)

And then, before taking questions, Calipari ended his introductory comments by once again becoming Cupid with a clipboard: "My goal is to create a love affair. . ."

•

UMass had signed five recruits for the 1996–97 season, a group considered perhaps the finest incoming class in school history. All had expected Calipari to be their coach when they signed letters of intent. Because the NCAA interprets the letters as commitments to the school rather than to the coach, players who want to go to another school are considered transfers who must take a year off from competition. Even so, six–nine Ajmal Basit from New Jersey, perhaps the most highly regarded of the bunch, went back and forth for weeks about whether or not to enroll at UMass.

Returning players were also startled by Calipari's departure. Every year they had heard the rumors. They knew he was a hot commodity. But they had expected him to stay.

When the shock wore off, though, most admitted they would have made the same choice. For one thing, it was an enormous amount of money. For another, Calipari would be coaching in a league with the world's best players. "He's going to the NBA," said Carmelo Travieso. "We all have the same dream."

In late June, the dream was also realized for Marcus Camby.

Ironically, the NBA draft was held at the Continental Airlines Arena at the Meadowlands. Before the selections were made, Camby stopped by the "War Room" of the Nets and exchanged a hug with Calipari. "He wished me all the best of luck," said Camby. "And I wished him all the best of luck."

With the first pick in the draft, the Philadelphia 76ers chose Allen Iverson, the sophomore point guard from Georgetown who had been stymied by UMass in the Elite Eight game. Iverson, who had aroused mild controversy by driving a Mercedes around the Washington area in the weeks prior to his announcement to join the NBA draft, became the first player in coach John Thompson's distinguished career to leave for the NBA before the beginning of his senior year.

Camby was picked next by the Toronto Raptors. Smiling broadly and towering over league commissioner David Stern, Camby held a huge purple jersey with the Number 21 aloft for the cameras. His wild seven–month saga—a consensus National Player of the Year season, a Final Four berth, a frightening collapse and a swirling controversy regarding his dealings with agents—had come to an end.

"It's finally over," Camby said. "And I'm just so happy right now."

Before the summer was out, he would sign a three–year contract for $8.4 million.

●

For others, the dream sat in various states of being deferred or surrendered. Three former UMass players earned invitations from NBA teams to attend "veterans camp" in October, where they stood slim chances of making it as free agents.

While not picked in the draft, Donta Bright accepted an offer from John Calipari to come to veterans camp with the New Jersey Nets. If he did not stick with the team, he was planning to play in either the Continental Basketball Association—the top American minor league for hoops—or in Europe.

Lou Roe floundered through the 1995–96 season on the end of the bench for the Detroit Pistons, and was not offered a contract for the 1996–97 season. He reported to veterans camp with the Golden State Warriors.

Mike Williams had been drafted by the San Diego Wildcards of the Continental Basketball Association in 1995, but he was cut from the team. After a short playing stint in Ukraine, he returned to Hartford and worked out frequently in the late spring of 1996 with Marcus Camby at the University of Connecticut. He played very well in a Colorado summer league for a team sponsored by the Denver Nuggets, earning an invitation to their veterans camp.

Others had their sights set on a different level.

Dana Dingle was looking to play overseas. He was hoping to get offers in the fall from teams in Israel and Brazil.

Ted Cottrell hoped to catch on with a Delaware team in the fledgling Atlantic Basketball Association.

Giddel Padilla worked out with a couple of teams in the Continental Basketball Association, but was not picked in the league's draft. His sister Millie, expected to graduate with Edgar in 1997, said the whole family might move back to Puerto Rico at that time.

Other players moved on to a life after basketball.

Rigo Nuñez took a community development job in Springfield, directing a minority employment program in a social service agency.

Derek Kellogg's professional career consisted of his brief stint with the Converse All-Stars in November of 1995, when he helped pin a memorable loss on the University of Massachusetts. After working in the state treasurer's office for a year, Kellogg returned to UMass to pursue a Master's in education.

•

Four of five UMass basketball seniors graduated with their class in 1996. Bright, the one who didn't, says that he plans to return for his degree after his playing days are over.

During the summer of 1996, the latest NCAA graduation report was published, the one that had UMass's four–year average rate (for entering freshman classes in the years 1987–90) at seventy–five per-cent. That figure was third–best among teams that finished the year ranked in the Top 25. UMass administrators were angered that the news was all but unreported in *The Boston Globe.* Indeed, it was confined to one paragraph at the bottom of Jack Craig's media column, a few pages into the sports section, and only then in the context of CBS commen-tator Billy Packer's public criticism of the paper about the grades story.

A slew of other stories about UMass filled the front page of the *Globe* in the weeks after the season: the school's dispersal of Final Four tickets to various VIPs, Calipari's gift of tickets to alleged scalper Michael Toney, UMass's spending of $200,000 at the Final Four week-end, Camby's dealings with agents, Calipari's departure, the "Refuse to Lose" trademarking, UMass's financial settlement with players whose grades had been leaked. To report some of the stories, the *Globe* had to file requests through the Freedom of Information Act.

On campus, school officials spent a good chunk of the summer defending their policy of dealing with agents. They detailed the pro-cess of registration, the type of presentation each agent was required to make, the number of guest speakers brought in to talk to players. It was impossible to police all types of contact, school officials main-tained. In their eyes, Camby was mostly the victim of exploitation.[4]

*The Hartford Courant,* also using the Freedom of Information Act, reported that UMass had given agents free tickets to games at the Mullins Center. For some people, this practice suggested a coziness with the very elements school officials were decrying as repugnant. UMass athletic director Bob Marcum claimed that the policy repre-sented merely a way of monitoring player contact with prospective agents. By only offering access to "good" agents, he thought the school could avoid problems.

An internal committee at the school worked through the summer investigating the Camby case, and was expected to file its report to the NCAA in the fall of 1996. NCAA penalties might, or might not follow.

Really, there was no off–season.

•

In September, school began at the University of Massachusetts. All five recruits, including Ajmal Basit, enrolled. They began a grueling series of conditioning exercises with the returning players, starting with weight lifting before sunrise. After classes, they played spirited scrimmages at the Mullins Center. The scrimmages were led by two players who had played for Puerto Rico in the Summer Olympics, Edgar Padilla and Carmelo Travieso, a pair billed by the school's Media Relations department as "the best backcourt in America."

Though he was not looking forward to the travel, Jack Leaman prepared for another year of doing color analysis on the radio broadcasts. His 217 victories still made him the winningest coach in UMass history.

The first NBA game ever played at the Mullins Center was scheduled for October 13. The Washington Bullets would be taking on the New Jersey Nets in an exhibition game. John Calipari was hoping to break his one–game exhibition losing streak in the building.

The following night, as the clock struck midnight, the Bruiser Flint Era was scheduled to begin with the first official practice for the 1996–97 Minutemen.

At just thirty years old, Flint was the second youngest head coach in Division I when he accepted the UMass job two days after Calipari's decision to leave for the Nets. Looking dapper and confident, the former financial management major stood in the Green Room that Saturday in June and spelled out his goals for his first head coaching job. "I want to win the national championship," he said. "I don't want to get as far as John Calipari did—I want to win it."

## Chapter 1

1. Sponsored by adidas, which pays all expenses, ABCD is one of the elite summer showcases for top–notch high school talent. These camps are widely watched by college coaches, who get the opportunity to see how young players fare against serious competition.

## Chapter 2

1. Deeming the name Redmen offensive, UMass officials changed the name of the school's teams to the Minutemen in the spring of 1972, well ahead of the politically correct curve.

## Chapter 3

1. This confluence of strong–willed point guards had yet another twist for UMass basketball that no one could have foreseen at the moment. Just seven months later, Pitino lectured at the Five–Star Basketball Camp before a transfixed John Calipari. When Calipari hit *his* sophomore year of college a few years later, he too locked horns with his coach and left school.

## Chapter 4

1. Division I programs are now allotted thirteen scholarships.
2. Citadel's teams from the mid–1950s still hold the dubious mark with thirty–seven straight losses.
3. The infusion of big television money led to changes in the way the NCAA allots tournament funds to member schools. Prior to 1990, schools received a set amount of dollars from the NCAA "basketball fund" for every game their teams won in the tournament. Maintaining that policy under the new billion–dollar TV contract would mean that millions of dollars could be riding on a team's postseason performance. To ease the pressure to perform and temptation to cheat, the NCAA started funneling a school's tournament earn-

ings through its individual conference. Most conferences, including the Atlantic 10, have a revenue–sharing agreement. Thus, a Final Four appearance by one school is a boon for the league, but for the school it actually generates less of a direct one–year payoff than it did ten years ago.

## Chapter 6

1. The NCAA then allowed two full–time assistant coaches to be paid as the university saw fit. The third, still full–time in most cases, was limited to an annual salary of $16,000.
2. Neuharth is the former CEO of Gannett. The summary of the book on the title page says, "A maverick CEO reveals how you can outfox your enemies, outcharm your friends, outdo yourself . . . and have a helluva lot of fun."

## Chapter 7

1. The injury, a slightly torn meniscus, kept Camby out of action for three weeks.
2. Chaney was apparently tipped off about Calipari's interaction with the referees, though whether he was given an accurate picture remains questionable. Some have speculated that he was told by an assistant coach at Temple; others feel the tip came from a member of the media.

## Chapter 8

1. The culprit, Calipari remains convinced, was a former tutor who had grown disgruntled with the coaching staff. In an electronic age of fingerprint–free thievery, though, Calipari would never be able to pin it conclusively on anyone.
2. Proposition 48 is a piece of academic legislation of the NCAA which establishes minimum guidelines for freshmen to be allowed to compete in varsity sports. Part of those guidelines at the time included a baseline SAT score of 700.
3. Precise comparisons are difficult because colleges do not always provide standardized test data in consistent fashion. The UMass average SAT score of 1005 comes from the entering class in the fall of 1991, as published in the university "Factbook" put out by the Office of Institutional Research and Planning. The student body figures for Cincinnati and Georgia Tech, also from the incoming class in the fall of 1991, come from the 14th Edition of *American Universities and Colleges*, published by the American Council on Education.
4. Some leagues, such as the Atlantic Coast Conference, and some schools do not accept Proposition 48 athletes. Many leagues and schools do. The practice is widespread in the Atlantic 10.

5. Even Calipari sometimes played a race card when talking about the *Globe* story. In an "Up Close" interview on ESPN in the summer of 1995, he said, "Forget about me. I'm a big guy. I'm paid to take the heat that way and the shots you take. But for players—for those six black kids to take the shots they took—it wasn't fair."

6. NCAA information director Ursula Walsh confirmed that the organization does keep records of academic performance by demographic groups.

7. There was no shortage of basketball programs willing to dive into the fray for Blount, who, as it turned out, did well enough on his SAT to qualify for freshman participation. He ultimately chose Pittsburgh.

8. During home games over intersession, the dorms were closed and UMass stayed in the Campus Center hotel.

9. In an intriguing twist on the UMass–UConn hype, Camby took his crutches down to Storrs that night as the invited guest of his good buddy Ray Allen. Sitting behind the UConn bench, Camby cheered for the Huskies in a blowout of Pittsburgh.

10. Calipari himself was particularly belligerent, directing a stream of vitriol and sarcasm at Art McDonald, the same official he had felt wronged by in the first GW game. After getting a technical in the first half, Calipari charged the court and had to be physically restrained by assistant coach Bruiser Flint and administrative assistant Brian Gorman. The next night on his radio show Calipari admitted, "I was as bad as I've ever been. I should have been thrown out. I went crazy this whole game. But you know that's not me."

11. Months later, Jeff Meyer said, "Mike had put a lot of straw on Calipari's back." Lou Roe added, "Mike's a great person, and he definitely was a great player, but we wanted to win. We all agreed, even when Mike was there, if we had problems out of anybody, we had to get rid of [that person]. This was too risky for us and too risky for our ball club. We couldn't risk having a cancer on our squad."

12. At Calipari's annual "Selection Sunday" party on Sunday, March 12—a gathering of team members and reporters to watch the NCAA tournament brackets and pairings on CBS—*Globe* beat writer Joe Burris was conspicuously absent. While Calipari acknowledged that Burris had nothing to do with the academic stories, he maintained that his players didn't feel comfortable with representatives of the newspaper. On his weekly radio show the next night, Calipari said of the *Globe*, "They've been throwing grenades at us all year."

13. His base salary, the one paid by taxpayers, was $132,000. Other money came through a variety of sources: his television and radio shows, revenue from a basketball camp, sneaker and apparel contracts, motivational speaking, NCAA tournament money and proceeds from ticket sales at one road game of his

choice. The overall package was consistent with what other top–level coaches were earning.

## Chapter 9

1. Historically, per–pupil funding for higher education in Massachusetts ranked at or near the bottom of the fifty states. From Fiscal Year 1988 ($351.8 million) to FY 92 ($270.7 million), the Total Available Funds for UMass were reduced every year, according to university budget director Valerie Uber. Since then, they have increased every year, up to $372.3 million for FY 97.

2. Of the twelve coaches in the Atlantic 10, only two—Temple's John Chaney and La Salle's Speedy Morris—began the year with a greater tenure at their school than Calipari.

3. The American Dream image is somewhat exaggerated. Calipari's grandfather did work in coal mines in West Virginia as a young man, but actually died at fifty–seven, not forty–four.

4. The widespread college basketball scandals of the early fifties involved pay-offs to players for "shaving points" (deliberately trimming the margin of victory to benefit people who bet on the games).

5. The recruiting shortfall accounted for the low scholarship numbers. In fact, one of the ten players on scholarship, Rigo Nuñez, had been a walk–on for his first three seasons.

## Chapter 11

1. Having transferred from UNCW, after the first semester of his sophomore year, he had to sit out his first two semesters at Clarion. Thus, Calipari had the option of taking graduate courses and playing another season.

2. Longtime coach Owens was fired after Calipari's first year. Not expecting to be retained by his as–yet–unnamed successor, Calipari took a job for a few months as the assistant coach at Vermont. Brown then hired him back as the "restricted earnings" coach: one step below a full assistant.

3. In the summer of 1996, an out–of–court settlement was reached in which UMass agreed to pay Marcus Camby, Donta Bright, Dana Dingle, Tyrone Weeks, Ted Cottrell and Mike Williams a reported $12,000 apiece for not safeguarding the records.

## Chapter 12

1. Of 3,639 Division I college basketball players receiving athletics aid in the 1995–96 season, only 47 were characterized by the NCAA as Hispanic. Three of those—Edgar Padilla, Carmelo Travieso and Rigo Nuñez—went to UMass. Throw in walk–on Giddel Padilla, and UMass had more Hispanic players than any team in the country.

2. Burks was out late with Mike Williams on the team trip to his home state of Louisiana in February of 1995, an incident that set the wheels in motion for Williams's eventual dismissal from the team. Subsequently, Burks ran into legal difficulties on a couple of occasions—once regarding an allegation of assault in the dorms and once regarding a check–cashing controversy that also involved Williams. He was never arrested in either incident.

## Chapter 14

1. Jim Baron is the St. Bonaventure basketball coach.
2. Calipari's grandmother died later in the year.

## Chapter 15

1. Dingle finished his career by playing in a UMass–record 137 games, every one in his four years. The Minutemen's record in that time was 116–21.
2. Both the University of Cincinnati and Xavier have tradition–rich programs and tremendously loyal followings.

## Chapter 16

1. Jarvis is right. Peter Bernard was the only black player on the UMass team at the time. As late as 1968, a U.S. Office of Education Census reported that only 64 out of 11,594 students at UMass (0.6 percent) were black. In the fall of 1995, 685 out of 17,559 undergraduates (3.9 percent) classified themselves as "Black, Non–Hispanic." A total of 593 students (3.4 percent) did not respond to the question.
2. A year later, Jarvis referred repeatedly to "the game that we won, but not on the scoreboard."
3. Calipari was hurt by the lack of public support he received in the aftermath of the Chaney incident. He complained to Joe Burris of *The Boston Globe* about a mostly flattering profile he wrote about the Temple coach. Few coaches publicly backed Chaney, but St. Joseph's coach John Griffin said that he hadn't lost respect for the Temple mentor. During St. Joe's next visit to UMass, Calipari continued to press very late in a twenty–six–point UMass win.
4. Asked by a Boston reporter if he had shaken hands with Jarvis afterward, Calipari replied, "No, he was doing his fucking dance."
5. The uniforms appeared just once in the 1995–96 season, a poorly played victory over lowly Fordham at Madison Square Garden.
6. In 1995–96, the Atlantic 10 expanded to twelve teams and began divisional play for the first time in its twenty–year history. Teams in the "East" like UMass and the "West" like GW met only once during the regular season.
7. In 1991, freshman Scott Drapeau left after a few games, ultimately winding up at New Hampshire. Jerome Malloy transferred to Jacksonville after his sopho-

more year of 1992–93. Andre Burks left after his freshman year of 1994–95 to play at McNeese State.

8. In Calipari's first game against George Washington in 1989, he walked off the court after getting one technical foul for his infamous partial striptease. He never got a second technical, and was not required to leave.

## Chapter 19

1. According to a Newhouse News Service feature in March, more than $3 billion of illegal betting was expected for the 1996 NCAA tournament, plus another $60 million of the legal variety. Of all sporting events, only the Super Bowl generates a larger sum.

2. Indeed, the dreams of professional stardom are less realistic in basketball than in any major professional sport. The 336 players in the NBA represent a far smaller labor force than the NHL (624), Major League Baseball (700) and the NFL (1590).

3. In the *Courant* story, Camby admitted accepting other gifts from Spears. Those gifts included a diamond necklace with a Number 21 pendant that he wore for the second half of the season—a gift that he claimed was funneled from Spears through Camby's friends. Camby also acknowledged accepting $1,000 from Spears after the season. In addition, he was quoted as saying he accepted "a couple thousand" from agent John Lounsbury before his junior year even began.

## Chapter 21

1. In the foreseeable future, The Road to the Final Four will not lead to the New York area. The NCAA has decreed that all future Final Fours have to be staged at arenas that seat at least thirty thousand fans. The Continental Airlines Arena seats just over nineteen thousand.

2. A total of 18,500 tickets (of the crowd of 19,224) were "made available." Only 1,000 tickets were put on sale to the general public. Approximately 2,800 were given to college basketball coaches, who have their convention at the Final Four. Some 4,700 went to a variety of VIPs, including administrators from the NCAA, college presidents and members of the Meadowlands Organizing Committee. The remaining 10,000 seats were dispersed in blocks of 2,500 to the participating schools, who were permitted to distribute them as they saw fit. UMass's ticket list was obtained by *The Boston Globe* using the Freedom of Information Act.

## Afterword

1. Though the deal was done within a week of the initial meeting, both sides

later indicated that negotiations had an on–again, off–again quality. Perhaps this accounts for some of the inconsistencies in public statements during the next several days.

2. The basketball part of the camp is intended for players like Bright, whose ability to play in the NBA is considered debatable. Someone like Camby, a certain high draft pick, was not expected to play.

3. Rowe later explained to *The Record* that he thought he was responding only to a question about whether he had spoken directly to Calipari in Chicago. The lead of the story reads, "The Nets should have a head coach in place by next week, team president Michael Rowe said Wednesday. And, Rowe said, John Calipari has not been considered for that opening." Rowe is not explicitly quoted as saying that Calipari wasn't considered for the position, but staff writer Ken Davidoff stands by his interpretation of the conversation.

4. Another lengthy front–page *Globe* story in the summer detailed some of the ways in which agents tried to make money off Camby's talent. One confessed, "This almost ruined my marriage. Every night when I went to bed, I was dreaming of a six–foot–eleven black guy instead of my wife."

# Index